Library of
Davidson College

ARCHITECTURE IN ENGLISH FICTION

BY
WARREN HUNTING SMITH

ARCHON BOOKS
1970

Copyright, 1934, by Yale University Press
Reprinted 1970 with permission of Yale University Press
in an unaltered and unabridged edition

823.09
S663a

[*Yale Studies in English, Vol. 83*]

72-8706
SBN: 208 00916 7
Library of Congress Catalog Card Number: 73-91191
Printed in the United States of America

PREFACE

The architecture and the literature of English-speaking countries have had unusually close connections since the origin of architectural description in English fiction of the eighteenth century. The "Gothic romances" of that period, together with later developments of literary architecture in England and America, are the subject of this book. The earlier novels have been emphasized because they are so obscure and so inaccessible; Scott and his followers are too well known to need such detailed treatment.

Since a complete bibliography would fill an inordinate space, the index must be its substitute. Complete foot-notes would also tend to overwhelm the text; unannotated quotations can often be found either in the opening pages of the book cited, or in proximity to the annotated quotations from that book. Unless the notes specify otherwise, the references are to editions published in London at the date given. The original spelling and punctuation of the novels are retained in the quotations. The lino-cut decorations are based on old engravings: the frontispiece is Fonthill Abbey (after J. Martin); the other illustrations, in succession, are Strawberry Hill (from a vignette in Walpole's *Works*, 1798), the entrance hall of Fonthill (after Rutter's *Delineations*), Otranto (from the frontispiece to the Italian edition, 1795), and Warwick Castle (after J. Rowe).

This study, in its original form, was accepted by the Graduate School of Yale University as a dissertation for the degree of doctor of philosophy. I am indebted to Professor C. B. Tinker for his supervision, for the use of his library, and for innumerable courtesies; it would be presumptuous to add this book to the many impressive volumes already dedicated to him. Dr. J. W. Ruff of Yale corrected my original version; Dr. Eugene Finch, formerly of Yale, gave me his bibliography of American fiction; Professor Man-

Preface

waring of Wellesley College and Mr. Christopher Hussey of London provided useful information when I was studying in England; Mr. Michael Sadleir brought his unique copy of *The Orphan of the Rhine* to London for my perusal. Professor W. S. Lewis maintains that the Castle of Otranto *is* Strawberry Hill, and my remarks on that subject in Chapter III must be compared with his monograph on the genesis of Strawberry Hill. To these and many others, to the Yale Library staff, and, above all, to my parents, my thanks are due—and now I must make my bow to those dear sentimental ladies of eighteenth-century fiction, with whom I have "kept company" for three pleasant years.

W. H. S.

*Yale University,
June 3, 1934.*

CONTENTS

I. The Use of Architecture in Fiction.......... 1

II. Sources of the Architectural Interest Shown in the Eighteenth-century Novel............. 6

III. Castles, Manors, and Abbeys............... 79

IV. Temples, Villas, and Pavilions............. 145

V. Realism Displacing Romance............... 159

VI. Later Architectural Developments in the Novel
   1. *Architecture in Early American Fiction* 191
   2. *The House Personified*............... 202
   3. *The Bizarre House*.................. 210

VII. The Contributions of Architectural Fiction.... 217

CHAPTER ONE

THE USE OF ARCHITECTURE IN FICTION

Buildings are visible enough to ordinary eyes, but many people seem to use literary eyeglasses when they judge architecture. What they see is colored, focused, or distorted by what they have read. With these glasses perched on their noses, some of them have even written books to furnish other people with similar glasses, or have designed buildings to satisfy a vision thus assisted (buildings which seem very queer through the wrong lenses), or have demolished the books and buildings of differently equipped persons. Reading, to be sure, influences all our reactions, but perhaps no subject of aesthetic reaction has had greater literary entanglements than architecture has.

The literary eyeglasses of most people are furnished by fiction. Very few readers can endure straight architectural criticism, but a great many unconsciously adopt such criticism from novels that describe buildings. The effect of these novels has been to inculcate architectural prejudices, to invest certain styles and buildings with a glamour quite independent of their physical structure, to reclothe historic edifices with the apparel of their vanished youth, and even to revive past styles of design. In such ways, English fiction has been unusually effective, and a knowledge of architecture as popularized in the novel is essential for a thorough understanding of English architectural history.

Literature, concerned as it is with people civilized enough to live in houses, has always made allusions to architecture. English literature, from Beowulf onwards, has made such allusions in varying abundance, but not until the eighteenth century do we find architectural setting as a dominant feature of any important branch of literature, and this dominance is most apparent in the novels of the end of the century.

Earlier writers seem to have entered the homes of their characters (just as many people still enter the homes of their friends) with indifference to architectural surroundings. They assumed that people lived in habitations of some sort, and they did not care what sort it was. The literature of pure action does not pause to observe scenery; it is the literature of introspection, of subjectivity, or of psychological analysis that considers such things. Obviously, such literature is a product of intense civilization; it need not be sought among ancient bards and medieval troubadours.

The novel of the eighteenth century brought architectural setting from its ordinary position as an unobtrusive background to a place of prime importance in the narrative. There is, for instance, a great difference between Mariana's moated grange, casually mentioned by Shakespeare in *Measure for Measure*, and the desolate structure described by Tennyson, who seems more interested in the house than in the lady. Pope's Eloisa complains of the "moss-grown domes," "spiry turrets," and "awful arches" of her convent; but the convents of Ann Radcliffe and "Monk" Lewis are furnished with secret passages and subterranean dungeons, far more awful and certainly more complicated than any thing which Eloisa mentions. Dr. Johnson's Rasselas is reared in a palace full of secret vaults and passages which play no part in the story, but S. J. Arnold's imitation of *Rasselas*, published in 1796, makes the palace a castle, and leads us through the secret passages to a hermit's cave below. Richardson's Pamela is confined in a "handsome, large, old, and lonely Mansion," and his Clarissa is threatened with imprisonment in her Uncle Antony's moated house, but it remained for the followers of these novels to provide their imprisoned Pamelas with exits hidden behind the tapestry, and to send their Clarissas to houses which were not only moated but ruined and haunted.

In the nineteenth century, certain novelists described

The Use of Architecture in Fiction

architecture not only in its relations to their characters, but purely for its own sake. Harrison Ainsworth wrote a romance about the Tower of London, with the avowed intention of contriving "such a series of incidents as should naturally introduce every relic of the old pile—its towers, chapels, halls, chambers, gateways, arches, and drawbridges—so that no part of it should remain un-illustrated." Other novelists personified their buildings, and made the house itself a character. In the present century, writers of detective stories have found architectural exposition so essential that they sometimes include floor-plans of the houses where their murders take place.

The best architectural descriptions are the fruit of that sensitiveness to environment which results also in a love of nature. The two qualities are usually found together; in fact a really good description of a building seldom fails to make some reference to the surrounding landscape, for the best descriptions come from vivid mental pictures, and it is hard to visualize an object apart from its setting. Furthermore, the boundary line between art and nature becomes very indistinct in the case of the old castles of the Gothic romances; the buildings are so weather-beaten, so mantled with moss and ivy, that nature has really claimed them for her own, and they seem to have renounced all connection with human hands and minds. To some writers, they really seem to be sublime phenomena of nature, like sunsets and thunderstorms; to class them as architecture would be almost an insult.

As evidence of the sensitiveness of some writers to their environment, their homes are as interesting as their descriptions. Not content with creating buildings on paper, they tried to construct in slightly more substantial materials the environment that they craved. Fortunately, they were easily satisfied with the results, though we of later times are amused to see Walpole making Strawberry Hill into a miniature castle, Beckford rearing a colossal "abbey" which presently fell down, Scott building a baronial mansion, Irving Gothicizing his Dutch cottage, and even Fenimore Cooper stretching medieval rood-screens across the too-Protestant interior of his church in Cooperstown. It was once the fashion to sneer at these early products of the Gothic revival; it is now customary to find them rather charming. They are really unsuccessful attempts at a sort of poetry—poetry which the architectural descriptions of the Gothic romances sometimes achieved. It is hard, however, to express any thing poetic through the medium of poor architects and unskilled masons; the buildings remain as evidence that these authors tried to live in the environment of which they wrote.

Mere allusions to buildings do not constitute architectural setting in a book, any more than mere construction constitutes architecture. When one reads: "She walked through the door of the house into the front room," there is no architecture because doors and rooms are common to all buildings. If, however, the sentence reads: "She entered the arched door of the Tudor mansion, and found herself in a panelled hall," there is decided architectural setting. Still further development comes in the sentence: "She entered the arched door of the Tudor mansion, opened a panel in the hall by a hidden spring, and, snatching a casket of jewels, she escaped by a secret door behind the tapestry." Here the architecture serves a purpose in the narrative: by means of the sliding panel and the secret door, the lady is enabled to do things which otherwise she could not have done. The sentence, however, can acquire yet more significance: "The tottering turrets of the dismal Tudor mansion seemed about to annihilate her with an avalanche of masonry, and the arched door creaked mournfully, as she entered the gloomy hall, where mysterious banners made her shudder as they rustled in ghostly whispers." Here, an emotional element has been introduced. The lady (and presumably the reader) is made to shudder.

There are, then, three main types of architectural setting: the purely decorative type, used for ornament and "local color"; the structural type performing a service in the narrative; and the emotional type, explaining the reactions of the characters and arousing the feelings of the reader. In the most highly developed architectural settings, all three kinds are combined, and the narrative sometimes suffers from the overwhelming masses of architectural exposition imbedded in it. The intrusion of architecture into literature, as we shall see, was not always beneficial; it was brought about, not by logical and necessary growth within the novel, but in compliance with certain popular enthusiasms of the eighteenth century. These fancies must be examined before the resulting literature can be studied.

CHAPTER TWO

SOURCES OF THE ARCHITECTURAL INTEREST SHOWN IN THE EIGHTEENTH-CENTURY NOVEL

The novelists of the eighteenth century would not have provided architectural descriptions unless they and their readers had really been interested in buildings. Before examining the development of architectural setting in the novel, one must understand why it should ever have developed at all, and so it is necessary to study the various causes which were at work during the century to bring about this interest in architecture. The causes may be roughly divided into two main groups: the purely literary sources, and the contemporary architectural tendencies. Obviously, it is impossible to include here a complete discussion of the Gothic revival, much less of Georgian architecture, so that the sources of the novelists' architectural tastes will be discussed only in their relation to the novels themselves.

The middle of the eighteenth century witnessed the end of that slow progress in architectural style which had been continuing through the preceding centuries, and the beginning of the modern architectural chaos. From 1750 on, a series of revivals, Gothic, Greek, Roman, and even Oriental, disturbed and finally supplanted the existing Georgian style. New facilities for transportation and for pictorial representation made all the past styles available for present use. The age of eclecticism set in.

During the first half of the century, however, only two styles of architecture were well known in England, and only one of them was popular. This favored style was, of course, the style of the Renaissance, in the form which we now call Georgian. The only other style of construction in England was the outmoded medieval form, contemptuously called

Gothic, and seldom used. Gothic was not completely abandoned, nevertheless, because the existing buildings in that style had to be kept in repair, and because there were always people who continued to admire medieval architecture and even to imitate it. In the remoter provinces, Gothic construction continued almost to the end of the seventeenth century, and there were doubtless obscure masons, even in the eighteenth century, who still built in the traditional style of their ancestors. The world of fashion, nevertheless, regarded Gothic architecture as something rather barbarous.

Indeed medieval architecture was regarded in the early eighteenth century much as Victorian architecture is regarded in the early twentieth century. The objections to the typical Gothic castle sound exactly like the objections to those large and elaborate mansions of the 1870's and 1880's which are to be found amid lawns and shrubbery on the outskirts of most American towns. These houses are gloomy; they are full of waste space; they are expensive to repair and maintain; and they are over-decorated in a heavy and fantastic way. Exactly the same objections were made in the eighteenth century to the medieval castle or manor-house. A Georgian mansion with its cheerful paint and paper, its broad windows, its compact arrangement, and its more chaste ornament seemed in its day infinitely preferable to the Gothic castle, just as the houses of today seem to us more satisfactory than their Victorian predecessors. The Victorian mansion has one advantage, however; if it is still in the possession of its builders, it shows that for at least half a century this particular family has possessed wealth, and presumably, prestige. Parvenus do not usually buy Victorian villas, they prefer a more fashionable style. The Victorian house is, then, a symbol of family background and conservatism. Even more so was the Gothic castle in the eighteenth century, when tradition and conservatism were more highly regarded than they are now. Upstarts might have mansions by Vanbrugh or Adam or Chambers; they might even indulge in imitation-Gothic styles, but the old castles of the nation were still in the hands of the nobility, who were proud of them, not because of their architecture, but because they testified to the importance and antiquity of the family.

Gothic architecture, therefore, was cherished as a symbol of family pride even before it was found to have charms of its own. Its heraldic emblems, carved in stone or painted in glass, were interesting to people for no other reason than that they were emblems of family history. The first stage of the Gothic revival was this appreciation of Gothic architecture merely because of its antiquity and its historical associations. Horace Walpole, writer of the first Gothic romance, and builder of the most famous example of eighteenth-century Gothic architecture, seems to have been led into his taste for Gothic largely through his genealogical and heraldic interests. His references to famous castles are principally references to the family portraits, heraldic emblems, and tombs which they displayed. He writes George Montagu that he would like to visit the latter's ancestral castles in Wales, and Picton Castle, the seat of his own ancestors. While Strawberry Hill is under construction, he refers to it as "the castle (I am building) of my ancestors."[1] In the same letter he remarks that "the armoury bespeaks the ancient chivalry of the lords of the castle." On September 23, 1755, he writes to Henry Conway:

> I do not so much consider myself writing to Dublin Castle, as from Strawberry Castle, where you know how I love to enjoy my liberty. I give myself the airs, in my nutshell, of an old baron . . . .

Walpole was merely joking, of course, but beneath the whimsicality of his statements, there is a real enjoyment of his

[1] *Letters*, ed. Toynbee, III, 163.

position as lord of a castle, surrounded by emblems of his family history.

William Beckford, who, like Walpole, was the author of a famous eighteenth-century romance, and the builder of a notorious example of eighteenth-century Gothic architecture, likewise had genealogical and heraldic interests. His "abbey" at Fonthill was profusely decorated with heraldic emblems, and Melville quotes two letters from Beckford to Isaac Heard, relating to the arrangement of these details. In one letter he says:

> What think you of four Catisbys; all of a row, with their Beasts' Heads and battle axes entwisted with their own snug comfort-breathing scroll? Chuse 4 of their best connections—begin, if you like, with Montfort, then some other decent match—then—ditto—then quarterings Montfort, &c., as settled before . . . .[2]

Beckford is reported to have said of Walpole that "He would have abused my heraldic emblazonments at Fonthill."[3] Certainly these emblazonments received plenty of abuse in their day, for a very sarcastic reference to them is to be found in William Cobbett's *Rural Rides*:[4]

> .Talking of *Normans* and *high-blood*, puts me in mind of BECKFORD and his "ABBEY"! The public knows, that the tower of this thing fell down some time ago. It was built of *Scotch-fir* and *cased with stone*! In it there was a place which the owner had named, "The Gallery of Edward III., the frieze of which, (says the account,) "contains the achievements of *seventy-eight Knights of the Garter*, from whom the owner is LINEALLY DESCENDED"! Was there ever vanity and impudence equal to these! the negro-driver brag of his high blood! I dare say, that the old powder-man, FARQUHAR, had as

---

[2] Lewis Melville, *Life and Letters of Wm. Beckford*, 1910, p. 259.
[3] Lewis Melville, *op. cit.*, p. 299.
[4] Ed. Cole, 1930, II, 406.

good pretension; and I really should like to know, whether he took out Beckford's name, and put in his own, as the lineal descendant of the seventy-eight Knights of the Garter.

Fonthill and Strawberry Hill were by no means the only castles to be erected in the eighteenth century. The Duke of Roxburghe built Floors Castle in 1718; the Duke of Argyle erected Inverary Castle between 1744 and 1762; much of Arundel Castle was built in the 1790's; and most of Milton Abbas in 1771. All these castles, and numerous humbler country seats, were made to appear more or less Gothic. They witness to the "castellated" style which seems to have been traditional for the residences of the English nobility. Many of Vanbrugh's buildings, such as Blenheim, present the towered outlines and broken masses of a medieval castle, even though the actual forms are Renaissance. Early in the eighteenth century, Vanbrugh built himself a miniature Gothic castle near Greenwich. Evidently castles were regarded as appropriate homes for ancient families, even though many of the nobility deserted them for more modern and commodious houses.

This association of the Gothic castle with family pride is reflected in many of the eighteenth-century novels. Thus 'Lady' O'Shaughnessy in *The Story of Lady Juliana Harley* (1776) by Mrs. Elizabeth Griffith, writes that "I love the grandeur of an ancient family-mansion."[5] In the story of *Kruitzner*, by Harriet Lee, in Harriet and Sophia Lee's *Canterbury Tales* (1797-1805), we find a nobleman who "loved . . the petty dignity attached to his family and alliances; and surveyed with much satisfaction a Gothic chateau, situated in a marsh, and flanked with avenues of worm-eaten timber, because its precincts were his own." In Mrs. Agnes Maria Bennett's *Beggar Girl* (1797) is a similar

[5] II, 102.

character: "whose veneration for the ancient feudal system of the country was evinced by a respect for every object that kept up the recollection of past times, even to the tapestry hangings and furniture of his Castle."[6] *Ellen, Countess of Castle Howel* (1794), by the same author, describes an old abbey which is preserved because, although "the Ladies had insuperable objections to living in the gothic apartments of the abbey, their family pride did not object to the display of its antiquity."[7] T. P. Lathy says that a medieval house "is reckoned an honour amongst the breed of country 'Squires, whose greatest pride is to inform their guests how many generations of their family have *vegetated* in one spot like cabbages."[8]

Mr. Delvile, in Fanny Burney's *Cecilia* (1782), is very proud of his ancestral castle. He reproves the pert Lady Honoria for speaking slightingly of "any gentleman's ancient family seat,—a thing, Lady Honoria, always respectable, however lightly spoken of." He adds that "such a thing, belonging to a man from his own ancestors, is invaluable." When she makes contemptuous remarks about a particularly dilapidated tower, he retorts:

> ". . . . . that old tower, of which you are pleased to speak so slightingly, is the most honourable testimony to the antiquity of the castle of any now remaining, and I would not part with it for all the new boxes, as you stile them, in the kingdom."[9]

Mr. Delvile's defense of the tower is significant—he does not praise it for its beauty, its sublimity, or its picturesqueness, but merely for its antiquity, testifying as it does to the antiquity of his family. Men like Mr. Delvile really existed

[6] 1799, II, 37.
[7] III, 144-5.
[8] *Paraclete*, 1805, I, 41.
[9] Book VI, Chapter VII.

in the eighteenth century; for instance, Horace Walpole's nephew, the Earl of Dysart, was so conservative that he disgusted even his antiquarian uncle. On returning from a visit to his nephew, Horace writes:

> In this state of pomp and tatters my nephew intends it [the mansion] shall remain, and is so religious an observer of the venerable rites of his house, that because the gates never were opened by his father but once for the late Lord Granville, you are locked out and locked in, and after journeying all round the house, as you do round an old French fortified town, you are at last admitted through the stable-yard to creep along a dark passage by the housekeeper's room, and so by a back-door into the great hall.[10]

This veneration for castles merely as symbols of family dignity was usually supplemented by other attitudes towards medieval architecture. One stage in the Gothic revival was marked by a regard for buildings because of their historical and genealogical associations; the next stage was that of valuing the castle for its pictorial effect. The eighteenth century regarded Gothic buildings as "picturesque"—meaning that the irregularity of form and outline, the discolorations of time, and the vegetation which usually clothed such ancient structures made good subjects for the brush and pencil. Classical buildings were picturesque only when in ruins, but Gothic architecture was always picturesque.[11] The use of picturesque buildings in painting was largely inspired by the landscape of Claude Lorrain and Salvator Rosa, painters who exercised an immense influence upon English taste.[12] The buildings in these paintings were usually

---

[10] *Letters*, ed. Toynbee, VII, 385.
[11] Cf. Christopher Hussey: *The Picturesque*, 1927.
[12] Cf. Elizabeth Manwaring: *Italian Landscape in Eighteenth Century England*, New York, 1925.

classical ruins, but it was easy for the English to perceive that their own antiquities, which were Gothic, were fully as picturesque as those of Italy. Hence came the love of ruins which played so prominent a part in the history of eighteenth-century landscape gardening, witnessed by the abundant references to ruins in literature, and by the erection of sham castles and abbeys in the grounds of every fashionable country house of the time.

The devotees of the "picturesque" school valued the castle, not for its historical associations, but for itself; nevertheless, they were not so much interested in the castle as a work of architecture as in the castle as an ornament to nature. The ruin provided a point of interest in the landscape, much as a crag, or a mountain might do; indeed, from the standpoint of the picturesque, the ruin itself might just as well have been a product of nature.

In the novels of the century, buildings frequently appear in this capacity of landscape ornaments. The number of examples is so great, that only a few specimens can be included here. In *Ranspach,* or *Mysteries of a Castle* (1797), a character says:

> ". . . . observe this valley, bounded on one side by the craggy declivity of a mountain, on the opposite by a thick forest, the trees of which appear nearly as ancient as the soil; while the dismantled turrets of an old castle, appearing amidst them, render the view truly picturesque."[13]

In Thomas Holcroft's *Anna St. Ives* (1792) we read that Sir Arthur "did not forget to point out to us . . . . . how picturesque a temple, or a church steeple, would look in this place."[14] His gardener writes him about the "extenshun

---

[13] Uttoxeter, I, 17.
[14] I, 36.

and ogmenshun of the new ruins." The heroine of Mrs. Charlotte Smith's *Ethelinde* (1789) has similar tastes:

> Sitting down on a rustic and half ruined tomb, she contemplated with mournful pleasure the picturesque appearance it made adjoining the church . . . . .[15]

In *Desmond* (1792), the same author describes a ruin, "than which, nothing can be more picturesque: when of a fine glowing evening, the almost perpendicular hill on which it stands is reflected in the unruffled bosom of the broad river, crowned with these venerable remains. . ."[16] In Mrs. Kelly's *Ruins of Avondale Priory* (1796), we read that in a garden stands "a half ruined gothic temple, dedicated to innocence" (!) which was "left there as a good point of view from the windows in the eastern wing of the castle."[17] Mrs. Agnes Maria Bennett, in *Anna, or Memoirs of a Welch Heiress* (1785), says that the situation of Llandore is "beautifully picturesque and romantic" because it stands in a "vale, which is irregularly interspersed with various old ruins, the sad memento of the faded glory and sunk dignity of the ancient inhabitants of Cambria." The Castle of Hardayne, in the romance by that name, written by John Bird (1795), has very picturesque coloring:

> The shattered walls were stained with a variety of beautiful mosses, or shadowed with the broad masses of ivy, through which the grey tint of Gothick ornaments would sometimes peep, and give a pleasing relief to the deep green shades.

Later novelists are equally devoted to the picturesque. Horsley Curties describes ruins, to which time has given "a

---
[15] V, 217.
[16] I, 171.
[17] I, 131.

more picturesque aspect."[18] R. C. Dallas says that a ruined castle "heightened the pleasing landscape into a picturesque scenery."[19] A ruined abbey in Mrs. Damer's *Belmour* has "an air of picturesque grandeur."[20] Mrs. Roche remarks that a Roman arch, "from its picturesque effect, amidst the surrounding scenery, had been allowed to remain,"[21] and she calls a ruined abbey "a grand and interesting object to the lovers of the picturesque."[22] A Gothic building of heterogeneous construction seems to her "extremely picturesque," and she thinks it "perhaps, better harmonizing with the scenery around, than one of more recent date or regular construction."[23]

Not only was Gothic architecture considered harmonious with natural scenery; it was itself considered the most natural style. The similarity of forest avenues and cathedral aisles was obvious, and it occurs often in the novels. Dallas says that "the social and beautiful intertwining" of linden branches, "it has been said, gave the first idea of those Gothic structures that are the pride of former days, and the admiration of the present."[24] Anna Maria Porter describes an avenue of trees which, "with their high intermingling tops, and spreading branches below, bore a striking resemblance to the aisles of Gothic churches."[25]

Associated with the "picturesque" attitude towards Gothic architecture is the standpoint of the "sublime." Sublime objects, in the eighteenth century, were supposed to have an overwhelming effect upon the beholder, arousing fear and

[18] *St. Botolph's Priory*, 1806, I, 130.
[19] *Aubrey*, 1804, III, 115.
[20] 1801, II, 124.
[21] *Houses of Osma and Almeria*, Philadelphia, 1810, 204.
[22] *Contrast*, New York, 1828, I, 115.
[23] *The Munster Cottage Boy*, 1820, I, 168.
[24] *The Morlands*, 1805, I, 215.
[25] *Honor O'Hara*, 1826, I, 91.

awe, and therefore differing from picturesque objects, which merely appealed to the eye. Buildings, obviously, could well be picturesque and sublime at the same time, but the cult of the sublime presented a new attitude towards Gothic architecture, because it stressed the vertical aspect of buildings. Sublimity was usually the effect of towering masses, and implied a sense of great height, although it was sometimes used as an attribute of wildness or mystery. Mrs. Radcliffe, in her journal remarks: "Why is it so sublime to stand at the foot of a dark tower, and look up its height to the sky and stars?"[26] and Mrs. Charlotte Smith begins a sonnet with the words, "Ye towers sublime." Mr. Michael Sadleir has suggested[27] that the Gothic revival in the eighteenth century was largely caused by a revulsion in taste from the horizontal to the vertical line in architecture. The classical building, though displaying some vertical accents, is terminated by the horizontal lines of the cornice and the low-pitched roof. There is, therefore, a certain squareness and squatness in classical architecture, as contrasted with Gothic architecture, in which everything from windows to statuary is tall and narrow, and where buttresses, tracery, towers, battlements, and pinnacles soar upwards, emphasizing the vertical effect. Classical architecture regained this vertical effect, however, when it was in ruins, because the gaps in the roof broke the horizontal lines, and the separation of the building into tall fragments gave the structure a vertical emphasis.

The psychological effect of height in architecture is very evident. In a lofty building, there is always a sense of the overpowering which is lacking in a low structure, even though the relative size of the two be the same. When the

---

[26] *Gaston de Blondeville*, 1826, I, 98 (Memoir).
[27] *The Northanger Novels*, Oxford, 1927, p. 7.

lofty building is split into fragments, the height of these surviving portions seems even greater than before, and consequently the towering vestiges of ruined castles and abbeys were a constant source of "sublimity" in the eighteenth century. The vertical accent, providing a "thrill" to the beholder, was a welcome relief from classical architecture with its monotonously horizontal lines. Certainly the early Gothic revival cultivated vertical effects with amazing assiduity. The only style which was thought worthy of revival was Perpendicular Gothic, which, with its myriads of buttresses, mouldings, and pinnacles all pointing upwards, was the most vertical of all the Gothic styles. Fonthill Abbey carried the vertical effect to the extreme, and, lacking proper foundations, collapsed. The entrance hall of this astounding structure was a miracle of loftiness and narrowness.

The association of "sublimity" with vertical effects is often noticeable in the Gothic romances. Mrs. Radcliffe, for instance, who specializes in "sublime" effects, is constantly emphasizing the height of her buildings. Her first novel, *The Castles of Athlin and Dunbayne,* contains an interesting description of Dunbayne: "Its lofty towers still frowned in proud sublimity." In her next work, *The Sicilian Romance* (1790), she states that "the abbey of St. Augustin was a large magnificent mass of Gothic architecture, whose gloomy battlements, and majestic towers, arose in proud sublimity." In the same novel is a hall, "whose lofty roof rose into arches," and whose "windows were high and gothic." Of this she says that "an air of proud sublimity, united with singular wildness, characterized the place."[28] The castle of Udolpho is described as "silent, lonely, and sublime."[29] In other novels, we find the same word used for the same pur-

---

[28] I, 104, II, 27.
[29] *Mysteries of Udolpho,* 1794, II, 170.

pose. The towers of Hollodale Castle, according to Horsley Curties, "reared in sublime altitude their grey battlements," and were "surrounded on every side by precipitous mountains, whose varied and lofty pinnacles towered in horrible sublimity."[30] The heroine marvels at the "sublimity of the turrets." One of Edward Ball's mansions "seemed to soar, awfully sublime, prince of the imposing landscape,"[31] and one of J. N. Brewer's castles is "towering in sublime grandeur."[32]

Closely associated with the sense of sublimity is the sense of mystery, both of which have an emotional appeal, though the former was aroused by height, and the latter was usually the effect of gloom. Classical architecture was flooded with light, leaving nothing to the imagination, but Gothic architecture was filled with impenetrable shadows and mysterious vistas, which might conceal anything of an exciting nature. The ends of great halls and chapels, and the roofs of high-vaulted rooms were often lost in darkness. William Beckford says of Canterbury Cathedral that he "had always venerated its lofty pillars, dim aisles, and mysterious arches."[33] The effect of darkness and mystery is used very frequently in the Gothic romances, especially by Mrs. Radcliffe. She describes the "highly vaulted aisles, extending in twilight perspective"[34] of San Stefano. At the end of a hall in the castle of Mazzini "arose several gothic arches, whose dark shade veiled in obscurity the extent beyond."[35] In the banqueting-hall of Udolpho, "long colonades retired in gloomy grandeur, till their extent was lost in twilight."[36]

[30] *Scottish Legend*, 1802, I, 106, 97.
[31] *Black Robber*, 1819, II, 449.
[32] *Winter's Tale*, 1799, I, 73.
[33] *Travel Diaries*, 1928, I, 2.
[34] *The Italian*, 1797, I, 303.
[35] *The Sicilian Romance*, 1790, I, 104.
[36] *The Mysteries of Udolpho*, 1794, II, 401.

Sources of the Interest in Architecture 19

Other novelists use the same effects; for instance, Catherine Selden thus describes a nuns' chapel:

> The high windows of painted glass dimly admitted the rays of fading light; and in the long aisles, only the darker shade of a pillar here and there shewed through the gloom ....[37]

Mrs. Kelly describes a sunset, shedding "a softened and mysterious light upon the Gothic turrets of the castle."[38] Mrs. Roche says that a peaked roof, "half lost in air, and half, by straining her sight, kept in view, excited mingled passions—a sensation of terror and delight."[39]

Both mystery and sublimity were impressive in architecture because they gave the effect of infinity. Sublime towers seemed endlessly high, and mysterious vistas endlessly long. Gothic architecture, tapering off in pinnacles and spires, or extending in interminable aisles, was thus more satisfactory than classic architecture, where terminations were more emphatic and more visible. The cathedral, like the forest, seemed to stretch on for ever, and this illusion furnished another analogy between nature and Gothic architecture.

After the historical, pictorial, and emotional effects of Gothic architecture, we come to its sentimental aspect. The sight of "grandeur in decay" inspired the more sensitive spirits of the eighteenth century with a great deal of "melancholy pleasure." Ruins suggested the transitory nature of human pomp, the futility of human accomplishments, and emphasized the fact that

> "The paths of glory lead but to the grave."

The ruin might be both picturesque and sublime, but its principal attraction lay in its melancholy associations. The

---

[37] *The Count de Santerre*, Bath, 1797, II, 187.
[38] *The Baron's Daughter*, 1802, I, 139.
[39] *Trecothick Bower*, 1814, II, 126.

popularity of Netley Abbey, for instance, was astonishing. Horace Walpole visited it in 1755 and exclaimed: "they are not the ruins of Netley, but of Paradise.—Oh! the purple abbots, what a spot had they chosen to slumber in!" An anonymous poem entitled *The Ruins of Netley Abbey* appeared in 1765. Charlotte Smith mentions Netley in one of her *Rural Walks,* and *The Rival Friends* (1776) describes the wanderings of a recluse "where the majestic ruins of Netley Abbey shew the instability of human works."[40] Richard Warner's *Netley Abbey, a Gothic Story* appeared in 1795; the abbey figures also in Miss Warne's *Herbert Lodge* (1808). Gilpin gives an extended description of Netley in his *Observations on the Western Parts of England.* Gray visited the ruins in 1755 and again in 1764. On November 19th of the latter year, he wrote to Norton Nicholls:

> there may be richer and greater houses of religion, but the Abbot is content with his situation. see there, at the top of that hanging meadow under the shade of those old trees, that bend into a half-circle about it, he is walking slowly (good Man!) & bidding his beads for the souls of his Benefactors, interr'd in that venerable pile, that lies beneath him.

Abundant evidence of this sentimental attitude towards medieval architecture is to be found in the eighteenth-century novel. *Count di Novini; or the Confederate Carthusians* (1799) states that:

> Ruins, even when the broken capitals, prostrate columns, and mutilated statues, evince the lighter graces of architecture and employ the pleasing powers of fancy and judgment, seldom fail to inspire melancholy and pensive ideas.[41]

Lady Boyne, in Mrs. Parsons' *Lucy* (1794), says that "I doat on ruins; there is something sublime and awful in the sight

[40] III, 169.
[41] I, 173.

of decayed grandeur, and large edifices tumbling to pieces."[42] Mrs. Roche's *Vicar of Lansdowne* says that "The fine old ruin impresses the mind with the most pleasing, the most awful, the most soothing sensations."[43] The heroine of *Adeline de Courcy* (1797) remarks, of a ruin, that: "These quiet sort of scenes [*sic*] soothe and dispose the mind to melancholy reflections."[44] Ruins give to Allan Cunningham "a lesson to earthly hope and human vanity,"[45] to Edward Ball "a melancholy emotion for the fallen grandeur of ancient times,"[46] and to Mrs. Parsons "many reflective hours, on the instability of fortune, power, and grandeur, in this sublunary world."[47] They make C. R. Maturin "tremble with a delicious dread,"[48] and they present "that mixture of deviation and decay that combines our admiration of greatness with our interest in debility."[49] They make Mrs. Edgeworth's Adelaide reflect "with a melancholy awe on the mutability of all earthly happiness."[50] Lady Morgan says that they add a moral interest to natural scenery.[51] In Charles Johnstone's *Arsaces*, extensive Roman ruins are described, and a character observes that "Imagination wearied itself, in the present contemplation, in reflection on the former grandeur of this scene of desolation." Later in this novel are more extensive reflections upon ruins:

> The scenes, through which he led me were sufficient to humble human pride: and damp the ardour of ambition, in their highest flights. Every effort of art to elude oblivion, and guard against the waste of time, was

[42] II, 223.
[43] 2nd edition, 1800, II, 27.
[44] I, 56-7.
[45] *Paul Jones*, Philadelphia, 1827, I, 189.
[46] *Black Robber*, 1819, I, 2.
[47] *The Convict*, 1807, II, 197.
[48] *Fatal Revenge*, New York, 1808, I, 18.
[49] *Milesian Chief*, 1812, I, 11.
[50] *Adelaide*, 1806, II, 206.
[51] *Wild Irish Girl*, 1808, I, 156-7, III, 70-1.

here defeated in the most mortifying manner. Statues, whose remains shewed traces of the most exquisite workmanship; and columns, which seemed to have been built as firm, as the foundation of the earth, lay defaced and tumbled on each other, in heaps of promiscuous rubbish.[52]

A fondness for the more decorative side of Catholicism is an important part of the sentimental attitude towards Gothic architecture. The cathedrals and monasteries suggested choirs of chanting monks, rich vestments, incense, and all those ornamental accessories which the ceremonial of the Anglican church so sadly lacked in the eighteenth century. When Walpole visited Barrett's new Gothic house at Belhouse, he wrote: "I carried down incense and mass-books, and we had most Catholic enjoyment of the chapel." Beckford, according to Samuel Rogers, was said to pay his devotions to a statue of Saint Antonio, placed in one of the galleries of Fonthill Abbey. Beckford's descriptions of the Portuguese monasteries in his travel diaries furnish ample proof of his appreciation of Catholicism as a decorative asset.

In the novels of the eighteenth century, this sentimental leaning towards Catholicism is very marked. M. G. Lewis begins *The Monk* (1795) with a description of mass in a magnificent Gothic church. Mrs. Radcliffe, though she abhors the authoritative aspect of Catholicism, is strongly influenced by its aesthetic appeal. Music always enchanted her, and she heightens the effect of many of her architectural descriptions by the introduction of choral services. This tendency is especially marked in *The Italian*, where the nuns of San Stefano are shown singing vespers. Since many similar descriptions occur in Mrs. Radcliffe's *Journey*, it is

[52] Dublin, 1774, I, 48.

probable that her contact with Catholicism on her travels gave her suggestions for the use of religious music in her descriptions, because *The Italian*, with the exception of the posthumous *Gaston de Blondeville*, was the only one of her novels to be written after her trip down the Rhine. The association of Catholic ceremonial with Gothic architecture can be seen in practically all the Gothic romances, so it is needless to multiply instances of its use.

Gothic buildings provided, for the eighteenth century, a welcome change from the classical sobriety of contemporary architecture, and, like the Gothic romances, they also offered an imaginative escape from the dull monotony of contemporary life. Mr. Kenneth Clark has suggested[53] that many buildings of the early Gothic revival were the result of a self-dramatization on the part of men who pictured themselves as monks, crusaders, or medieval barons, and consequently built houses of a style which would encourage such daydreams. Walpole's statement that "I give myself the airs, in my nutshell, of an old baron" is typical of this attitude. The connection of Walpole's dreams with the eighteenth-century novel is highly important, because it was in a dream that the suggestion for *The Castle of Otranto*, the first Gothic romance, came to him. William Beckford also had a high regard for the setting of his day-dreams, and he dramatized himself to an extent which surpassed any of Walpole's achievements in that respect. His earlier letters are full of weird rhapsodies, in many of which architecture plays a part. On December 4th, 1778, "being the full of the Moon," he writes:

> The Dusk approaches. I am musing on the Plain before the House which my Father reared. No cheerful illuminations appear in the Windows, no sounds of

[53] *The Gothic Revival*, 1928, p. 53.

> Musick issue from the Porticos, no gay Revellers rove carelessly along the Colonades; but all is dark, silent and abandoned. Such Circumstances suit the present tone of my mind.[54]

In another letter he writes:

> I walk to and fro in my Cell and fancy myself in the Caverns of *Chehabeddin* where every volume contained a Spirit.[55]

For poses of this sort, Fonthill Abbey was erected as a congenial background, while their literary expression is the Hall of Eblis in *Vathek*.

The extent to which the more susceptible people of the period dramatized their contacts with Gothic architecture can be seen in Jane Austen's *Northanger Abbey*. Catherine Morland, the heroine of this novel, is so overcome by romantic reading that she imagines her host, General Tilney, to be a fierce baron of the type portrayed in Mrs. Radcliffe's *Sicilian Romance,* and she thinks that Northanger Abbey, despite its distressingly modern appearance, conceals a hidden crime. In *Caroline Merton* (1794) the timid Lady Fairford dreams that ogres will spring upon her at any moment during her stay at C— Castle, while the more enthusiastic heroine imagines herself carried back to the days of chivalry and tournaments.

Many buildings of the early Gothic revival are thus attempts on the part of the builders to materialize their flights of imagination. It is certainly much easier to dream that one is a medieval baron when there are battlements at hand to encourage the illusion, and the presence of a cloister would go far to sweeten the reveries of a would-be monk. The psychological effect of environment is very important, and

---

[54] Lewis Melville: *op. cit.*, p. 60.
[55] *Ibid.*, p. 75.

in the eighteenth century, people like Walpole and Beckford created an environment that suited them. The effect of Newstead Abbey upon Byron's opinion of himself is a subject well worth considering.

Gothic architecture, when it came to be appreciated at all in the eighteenth century, was appreciated for almost any reason except its intrinsic merits. The fact that Gothic construction at its best was good construction seems scarcely to have occurred to the eighteenth century. Certainly such an idea did not occur to the architects of the early Gothic revival, who plastered medieval ornaments upon a structure which in form was classical. The principles of Gothic vaulting, with its thrusts and counterthrusts, were unknown and uninteresting to most people then. Even archaeologists were more concerned with ornament than with construction. The favorite form of medieval vaulting in the eighteenth century was the elaborate fan vaulting of the late Perpendicular Gothic—in its original form the most unstructural of Gothic vaults, and made still more unstructural in the Gothic revival by being imitated in plaster. The vaulting of the great gallery at Strawberry Hill, copied in plaster from the vaulting of Henry VII's chapel in Westminster Abbey, is the most notorious example of this cheap sort of imitation. The architects of the early Gothic revival used shoddy materials only too often: the walls of Strawberry Hill are lath and plaster; the pinnacles of Fonthill Abbey were so flimsy that they were held in place by tie-rods; Walpole is said to have out-lived three sets of his own (wooden) battlements; and such phenomena as cast-iron tracery, and wooden tracery early made their appearance.

Structural soundness, therefore, was but little regarded in the eighteenth century. People were interested in Gothic architecture because it preserved ancestral traditions, because it adorned the landscape, because it inspired awe, because it induced melancholy reflections, or because it gave them a congenial background — of these various aspects the "romantic" attitude towards medieval construction was composed. It would be difficult to say that any of these separate attitudes antedated any other, or that any one ever prevailed to the utter exclusion of any other. Exact definitions are hard to apply to such nebulous things as aesthetic theories, because the terms "picturesque," "sublime," etc., were loosely used to express a great many varying shades of meaning. Such theories are necessarily vague, and when they become more precise they too often become more misleading.

The growing appreciation of Gothic architecture from these various standpoints expressed itself in several ways—in archaeological research, in the revival of medieval architecture, and in the use of Gothic setting in literature. All these forms of expression acted in turn as sources of Gothic influences, so that the effect was cumulative. The earlier archaeological research of the century was mostly upon classical antiquities, and this classical research probably suggested to the English the desirability of investigating the Gothic antiquities of their own country, just as the classical ruins in the landscape paintings of Claude Lorrain and Salvator Rosa suggested to the English the availability of their own ruins for picturesque purposes. Sir William Chambers, perhaps the most influential architect of his day, remarks in his *Treatise on the Decorative Side of Civil Architecture* (1759) that English archaeologists would do well to investigate their own antiquities before studying those of other nations.

The result of the intense archaeological interest of the middle part of the century was the breakdown of Georgian Renaissance architecture and the beginning of various revivals. With so many detailed drawings of ancient buildings available, it was only natural that the architects should turn to them for suggestions. Consequently the Greek and Gothic revivals, and the Oriental craze were soon in full

Sources of the Interest in Architecture 27

swing. The researches of the archaeologists made possible the constructions of the Gothic revivalists.

The very formidable list of archaeological publications appearing after 1750 is too long to discuss in detail here,[56] but in the novels of the eighteenth century, Roman and Greek ruins are frequently mentioned, and a discussion of their use will be found at the beginning of Chapter IV. Some of the novels even mention the archaeological researches; for instance, *The Sentimental Spy* (1773) satirizes the feverish activities of a lady who has discovered Roman ruins on her grounds, and in John Shebbeare's *Lydia* (1755) we meet Lord Nicknackerton who "had been at Balbec to measure the Proportions of the various Remains of architecture to be found in that City, and compare them with what is yet to be seen at *Rome* and *Athens*."[57] A similar archaeologist, in Alicia Lefanu's *Strathallan*, is so fired with enthusiasm by the discovery of Roman remains that "his conversation now ran on nothing but medals, urns, vases, and inscriptions."

The immediate result of these researches in classical fields was the Greek revival, of which the principal apostle was James Stuart. The work of the Adam brothers, especially their decorative detail, shows strong Greek influence, and in the frontispiece to *The Works of Robert and James Adam* (1778) Minerva points to Italy and Greece as the sources of architectural inspiration. The inclusion of Greece is sig-

---

[56] Robert Wood: *Ruins of Palmyra* (1753), *Ruins of Balbec* (1757).
LeRoy: *Ruins of Athens* (1759).
Stuart and Revett: *Antiquities of Athens* (1762, 1788).
Robert Adam: *Ruins of the Palace of the Emperor Diocletian at Spalatro* (1764).
Thomas Major: *Ruins of Paestum* (1768).
Nicholas Revett: *Antiquities of Ionia* (1769).
[57] IV, 138.

nificant. A secondary result of this archaeological work was the aroused interest in Gothic antiquities, which had the advantage of being much more accessible to the English than were the ruins of Balbec and Palmyra.

Although there had been a slight amount of research upon these native antiquities back to the time of Dugdale's *Monasticon*, it was not until after 1770 that publications on the subject became really numerous. A discussion of Gothic tracery by Aubrey was appended to Perry's *English Medals* (1762). James Bentham's *Ely* appeared in 1771. In 1774 came Buck's *Antiquities or Venerable Remains of above 400 Castles in England and Wales*. From 1773 to 1787 appeared Captain Grose's *Antiquities of England and Wales* (4 vols.), which was followed in 1789 by his *Antiquities of Scotland*, and in 1791 by his *Antiquities of Ireland*. Henry Boswell's *Antiquities of England* (1785) was followed, the next year, by T. Hearne's *Antiquities of Great Britain*, Gough's *Sepulchral Monuments*, and Carter's *Specimens of Ancient Sculpture and Painting*. "An introductory discourse on the principles of Gothic architecture" by James Murphy was prefixed to Fr. de Sousa's *Plans Elevations Sections and Views of the Church of Batalha* (1795), a work to which both Horace Walpole and William Beckford are listed as subscribers, and in the same year appeared Joseph Halfpenny's *Gothic Ornaments in the Cathedral Church of York*. Bentham and Willis's *History of Gothic and Saxon Architecture in England* was published in 1798, and two years later appeared a reprint of four essays (by Bentham, Warton, Milner, and Grose respectively) on the history of Gothic architecture. There is architectural material in Bishop Milner's *History of Winchester* (1798), as there had also been in Thomas Warton's work on the same subject a half-century earlier. Dr. Nathan Drake, in foot-notes to Gothic romances in his *Literary Hours* (1798-1800), quotes fairly technical descriptions of Gothic buildings from Henry's

History of England and Thorpe's *History and Antiquities of Rochester*. Moreover, the *Gentleman's Magazine*, always fond of archaeology, became after 1780 very decidedly interested in Gothic antiquities, which, in the 1783 volume, were the subject of articles appearing nearly every month.

Most of these archaeological works were published in huge tomes, full of engravings. Since they were expensive to prepare, they were issued by subscription, and their circulation could not have been very large. People of modest means had to find their archaeology in the less expensive magazines, which were less elaborately illustrated. Consequently, the general public did not often see the magnificent engravings of such works as Stuart's *Antiquities* or Wood's *Palmyra*, where imposing views are given of the ruins in their dilapidated state, with long grass waving from the crevices of the masonry. Natives in turbans, accompanied by extraordinary animals, give local color to the pictures. There are also detailed and less picturesque drawings of the ornament.

The early works on Gothic archaeology seldom possessed any semblance of accuracy. Murphy, for instance, derives the Gothic arch from the Pyramid, and all the early archaeologists attribute Norman architecture to the Saxons—so did the novelists, and we find Mrs. Radcliffe in *The Mysteries of Udolpho* describing a "Saxon-gothic" fortress,[58] situated in the Pyrenees, a region where anything Saxon would hardly penetrate. Dates meant little to these inaccurate writers. Late Gothic architecture was usually traced to Saracenic origins.

Although the general public could not afford to subscribe to the ponderous and expensive archaeological tomes, it could and did buy the numerous books of travel which appeared in the eighteenth century. Here it could find descriptions of buildings in great abundance—descriptions which were

---

[58] IV, 250.

usually more interesting and less technical than the writings of the archaeologists. The travelling propensities of the eighteenth-century Englishman and Englishwoman are well known, and the literary output of these travellers was considerable. Descriptions of castles and ruins are to be found in the works of Arthur Young, William Gilpin, and many of their contemporaries. The influence of such books on the English novel was probably far greater than the influence of archaeological works, because most of the novelists of the period were middle-class women who could not afford to subscribe to expensive publications, and whose interest in architecture was far from technical. Evidence of the indebtedness of the novelists to travel descriptions is by no means wanting. Charlotte Smith, in *The Solitary Wanderer* (1800), mentions Gilpin's description of Tintern Abbey,[59] and Ann Radcliffe's description of Venice is based upon Mrs. Piozzi's *Tour*.[60] For her descriptions of the Pyrenees, Mrs. Radcliffe seems to have relied upon the work of Ramond de Carbonières.[61] Mrs. Mary Robinson refers to William Coxe's *Views of Switzerland* as the source of a landscape description in a foot-note to *Hubert de Sevrac* (1796), and she has the audacity to suggest that many of her fellow-novelists had already availed themselves of the same source for their own scenery. Mrs. Hanway also comments upon the pillage of travel books by authors, and says that she will not descant upon architectural ruins.[62]

If one result of the awakening Gothic enthusiasm was archaeological research, the next step, logically, was the revival of Gothic architecture. As a matter of fact, how-

[59] I, 27.

[60] C. McIntyre: *Ann Radcliffe in Relation to her Time*, New Haven, 1920, pp. 58-61.

[61] J. M. S. Tompkins: *The Popular Novel in England* 1770-1800, 1932.

[62] *Falconbridge Abbey*, 1809, IV, 14.

ever, the Gothic revival started before Gothic archaeology, with the result that the earlier Gothic buildings of the eighteenth century are amusingly naive. Historians have some difficulty in deciding just when Gothic survival ended and Gothic revival began; no exact date can be set, because, in remote districts, Gothic lingered much later than in the centers of population. All the important Gothic buildings of the eighteenth century are undoubtedly products of the revival, however. The earlier Gothic of the century, done by Vanbrugh, Hawksmoor, and their group, was of a different type from the Gothic of Walpole in the middle of the century, and still more different from the Gothic of Beckford at the close of the century. All three varieties of Gothic, nevertheless, were distinctly bad. Vanbrugh and Hawksmoor were interested in the general forms and outlines of Gothic, the broken sky-line and irregular silhouette; Walpole was primarily concerned with Gothic ornament; and Beckford was engrossed with effects of height and grandeur. None of these various schools approved of the others; Walpole disliked Vanbrugh's work at Blenheim,[63] and Beckford called Strawberry Hill "a species of gothic mousetrap."[64]

Following the early Gothic of Vanbrugh and Hawksmoor, which need not concern us here because it had no influence on that which followed, we come to the craze for sham ruins in the 1740's, sponsored largely by William Kent and Sanderson Miller. The primary object of these absurd structures was to adorn the landscape, but they were sometimes used to perform the service of a cow-shed or horse-stable. They were very popular, and they were probably largely responsible for the great vogue of "rococo" Gothic in the middle of the century. This fashion encouraged Gothic furniture, summerhouses, and interior decoration, and its most notorious

[63] *Letters*, ed. Toynbee, IV, 409.
[64] Lewis Melville, *op. cit.*, p. 299.

sponsor was Batty Langley, whose *Gothic Architecture Improved by Rules and Proportions in Many Grand Designs* (1742) attempted to codify a system of rules for Gothic architecture. The Gothic of this rococo school was analogous to the Chinese fashion, which arrived slightly later under the auspices of Sir William Chambers. Walpole, Gray, and their circle had a profound contempt for this naive Gothic, although their own variety was little better, and possessed much of the same rococo quality.

Sanderson Miller is perhaps the most important figure of the Gothic school of the 1740's, although he has not achieved the notoriety which has fallen to Langley. Miller's first triumph was the sham castle at Edgehill, on his own grounds. Thereafter, commissions for Gothic designs poured in upon him from his friends, who were both numerous and influential. The sham ruin at Wimpole, another at Bagley, Lacock Abbey, Barrett's house at Belhus, and the tower of Wroxton Church are examples of his work. Horace Walpole, perhaps a little jealous of Miller's architectural fame, was delighted to hear that the Wroxton tower fell down a few months after its erection.

Horace Walpole himself was a leader in the Gothic revival, and, since he was the author of the first Gothic romance, his architectural tastes must be examined with some care. References to architecture in the *Letters*, accounts of architecture in the *Anecdotes of Painting*, and architectural details in *The Castle of Otranto* all provide material on the subject of his Gothic ideas. The illustrations to his *Description of Strawberry Hill* give the student a very clear idea of that remarkable edifice as it originally was, and a visit to Strawberry Hill, even today, has much to reveal, since the original house, though enlarged by additions, has not been materially altered. Though stripped of Walpole's furniture, it still retains its remarkable fireplaces, its stained glass, its fantastic book-cases, and its ornate ceilings.

Sources of the Interest in Architecture

The first glance at the engravings of Strawberry Hill shows that Walpole preferred the late Gothic to the earlier styles. The bristling pinnacles, the elaborate ceilings, and the abundant windows are all characteristic of the buildings of the Perpendicular, or late English Gothic. Everything is ornate, loaded with detail, and richly carved. Simplicity was evidently not a virtue in Walpole's estimation. Even the fireplaces in some of the rooms, especially that in the Great Parlour, are embellished with pinnacles of the most attenuated kind. The long gallery is roofed with fan vaulting, copied from the roof of Henry VII's chapel at Westminster Abbey. The book-cases in the library are topped by flamboyant arches between pinnacles, while the ceiling is most elaborately adorned with fretwork and medallions—painted on a flat surface! Even the wall-paper in the hall had Gothic decoration. Obviously, such elaboration is a far cry from the stern massive forms of the medieval castles.

Walpole, like the Elizabethans, considered his house as a mansion designed for comfortable habitation; structural considerations were of less importance. Windows had to be abundant to provide "prospects"; Walpole hated houses that shut themselves up behind walls. Consequently, the windows at Strawberry Hill are large and numerous. Stained glass was usually employed in the upper panes alone, leaving the lower ones available for observation of "prospects." Walpole sometimes contrasts the gaiety of his mansion to the gloom of genuine Gothic buildings; indeed nothing could be more dissimilar than the exuberance of Walpole's Gothic and the austerity of the medieval fortresses. In its lightness, therefore, Strawberry Hill resembles the Elizabethan mansion rather than the feudal fortress.

In its ornament, Strawberry Hill is predominantly Tudor. The panelling is almost exclusively Perpendicular; so is the fan vaulting; so are the canopies and niches. The fireplaces, particularly the monstrosity in the Holbein chamber, were copied from Perpendicular tombs in the cathedrals. The lavish use of rosettes and trefoil and quatrefoil forms and shields are all characteristic of late Gothic ornament. The façade of the chapel in the garden, copied from a chantry in Winchester Cathedral, is completely Perpendicular. The offices, erected after the completion of the main building, are almost pure Tudor in style. Square drip-stones cap the windows on the exterior, although the arches under the drip-stones are not always of the proper Tudor variety. The ogee arch was popular in the early Gothic revival.

Perpendicular architecture, though dominant in the design of Strawberry Hill, was by no means consistently used there. Walpole was nothing if not eclectic in his tastes. Consequently, we find him using a round tower of Flemish shape, and he even employed Robert Adam to design a fireplace, although the basis of the design was supposed to be the tomb of Edward the Confessor. Small lancet windows in the lower hall belong to the early English rather than to the Perpendicular style. The screen in the Holbein chamber is certainly not Tudor. Nevertheless, Walpole seems to have been inspired chiefly by the architecture of the very late Gothic period.

In Otranto, the castle of Walpole's imagination, this same late style seems to predominate, despite the location of the building in Italy. The great hall is lighted by an oriel window, a characteristic feature of Tudor buildings, and there is a great staircase, which certainly does not suggest the winding little stairs of the medieval castles. The towers are crowned with battlements, through which the wind whistles. The various parts of the castle are arranged around a central court—a later design than that of the earliest English castles, which were great keeps, encircled by protecting defenses.

Upon turning from Walpole's buildings, both real and imaginary, to his letters, one finds further expression of his love for late Gothic as contrasted with earlier styles, and for ornament as opposed to structure. He visited most of the English cathedrals and many of the French ones, besides innumerable castles and country houses, and abundant comments upon these buildings are to be found in his correspondence. Furthermore, in his *Anecdotes of Painting,* Walpole writes several paragraphs upon the development of architecture in the Middle Ages. He dislikes what he terms "Saxon" architecture,[65] by which, of course, he means Norman or Romanesque, and he presents Gothic architecture as developing to its perfection in the Tudor period, until it was replaced in the reign of James I by the "mongrel" architecture of the early Renaissance, as exemplified in the early work of Inigo Jones and his contemporaries. His letters contain frequent and contemptuous references to this "bastard" style of design, although Strawberry Hill itself contained forms dangerously akin to the hybrid productions of the early seventeenth century.

Walpole's criticisms of buildings, in his letters, are still more indicative of his tastes. At Gloucester cathedral he admires the "beautifully light" exterior of the cathedral, the cloister, and the tombs, but he despises the heavy Norman nave. At Worcester, which he describes as "pretty," he also admires the tombs. He likes the "smugness" of Winchester, where tombs again delight him. Bristol cathedral he describes as "neat," but he dislikes Bath Abbey because it is glaring and full of modern tablets. He prefers Lincoln to York in some respects, but he likes the screen at York. The ornaments of Canterbury please him, especially the tomb of Archbishop Warham, which he describes as "being, I believe, the last example of unbastardized Gothic."[66] The

[65] *Works* (1798), III, 93; *Letters,* ed. Toynbee, VII, 303.
[66] *Letters,* ed. Toynbee, VII, 304.

façade of Rheims meets with his approval, especially the "filigraine" towers.[67] He is interested in the enamels in the ante-chamber of the Sainte-Chapelle in Paris. He likes the spectacular façade of Peterborough cathedral.

Among English castles, he apparently prefers Warwick, a significant fact, because Warwick is really less medieval than Elizabethan. Kenilworth he considers "awful," but he dislikes its situation. Castle Ashby he describes as "magnificently trist," but he complains that the bad little panes of glass exclude all objects. The tombs at Arundel please him. He expressed a desire to see the Welsh castles, principally for genealogical purposes.

The abbeys which he visited seem, for the most part, to have pleased him. As we have seen, he was delighted with Netley. He also liked Newstead. One notices that Walpole, in his descriptions of these various buildings, is always interested in the details, and especially the tombs, probably because they were so elaborately ornamented. He did not love Gothic architecture for its structural qualities but for its exquisite detail, and therefore he preferred the late Gothic, where detail ran riot, to the more sober productions of the earlier styles.

In spite of his love for Gothic, Walpole was not intolerant of Renaissance architecture. The one period which he thoroughly detested was that of transition from Gothic to Renaissance, the "bastard" style of the reign of James I. He expresses great contempt for Hardwick because it belonged to that unfortunate period. Blenheim also aroused his scorn. Contemporary French architecture struck him as being unbearably monotonous,[68] and he criticizes the Tuscan villas because their architecture was too regular for their situation. On the other hand, he remarks that the Palladian

[67] *Works*, 1798, III, 99.
[68] *Letters*, VI, 376-7.

house of Meresworth almost lures him from the Gothic. His own constructions were not exclusively Gothic; he writes that the small cottage, across the road from Strawberry Hill, is to have nothing Gothic about it because it is separate from the main house. Nevertheless he seems to regard Gothic as the suitable style for small buildings:

> The Grecian is only proper for magnificent and public buildings. Columns and all their beautiful ornaments look ridiculous when crowded into a closet or a cheese-cake-house. The variety is little, and admits no charming irregularities. I am almost as fond of the *Sharawaggi*, or Chinese want of symmetry, in buildings, as in ground or gardens.[69]

Apparently he was not averse to Oriental architecture, since he remarks that English garden architecture is becoming charming through the addition of Gothic and Chinese forms. Indeed he comments upon some perspectives in the Alhambra that might be "improved into Gothic."[70] The creations of Batty Langley and Hallet at Latimers, however, fill him with contempt, and he says that "half the ornaments are of his [Langley's] bastard Gothic, and half of Hallet's mongrel Chinese." He considers even classical forms as capable of translation into Gothic, as he shows when writing to Sir Horace Mann that he is designing a tomb for Mann's brother. "The thought," he says, "was my own, adopted from the antique columbaria and applied to Gothic."

His conception of Gothic ornament is rather naive, since he says[71] that except for the pinnacle, it consisted simply in trefoil, quatrefoil, etc., forms. Apparently, however, he considers these decorations superior to the earlier ones of the Norman style, because, in his outline of a proposed history of

[69] *Ibid.*, II, 433.
[70] *Ibid.*, X, 394.
[71] *Ibid.*, VII, 304.

Gothic architecture, he says that he would show how the Saxons plastered and zig-zagged their arches, "and then how better ornaments crept in, till the beautiful Gothic arrived at its perfection."[72] Evidently he thinks that this perfection was attained in the fifteenth and sixteenth centuries, since it is the work of these centuries that he copies in his constructions and admires in his writings most lavishly. He was by no means consistent in his comments, however, for he remarks that "in Queen Elizabeth's reign there was scarce any architecture at all."

Consistency, indeed, is something which is not to be expected from Walpole, at least when he is dealing with architecture. He says of Strawberry Hill:

> We pique ourselves upon nothing but simplicity, and have no carvings, gildings, paintings, inlayings, or tawdry businesses.[73]

When one turns from this statement to look at pictures of Strawberry Hill, thick with ornament from the fretted ceilings to the elaborate floors, and when one reads the following paragraph in Paget Toynbee's edition of the Strawberry Hill Accounts:

> Besides the Mr. Smith to whom £49 3s. 1½d. was paid for gilding the Cabinet, Walpole employed several other gilders; namely, Guichard, who was paid £86 6s. on Aug. 26, 1763; the unnamed gilder, who was paid £95 8s. on Oct. 27, 1769 for gilding the Round Tower; Vial, who was paid £34 6s. 7½d. on April 27, 1771, and £57 11s. 6d. on Aug. 12, 1773; and Nicholls, who was paid £115 1s. 9d. in the spring of 1773; making a total for gilding alone of £437 16s.

one is inclined to be extremely suspicious of Walpole's veracity. The explanation is, of course, in this instance that

[72] *Ibid.*, VII, 303.
[73] *Ibid.*, III, 168.

the passage boasting of simplicity was written before Walpole's plans had developed to the ambitious form which they were later to assume.

If Walpole is inconsistent in his statements, he would be expected to be ten times more inconsistent in his practice; and such is the case in his constructions at Strawberry Hill. Incongruity reigns supreme in all his designs. He puts sharply pointed windows beneath square drip-stones, and classical furniture and ornaments in pseudo-Gothic rooms. He uses that most un-Gothic device, the skylight, in the hall and the Cabinet. The chapel in the garden has a magnificent stone façade and brick sides. The significant fact with regard to Walpole's tastes is that so much of the detail belongs to the late Gothic period. It is plain that the Perpendicular style was the one which he preferred, although he did not care for its latest and crudest productions.

In this respect, he was but following the taste of his time. Perpendicular Gothic was the only Gothic style to be used at all extensively by the architects of the early Gothic revival. Its vertical effect and its peculiar richness of ornament, constituted its principal attraction in the eighteenth century. The illustrators of the period frequently use Perpendicular buildings when they want to represent Gothic architecture, perhaps because the straight lines of Perpendicular tracery were easiest to engrave. Furthermore, such *tours-de-force* as Henry VII's chapel at Westminster, or the King's College Chapel at Cambridge were praised even when Gothic architecture itself was in disrepute.

The Perpendicular style is notoriously the least structural and the most ornate of the Gothic styles. Nothing could be more unstructural or ornate than the vaulting of Henry VII's chapel at Westminster, with its pendants moored to iron rods to keep them from crashing to the pavement below, yet this was vaulting which Walpole copied for the ceiling of his gallery. Because the Perpendicular style permitted light walls, numerous windows, and elaborate ornament, it was precisely the style to appeal to Walpole, who desired all those things. Moreover it was this style which produced most of the ornate cathedral tombs and chantries which provided Walpole with so many designs; the more elaborate the tombs, the more attractive they were to him. Fretwork and filigree of any sort delighted him.

His tastes were not completely stationary, however, for certain changes appear in his later years. As Yvon remarks,[74] the architecture of the garden chapel and of the offices shows that Walpole was acquiring a purer conception of Gothic style in his later years. It is also to be noticed that these buildings are not only purer Gothic but almost pure Perpendicular. Probably Walpole was learning from the work of abler contemporaries and from a study of genuine Gothic buildings. His break with Bentley, who assisted him in the designs for the earlier alterations to Strawberry Hill, probably accounted also for the change in style, because Bentley was not an archaeologist, and Walpole himself showed decided tendencies in that direction—tendencies which Mr. Kenneth Clark deplores because they turned the Gothic revival into unintelligent copying rather than free adaptation and design. As the years passed, Walpole began to lose interest in architecture, however. In 1771 he writes that he does not get half the pleasure which he used to derive from visiting churches and monasteries. In the last years of his life he did practically no building.

Knowing Walpole's nature, one would soon be able to guess what his architectural tastes would be. A careful student of his character, as revealed in his letters, would know, without being told, that Walpole would prefer elaborate and showy ornament to austere simplicity, that he would

---

[74] *La Vie d'un Dilettante*, Paris, 1924, pp. 548-9.

be more interested in obtaining an effect than in doing a careful and consistent piece of work. It was almost inevitable that his preference would be for one of the ornate styles; either late Gothic or Baroque. It was only to be expected that Gothic structure with its stupendous feats of engineering, and its intricate system of thrusts and counter-thrusts would mean less to him than would Gothic ornament. The creator of Strawberry Hill and *The Castle of Otranto* was more interested in the clothing of architecture than in its skeleton, and it was because Perpendicular Gothic furnished such elaborate clothing that it appealed to Walpole's taste. Also, he loved comfort, and so we do not find him erecting a desolate monstrosity like Fonthill Abbey. Strawberry Hill is essentially a snug little manor-house, dressed up in Gothic clothes. The limits of Walpole's imagination are well shown by the fact that he could get excitement from such feeble objects as Strawberry Hill and *The Castle of Otranto*.

Walpole's influence upon the Gothic of his contemporaries was doubtless great. His personal popularity and the accessibility of his home brought many visitors to Strawberry Hill. Direct proofs of his influence can be seen at such homes as Arbury, which was Gothicized by Sir Roger Newdigate about 1780. The fan vaulting of the dining-room ceiling is strongly reminiscent of the vaulting in Walpole's gallery, and the book-shelves of Newdigate's library obviously ape the absurd flamboyant arches in the library at Strawberry Hill. Walpole calls Lee Priory "a child of Strawberry prettier than the parent."[75]

By the end of the eighteenth century, English architecture was in a chaotic state. The Gothic and Greek revivals were in full swing, and they were accompanied by the Oriental

---

[75] *Letters*, ed. Toynbee, XV, 309.

fashion which was largely the result of Sir William Chambers' *Designs of Chinese Buildings* (1757) and *Dissertation on Oriental Gardening* (1772). Fortunately, the Oriental craze was largely confined to garden pavilions, such as the pagoda at Kew, but it occasionally invaded the house in the form of furniture design and interior decoration.

The Gothic enthusiasm of the century was such that nearly every architect, however opposed he might be in theory to the style, was called upon to design buildings in it. Sir William Chambers built Milton Abbey, and Robert Adam designed Gothic interiors at Alnwick for the Duchess of Northumberland. The interesting church at Croome is also attributed to him, apparently on good authority.[76] This tiny building has a good Gothic tower, but a disappointing interior with a low plaster vault. Wyatt, the architect of Fonthill Abbey, whose best work was done in the classic manner, was called upon to design many Gothic buildings. Ashridge is probably the most striking example which survives, although Wyatt is principally notorious for Fonthill and for his activities in the English cathedrals.

William Beckford's romance, *Vathek*, was suggested by the Egyptian Hall of Beckford's paternal mansion. In its stupendous and overpowering qualities, however, the Hall of Eblis in *Vathek* is closely akin to Beckford's new home at Fonthill Abbey, Wyatt's masterpiece. The peculiarly terrifying qualities of Fonthill must be attributed to Beckford's genius rather than to Wyatt's. The beginning of this amazing structure was in 1796, when Beckford commissioned Wyatt to build him a ruined convent. This structure was subsequently enlarged by the addition of a huge octagon tower, and various wings, and finally Beckford made it his

---

[76] Arthur T. Bolton: *The Architecture of Robert and James Adam* (1758-1794), 1922, I, 187.

permanent residence. It passed through many vicissitudes; the great tower blew down once, and on another occasion there was a fire. Vast armies of workmen were employed, and the building arose with a rapidity which endangered its safety. An unscrupulous contractor neglected to provide the foundations which had been specified and paid for. Great length, excessive narrowness, and towering height characterized all parts of the building. Kenneth Clark estimates that the north and south wings were about four hundred feet long and twenty-five feet wide, that the great hall was one hundred and twenty feet high, and that the tower was over two hundred and seventy-six feet in height. The style of architecture was, in the main, Perpendicular, although most of the arches had sharp points that are not usually found in late Gothic work. The exterior bristled with the usual turrets and pinnacles, all dominated by the vast octagonal tower—vast only in height, for its breadth was alarmingly small. The eight pinnacles which surmounted the tower were so slender and tall that a network of tie-rods was necessary to keep them from falling. The great western hall had an open-timbered roof of Perpendicular design, and it communicated with an inner hall by a great stairway leading to a vast arch, which, from the scale of the engravings, must have been at least six times as tall as it was wide. Similarly overpowering arches appeared in the distance, with some ribbed vaulting between them.

This astounding structure was indeed appropriate for the creator of the Hall of Eblis (one of the most "sublime" buildings in the eighteenth-century novel), and it must have been as uncomfortable as it was awe-inspiring. Visitors were probably terrified, not only by its stupendous architecture, but also by the fact that it looked ready to topple over at any moment. Finally, in 1825, it did, when Beckford had long since moved elsewhere, and the house was the property of a Mr. Farquhar. The wood and plaster of which the tower was composed were so light that its fall made scarcely any noise at all.

To sum up the architectural merits of Fonthill, one cannot do better than to quote Mr. Clark's paragraph:

> As scenery it is superb. All that the eighteenth century demanded of Gothic—unimpeded perspectives, immense height, the sublime, in short—was present at Fonthill, and present more lavishly, perhaps, than in real medieval buildings. Even we, who pride ourselves on classicism, cannot be quite dead to this sudden outburst of romantic rhetoric. We know very well that the plaster tower is mere trumpery, but its sudden vehemence sweeps away our judgment; as Berlioz may suddenly sweep us away from Haydn, and El Greco's nightmare vision of Toledo seduce our eyes from the judicious Poussin.

Beckford, as Mr. Clark suggests, was more interested in effects than in form. The architecture in *Vathek* is vaguely Oriental rather than Gothic, and Beckford's tower at Bath was not Gothic, but a pseudo-classical affair, one hundred and thirty feet high, ending in a cast-iron model of the Temple of Lysicrates at Athens. Stylistically, he was not so great a Gothic purist as Walpole.

To Beckford, as to Walpole, it has been necessary to give considerable attention, because they were such prominent figures in the Gothic revival, and because both wrote romances with important architectural setting. There are many parallels and contrasts between the two men: both were eccentric, both lived alone most of the time, both reached a good old age, and both were writers, amateur architects, and collectors. There the resemblance ends. Their architectural tastes were certainly very different. Walpole was concerned with ornament, while Beckford was interested in grandiose design. The rooms of Strawberry Hill are small

and low—even smaller and lower than they look in the engravings—whereas the halls of Fonthill were vast and lofty. The visitor to Strawberry Hill entered a low door into a cramped little hallway, while the few people who were permitted to disturb Beckford's privacy entered the portals of a lofty arch. The tower of Strawberry Hill (it has since been raised) was originally barely high enough to overlook the low roofs of the rest of the structure, but the tower of Fonthill soared high above the turrets of a building which was itself dangerously tall. No wonder that Beckford called Strawberry Hill "a species of gothic mousetrap!" Nevertheless, despite these differences, and the interval of nearly fifty years which elapsed between the two constructions, both buildings are stamped with the defects of the early Gothic revival. Both were built of shoddy materials, masquerading as masonry. Both had lean turrets and attenuated pinnacles, giving the exterior a pin-cushion effect. Both were mainly based on Perpendicular Gothic, and both were crowded with bad ornament. There was no attempt at good craftsmanship in either building. Walpole seems to have employed men whose customary work was in the Georgian style, though, with some trouble, he might have found provincial masons who were still accustomed to Gothic work. Gayfere, the mason of Westminster Abbey, seems to have been the only workman at Strawberry Hill who might possibly have had some traditional connection with genuine Gothic architecture.

The influence of Strawberry Hill on the Gothic revival was much greater than the influence of Fonthill, just as *The Castle of Otranto* is more important than *Vathek* in the development of architectural setting in the novel. Walpole had the advantage of time—he built and wrote when the Gothic revival was more of a novelty than it was in Beckford's day. Strawberry Hill was near London, and Walpole was usually hospitable to visitors, indeed he was proud to exhibit his miniature castle. Fonthill Abbey, on the other hand, was more remote, and its owner insured privacy by erecting a twelve-foot wall around his estate. Beckford did not encourage visitors. Also Strawberry Hill, though Gothic, was livable, and therefore was more widely imitated than Fonthill, which must have been an exceedingly uncomfortable residence. Walpole's social position as son of a Prime Minister, as a leader of fashion, and eventually as Earl of Orford was much higher than that of Beckford, who was the son of a Lord Mayor, a very unsocial person, and a commoner—moreover there was unpleasant gossip afloat about the mysteries of Fonthill.

The literary structures of both men resembled their actual buildings. Otranto is as tame as Strawberry Hill, and the Hall of Eblis is as terrifying as Fonthill Abbey. Moreover, both these imaginary buildings were suggested by the residences of their respective authors, though the Egyptian Hall which suggested the Hall of Eblis belonged to the original Georgian and not to the later Gothic Fonthill. In his preface to the *Description of Strawberry Hill*, Walpole says that his home is "a very proper habitation of, as it was the scene that inspired, the author of the Castle of Otranto." Similarly Beckford told Cyrus Redding of the Hall of Eblis that:

> You could scarcely find anything like the Hall of Eblis in the Eastern writings, for that was my own. Old Fonthill had a very ample, lofty, loud-echoing hall, one of the largest in the kingdom. Numerous doors led from it into the various parts of the house, through dim, winding passages. It was from that I introduced the hall—the idea of the Hall of Eblis being generated from my own. My imagination magnified and coloured it with the Eastern character.[77]

Walpole and Beckford in their capacity as architects have been given what may seem a disproportionate share of emphasis because they typified two phases of the Gothic

[77] Lewis Melville, *op. cit.*, p. 142.

revival. Of course, neither was wholly responsible for his extraordinary house, for Walpole relied upon Bentley and Chute, and Beckford employed Wyatt, but both men gave so much personal attention to the design of their respective residences that the work may in a sense be called their own. Also, the fact that both were authors, and that they were both creators of architectural setting in the eighteenth-century novel gives to their architectural careers an importance which those careers, in themselves, certainly do not deserve.

Since the principal sources and expressions of Gothic enthusiasm in the eighteenth century have been reviewed, it is time to add a few words about the general architectural interests of the century. The middle of the eighteenth century was a period of considerable prosperity in England, and there was plenty of money available for building purposes. The architecture of the time was mostly secular, because religion, except for unarchitectural Methodism, was in a dormant state. Great country houses, and magnificent town residences, not only in London but in the provincial centers, notably Bath, arose in profusion. Gentlemen took a personal interest in the architecture of their houses and the adornment of their grounds; they did not leave such matters entirely to hired artists; and the Gothic revival was largely the work of amateur architects. Indeed, if the Gothic revival had been left to professional architects, it would never have developed at all; for the great architects of the century turned to it only under compulsion. The builders of Gothic houses were men like Miller, Walpole, Newdigate, and Barrett—Adam, Chambers, and their fellows dabbled in Gothic only to please an insistent patron.

Moreover, the English public was generally interested in architecture in the eighteenth century. The erection of the Adelphi and of Somerset House aroused great controversies. Even so unaesthetic a person as Dr. Johnson made many comments upon the buildings which he saw. The frequent architectural descriptions in travel literature, the numerous archaeological publications, and, above all, the long architectural descriptions in the novel all testify to the widespread architectural interest of the time. When the public was thus awakened to the subject, it is not surprising that the Gothic, Greek, and Oriental fashions should achieve quick popularity, or that people should demand architectural descriptions even in fiction.

The novels themselves often recognize the extraordinary architectural activity of the time. For instance, *The Munster Village* (1778) says that:

> A love of play, and building, are the characteristics of this age—our sex imitates the other as far as they can in the former—and having no *terra firma* for the latter, and not contented with the ancient custom of castle-building, erect fabrics on their heads three stories high. The rage of building is so great, that nothing can check their ardour in it, although it has been the ruin of many individuals; and there are at present (it is said) fifteen hundred uninhabited houses in the two parishes of Saint Mary-le-bone and Pancras.[78]

Things architectural were supposed to be interesting to every fashionable gentleman, and Thomas Vaughan's *Fashionable Follies* (1781) describes the plight of the young Englishman at Rome who was "obliged, much against my inclination, to spend whole mornings in viewing statues, obelisks, and triumphal arches, without number."[79] The young man complains that:

> I was absolutely wearied, fatigued, and tired to death with seeing all these things, and would gladly have paid double the sum agreed on, to have been at rest, but must then have given up every hope of being looked upon as a man of taste and virtue. . . .

[78] II, 106. By Lady M. Walker.
[79] II, 184-5.

Sources of the Interest in Architecture 49

Henry Boswell, in the preface to his *Antiquities* (1785), says that "without a sufficient Share of this kind of Knowledge, no Person can make a respectable Figure in Life."

The Gothic revival and the Gothic romance were both products of the same general trend, and to some extent they paralleled each other. Mr. Clark is not precisely correct in saying that the two were utterly divergent, and that not until the time of Fonthill was architecture intended to "make one's hair stand on end." To be sure, the buildings of the early Gothic revival were livable and pretty, and, to modern eyes at least, not too full of horror and gloom (although Walpole writes that "one has a satisfaction in imprinting the gloomth of abbeys and cathedrals on one's house")[80]—but apparently the buildings of the early Gothic romances were the same. Otranto, with its oriel window and its great staircase, is more Tudor than medieval, while Lovel Castle, in Clara Reeve's *Old English Baron*, seems almost Renaissance, or at least Elizabethan. Even Mrs. Radcliffe's castles, gloomy as they sometimes are, have huge windows commanding "prospects" of mountain scenery, and Mrs. Radcliffe herself admired the "hoary" towers[81]—of Hardwick, a Renaissance building! Mrs. Charlotte Smith's best architectural works are Tudor manor-houses, and she wrote a sonnet about the "towers sublime"—of Penshurst! It was not that the novelists were consciously describing Tudor or Renaissance buildings, but that they often classed as medieval and terrifying, buildings which we consider to be comparatively modern, and quite unexciting. The novelists were not architectural experts, and when even the archaeologists made so many ridiculous blunders, we cannot expect architectural accuracy from writers of fiction. The same ignorance prevails today: to most people, anything plausibly old, with a tower and a

---

[80] *Letters*, ed. Toynbee, III, 151.
[81] *Journey made in the Summer of 1794*, 1795, p. 371.

few pointed windows, will pass for a castle, and, in America, anything painted white with a few columns on the front is called Colonial architecture.

In tracing the sources of the Gothic enthusiasm of the eighteenth century, the genealogical, picturesque, sublime, sentimental, and dramatic aspects of this enthusiasm were discussed, and two of the three main products of the Gothic fashion were described. These two were works on archaeology, and the Gothic revival in architecture. The third expression—the literary—remains, and also the literary sources which helped to foster the Gothic revival. The Gothic setting of Shakespeare and Spenser undoubtedly did much to encourage the Gothic revival, and so did the "romantic" poetry of the middle part of the eighteenth century, and the writings of Bishop Hurd, the Wartons, and others. Nevertheless, Gothic architecture is not so obtrusively prominent a part of these writings that the literary influences of the century can be called the main source of the Gothic revival. They were a contributing source, doubtless, but it is extremely improbable that the Gothic setting of Shakespeare or Milton, or the Gothic references of Thomson, Collins, Gray, and their fellows could have started a vogue for medieval architecture unless other factors, such as the ones discussed at the beginning of this chapter, had been at work. Although generalizations are necessarily somewhat inaccurate, it is perhaps best to say that the trend of contemporary taste, influenced by these various factors, turned towards an appreciation of Gothic architecture, and that the Gothic setting of the English poets suggested ways of turning this Gothic enthusiasm to literary purposes in the novel. The discussion of the purely literary sources of architectural setting will be limited to those authors whom the writers of Gothic romances certainly knew, and whose work is actually quoted in connection with their architectural descriptions. To enumerate all the architectural references which the novelists might have known would be futile, for such references are to be found in all literatures and in every period. It is enough to indicate the architectural descriptions which were certainly familiar to the novelists, and which may well have influenced their work.

The first literary source with which we are confronted is Shakespeare. This statement may seem absurd, at the first glance, because Shakespeare obviously was not keenly interested in buildings, and his actual references to them, all told, would scarcely fill more than a page of ordinary print. Nevertheless, these brief references have an importance quite out of proportion to their scanty numbers.

They are important, in the first place, because they make it clear that most of Shakespeare's tragedies and histories were supposed to take place in a medieval setting. This statement applies not only to such plays as *Macbeth*, where the background is obviously a castle, but even to *Julius Caesar*, where one would least expect to find anything Gothic. However, when one finds Shakespeare, in *Richard II*, attributing the tower of London to the Romans—"Julius Caesar's ill-erected tower"—it is not surprising to hear him describe ancient Rome in terms more appropriate to Elizabethan London:

> Many a time and oft
> Have you climb'd up to walls and battlements,
> To towers and windows, yea, to chimney-tops,
> Your infants in your arms, and there have sat
> The live-long day, with patient expectation,
> To see great Pompey pass the streets of Rome.[82]

In *Titus Andronicus*, a Goth indulges in a pastime which was to become very popular in eighteenth-century England:

> Renowned Lucius, from our troops I strayed,
> To gaze upon a ruinous monastery—

[82] *Julius Caesar*, Act I, Scene i.

Timon of Athens mentions the "great towers" of Athens, and more towers appear in *Troilus and Cressida*:

> Up to the eastern tower,
> Whose height commands as subject all the vale.

The towers of Troy are mentioned also in *The Rape of Lucrece*.

It was natural that Shakespeare should imagine Rome, Athens, and Troy to be bristling with towers, because the architecture with which he himself was familiar was almost entirely medieval. In the early Jacobean period, the Renaissance had barely appeared in England, and its earlier examples still retained many Gothic characteristics. Moreover, the greater part of his audience was acquainted with no cities which did not have a more or less medieval aspect, and the middle ages had left so many vestiges behind it, that there were few such cities to be seen. Consequently, towers and battlements appear in Shakespearean plays, regardless of time or place.

In *Hamlet* and *Macbeth*, the setting is, of course, entirely medieval, although the references to buildings are few and meager. The setting for much of *Othello* is a castle in Cyprus; Montano refers to "our battlements," and Othello exclaims: "Come, let us to the castle." Juliet cries:

> O, bid me leap, rather than marry Paris,
> From off the battlements of yonder tower.

—a quotation which is actually used for a chapter heading in one of the Gothic romances.[83] The historical plays of Shakespeare are all somewhat concerned with castles, and in two of them (*Henry IV*, Part II, and *Richard II*) the castles are in a ruinous condition.

---

[83] *The Castle of Beeston*, Chapter XVI.

Sources of the Interest in Architecture 53

These references to buildings are very slight, and they perform no important service in the plays where they are to be found. The architecture of Elsinore, apparently, is not among the causes of Hamlet's melancholy, and Duncan is so far from being depressed by the appearance of Macbeth's castle, that he says it "hath a pleasant air." Had *Macbeth* been the work of Mrs. Radcliffe, Duncan would have been seized with dismal forebodings at the first sight of the frowning towers; as it is, the only dismal reference to the castle comes from Lady Macbeth.

Evidently there is little resemblance between the architecture of Shakespeare and that of the Gothic romances, but lack of resemblance need not imply lack of connection. Shakespeare was very popular in the eighteenth century, and his popularity with the writers of Gothic romances, in particular, is shown by the quotations at their chapter headings. From nineteen Gothic romances[84] or novels with important architectural setting, representing the work of fifteen authors, I have compiled a list of 561 poetical quotations. Of these, 157, or more than a quarter of the total, are from Shakespeare. The author next in popularity is Thomson, with only thirty-seven quotations. This list does not prove conclusively that the novelists were thoroughly acquainted with Shakespeare, but it indicates, at least, that he was the author to whom they turned most readily for their quotations. For this purpose, *Hamlet* and *Macbeth*

[84] M. G. Lewis: *The Monk*; Mrs. Radcliffe: *The Romance of the Forest, The Mysteries of Udolpho, The Italian*; Mrs. Smith: *The Old Manor House, The Banished Man*; Mrs. Roche: *Clermont, The Children of the Abbey*; Mrs. Sleath: *The Orphan of the Rhine*; Francis Lathom: *The Midnight Bell*; John Bird: *The Castle of Hardayne*; Charles Lucas: *The Castle of St. Donats*; John Palmer: *The Haunted Cavern*; Mrs. Robinson: *Hubert de Sevrac*; *The Church of St. Siffrid*; *The Castle of Beeston*; *The Castle on the Rock*; Catherine Selden: *Count de Santerre*; and *Count di Novini*.

seem to have been most in demand, as well they might be, since their tragic themes, their use of the supernatural, and their implied Gothic setting made them particularly acceptable.

It is the atmosphere, rather than the actual architectural references, which seems to have attracted the novelists to Shakespeare; they loved the emotions of terror or awe so often associated with the great tragedies. To Mrs. Radcliffe, Shakespearean influence was more directly applied to architecture. She seems to have visualized the ghost of Hamlet's father at almost every castle she saw. On her visit to Windsor, she says:

> What particularly strikes at Windsor is the length of terrace in the east, thus seen by moonlight; the massy towers, four in perspective; .... Then the north terrace stretching and finally turning away from them towards the west, where the high dark towers crown it. It was on this terrace, surely, that Shakespeare received the first hint of the time for the appearance of his ghost.[85]

Of Warwick Castle, she says:

> Before those great gates and underneath these towers, Shakespeare's ghost might have stalked.[86]

Mr. Simpson, a character in Mrs. Radcliffe's *Gaston de Blondeville*, also couples Warwick with Shakespeare:

> "No, no; I do not recall any thing of what you tell me; but you were talking a little while ago of Hamlet and towers; now, if you want towers that would do honour to Hamlet, go to Warwick Castle."

Evidently Gothic castles were strongly associated in Mrs. Radcliffe's mind with the setting of *Hamlet*, and, since she uses Shakespearean quotations so often in her Gothic

[85] *Gaston de Blondeville*, 1826, I, 98 (*Memoir*).
[86] *Ibid.*, I, 60.

romances, the inference is that she found at least a little inspiration in Shakespeare for her architectural setting. From this very ghost scene she quotes a few lines at the head of the chapter in *Udolpho* describing the Count de Villefort's visit to the haunted wing of his castle.

This association of castles and ruins with tragic scenes and melancholy emotions is the only contribution of Shakespeare to the setting of the Gothic romances. It was probably an additional inducement to the novelists to use Gothic setting for their tales of terror, when such a setting was associated in their minds with the tragedies which they had read. Most of the great Shakespearean tragedies and histories, as well as Middleton's *Changeling*, Marlowe's *Edward II*, Webster's *Duchess of Malfi*, and other Elizabethan plays, had castles for their setting. Congreve's *Mourning Bride* has an important passage about a dismal and awe-inspiring temple. In the eighteenth century we find Gothic setting in such tragedies as Home's *Douglas* and Walpole's *Mysterious Mother*, which are both sometimes quoted for chapter headings in the Gothic romances. Consequently, when there were so many well-known precedents for the use of castles and ruins in tragic scenes, it would be natural for castles and ruins themselves to become associated with tragedy, and with the emotions of horror and awe. Of this vague nature is the influence of Shakespeare upon the setting of the Gothic romances, but although the influence is vague, it must not be ignored.

The connection of the Gothic romances with Shakespeare, though somewhat tenuous, is supported by the 157 quotations at chapter headings; in the same list, there are only seven quotations from Spenser. Consequently there is little basis for the statement, sometimes heard, that Spenser's castles influenced the Gothic romances. Indeed it is very doubtful if the eighteenth-century novelists possessed the patience to read much of Spenser; Dr. Drake, certainly one of the most erudite writers of Gothic fiction, remarks that many cantos of Spenser "must be pronounced both tedious and disgusting."[87] Other Elizabethans are even less often quoted than Spenser in the Gothic romances, although many of the dramatists were known in the eighteenth century, and Webster's lines:

> I do love these ancient ruins,
> We never tread upon them but we set
> Our foot upon some reverend history[88]

are quoted upon the title-page of *The Ruins of Netley Abbey*, published in London in 1765.

Milton, with thirty quotations, stands next to Thomson in the list of poetical extracts in the romances, but his references to architecture are few (the most famous one is that featuring the "storied windows, richly dight" in *Il Penseroso*), and they had little or no effect upon the novelists. Other seventeenth-century writers were seldom quoted—there are twelve quotations from Dryden, three from Butler, two from Congreve, and one each from Waller and Cowley. One passage from Congreve's *Mourning Bride* (the very passage which Dr. Johnson proposed for the honor of "most poetical paragraph" in English poetry) is interesting for its use of architecture:

> How reverend is the face of this tall pile,
> Whose ancient pillars rear their marble heads,
> To bear aloft its arched and ponderous roof,
> By its own weight made steadfast and immoveable,
> Looking tranquillity! It strikes an awe
> And terror on my aching sight; the tombs
> And monumental caves of death look cold,
> And shoot a chillness to my trembling heart.

[87] *Literary Hours*, 3rd ed., 1804, II, 155.
[88] *The Duchess of Malfi*, Act V, Scene iii.

> Give me thy hand, and let me hear they voice;
> Nay, quickly speak to me, and let me hear
> Thy voice—my own affrights me with its echoes.

Here, certainly, is a good example of the emotional use of architectural setting, and it is quoted in at least two Gothic romances.[89]

Another good example is Pope's *Eloisa to Abelard*, a popular poem throughout the eighteenth century. Its setting is Eloisa's convent:

> In these lone walls, (their days' eternal bound)
> These moss-grown domes with spiry turrets crown'd,
> Where awful arches make a noon-day night,
> And the dim windows shed a solemn light—

From this poem, the line "long-sounding aisles, and intermingled graves" is misquoted by Charlotte Smith in describing the abbey of Kilbrodie in *The Young Philosopher*,[90] while a couplet:

> Deepens the murmur of the falling floods
> And breathes a browner horror on the woods

is misquoted in Mrs. Smith's *Solitary Wanderer*,[91] and two other lines are quoted in the notes to her elegiac sonnets, showing that Mrs. Smith, who was one of the foremost creators of architectural setting in the eighteenth century, was well acquainted with *Eloisa to Abelard*. Horace Walpole, in one of his letters,[92] calls Strawberry Hill "Paraclete," after Eloisa's convent.

---

[89] *The Castle of Beeston* (1798) and Louisa Stanhope's *Treachery* (1815).
[90] 1798, II, 101.
[91] 1800, I, 3.
[92] Ed. Toynbee, III, 151.

Sources of the Interest in Architecture

The poetry of the middle part of the century is full of references to ruins, usually employed to adorn landscape descriptions.[93] This poetry is frequently quoted at the chapter-headings of Gothic romances, showing that eighteenth-century verse was well known to the novelists. Except for the quotations from Shakespeare, a few French and Italian and Latin quotations, and a very few from seventeenth-century poets, all the poetical quotations come from English verse of the eighteenth century. In our list, Thomson, with thirty-seven quotations, is second in popularity to Shakespeare alone, and Collins, with nineteen quotations, comes after Milton, in the fourth place. There are only three quotations at the chapter headings from Ossian, but numerous quotations and imitations of Ossian in the text show the popularity of the Ossianic poems. Ossian probably would have been quoted more frequently had the poems appeared in metrical form. It is evident that poetry of the so-called "romantic" school was the favorite verse of the Gothic novelists.

There are numerous connections between these quotations and architecture. Lines from Dyer about mouldering ruins head a chapter in Mrs. Charlotte Smith's *Banished Man*, while a passage from the same poet about "disparting towers" is quoted by Mrs. Regina Maria Roche in *The Children of the Abbey*.[94] A quotation from Warton, mentioning "Gothic churches, vaults, and tombs" heads a chapter in Catherine Selden's *Count de Santerre*. Mrs. Charlotte Smith parodies the opening lines of Gray's *Ode on a Distant Prospect of Eton College* ("Ye distant spires, ye antique towers") in *The Old Manor House*,[95] while another quota-

---

[93] Cf. Reinhard Haferkorn: *Gotik und Ruine in der Englischen Dichtung des Achtzehnten Jahrhunderts*, Leipzig, 1924.
[94] Exeter, 1826, I, Chapter XVIII (in text).
[95] 1793, III, 205.

tion from Gray, referring to "dim cloisters," heads a chapter in Mrs. Radcliffe's *Mysteries of Udolpho.* In a novel called *Emily, or the Fatal Promise,* a description of a ruined abbey[96] is embellished with the famous quotation from Gray's *Elegy:*

> The moping owl does to the moon complain
> Of such as, wand'ring near her secret bow'r,
> Molest her ancient solitary reign.

Dr. Nathan Drake, in the romance called *The Abbey of Clunedale* in his *Literary Hours* (1798-1800), quotes in a foot-note a long description of a typical abbey from Mason's *Notes on the English Garden.* Dr. Drake's attempts at accurate description are an interesting feature of the architectural setting of the novel, but his choice of Mason as an authority must be considered odd, to say the least. Mason's *English Garden* seems to have been well known to the novelists of the latter part of the century, as, indeed were all poems with landscape descriptions.

Two poetical productions of this century must receive special mention because of their connection with the architectural setting of the Gothic romances: the so-called Ossianic poems, published by James Macpherson, and Bishop Percy's *Reliques of Ancient English Poetry.* Both these compilations were alleged to be taken from manuscripts of ancient verse, and both contain much which is of modern authorship. It is useless to enter here into the famous controversy over Ossian, for we are interested, not in the origin of the poems, but in their effect upon the novel.

Ossian's heroes lead a strenuous outdoor life, which apparently affords little opportunity for architectural interests. Only at night do they retire to the banquet hall, to gather around the blazing fire of oak logs, and to listen to the

[96] 1792, I, 17.

strains of the minstrels. The background for their bloody adventures is indeed gloomy, but it is a background composed mostly of glens, caves, and hills, rather than of the works of man. In the few cases where buildings are mentioned, there is a notable absence of concrete detail, together with the implication that the dwellings of these heroes were of an extremely crude nature.

Architecture, in Ossian, is confined to towers, halls, and walls, all of which are distinguished by a luxuriant covering of moss. The towers are described as "mossy" and "windy." The walls are "mossy," "shaded," "dusky," and "mournful." The halls are "mossy," and either "ecchoing" or "silent." After these dismal descriptions, one does not blame the Ossianic heroes for preferring to stay out-of-doors. The buildings are usually placed in wild and picturesque situations. For instance: "We came to the hall of the king, where it rose in the midst of rocks,"[97] or "I came, in my bounding ship, to Balclutha's walls of towers."[98] We are told that: "High walls rise on the banks of Duvranna; and see their mossy towers in the stream; a rock ascends behind them with its bending firs."[99] The interior of the hall is adorned with ancestral weapons: "Go to Lamor's hall: there the arms of our fathers hang."[100] Apparently the roof is supported by columns, for the lovely Morna is told that her arms are like "two white pillars in the halls of the mighty Fingal."[101]

Ossianic architecture is frequently ruined, and almost always desolate. Considering that the poems describe events which took place in the infancy of the race, before the advent of Christianity, it seems rather strange that the build-

[97] *Temora*, 1763, p. 67.
[98] *Fingal*, 1762, p. 130.
[99] *Ibid.*, p. 247.
[100] *Ibid.*, p. 99.
[101] *Ibid.*, p. 8.

ings should at that early date be already in an ancient and dilapidated condition. In the poem called *The War of Caros,* we are informed that "their ancient halls moulder on Balva's bank." In *Calthon and Colmal,* we learn that: "they saw the fallen walls of their fathers; they saw the green thorn in the hall." An old chieftain prophesies: "This lofty house shall fall. Our sons shall not behold the ruins in grass. They shall ask of the aged, 'Where stood the walls of our fathers?'"[102] The perishable nature of Ossianic buildings is exemplified in the case of the deserted Balclutha:

> I have seen the walls of Balclutha, but they were desolate. The fire had resounded in the halls: and the voice of the people is heard no more. The stream of Clutha was removed from its place, by the fall of the walls.— The thistle shook, there, its lonely head: the moss whistled to the wind. The fox looked out, from the windows, the rank grass of the wall waved round his head.—Desolate is the dwelling of Moina, silence is in the house of her fathers.
>
> .... Why dost thou build the hall, son of the winged days? Thou lookest from thy towers today; yet a few years, and the blast of the desart comes; it howls in thy empty court, and whistles round thy half-worn shield.[103]

Dreary winds sweep through these ruined buildings, which must have been rather draughty even before they were ruined:

> Such were the words of Gaul, when he came to Dunlathmon's towers. The gates were open and dark. The winds were blustering in the hall. The trees strowed the threshold with leaves; and the murmur of night is abroad.[104]

[102] *Ibid.,* p. 256, footnote.
[103] *Ibid.,* p. 132.
[104] *Ibid.,* p. 242.

> The blast came rustling through the hall, and gently
> touched my harp. The sound was mournful and low,
> like the song of the tomb.[105]

Some of these quotations from Ossian are strangely reminiscent of the work of a much better known writer, and it is not improbable that in discussing Ossianic influence upon the English novel, we are dealing, not only with Macpherson, but also with the prophet Isaiah!

The melancholy architecture of Ossian was not without effect upon the architecture of the eighteenth-century novel. In Mackenzie's *Julia de Roubigné,* for instance, Ossian is evidently imitated in the lines:

> Where now are Roubigné's little copses, where his winding walks, his nameless rivulets? Where the ivy'd gate of his venerable dwelling, the Gothic windows of his echoing hall?[106]

Mrs. Radcliffe, in *The Romance of the Forest*, quotes directly from Ossian in describing the ruined abbey: "The thistle shook its lonely head; the moss whistled to the wind." Mrs. Roche uses the same quotation, with variations, in *The Children of the Abbey*, when she describes Castle Carberry. In *Clermont,* she quotes the lines beginning: "Why dost thou build the hall, son of the winged days?"[107] Mrs. Sleath, in *The Orphan of the Rhine*, uses another quotation about the thistle when she describes a ruined abbey:

> The thistle was there, on its rock, shedding its aged beard; the old tree groaned in the blast; the murmur of night was abroad.

[105] *Ibid.,* p. 168.
[106] 1777, II, 14.
[107] 1798, III, 116.

John Bird, in *The Castle of Hardayne*, quotes a document supposedly found in the castle, in which occur these Ossianic imitations:

> .... this castle shall mourn in ruins the fate of her injured lord, the owl shall scream round the desolated court, and the bat shall find her habitation in the ruined turret.[108]

The familiar lines: "The thistle shook there its lonely head" are quoted at a chapter heading in the same romance. Charlotte Smith mentions Ossian in her first novel,[109] and Dr. Nathan Drake quotes frequently from Ossian in his critical essays, though not in his Gothic romances.

The actual influence of Ossian upon architectural descriptions in the novel is hard to determine, but it certainly helped to emphasize the ruinous nature of the novelists' castles, and especially the vegetation with which the ruins were so plentifully covered. The authors who mention or quote Ossian are almost always interested in this vegetation: Mrs. Radcliffe decks Udolpho with briony, moss, and nightshade, while Charlotte Smith presents long botanical catalogues, including anything from moss to trees.

The castles of Percy's *Reliques* have a more cheerful air than those of Ossian. The writers of the ballads in this collection took their architecture as a matter of course; castles meant little more to them than apartment houses do to us. If the castle were deserted, it might seem somewhat ghostly and forbidding, but there are no mouldering walls or mournful winds in these buildings; above all, none of the moss with which Ossianic castles were so liberally shrouded. A description of a dungeon suggests the devices of the Gothic romances, but with the difference that the dungeon here

---

[108] 1795, I, 214.
[109] *Emmeline, the Orphan of the Castle*, 3rd ed., 1789, IV, 281.

64 Sources of the Interest in Architecture

pictured is horrible because of its physical discomforts, and not because it is ruined or haunted.

The ruins that were so absent from the text of Percy's *Reliques*, however, are amply supplied by the illustrations. On the title-pages of all three volumes of the first four editions is a vignette depicting a harp leaning against a stunted tree, which rises against a background composed of a Gothic arch, a broken column, and a gable containing a window with Perpendicular tracery. Rough stones in the foreground are partly concealed by vegetation. The frontispiece has Gothic towers in the distance. A battlemented castle with a huge chimney flanks the coat-of-arms at the beginning of the dedicatory epistle. Other Gothic structures, mostly with Perpendicular tracery, appear in the vignettes at the beginning of the different books. Evidently the illustrator was providing the atmosphere which was rather lacking in the text.

Although Percy's *Reliques* were occasionally quoted in the Gothic romances, their influence seems to have been negligible—at least in comparison to that of Ossian—and two of the quotations from Percy come from the modern rather than the ancient part of his collection. The first one is quoted by Charlotte Smith in *The Old Manor House*:

> Theirs nae licht in my lady's bowir,
> Theirs nae licht in the hall—[110]

while from the same ballad (*Hardyknute*), some lines are quoted by Harriet Lee in *Errors of Innocence*, in reference to Lord Melrose's castle.[111] Dr. Drake uses the passage:

> But when he reached his castle gate,
> His gate was hung with black.

at the head of a chapter in *Henry Fitzowen*.[112] There is far less evidence of imitation by the novelists in the case

---

[110] 1793, II, 302.
[111] 1786, III, 202.
[112] *Literary Hours*, 3rd Edition, 1804, I, 155.

of the *Reliques* than in the case of Ossian. It is significant that the novelists should find the gloomy, mossy, and ruinous buildings of the mostly fictitious Ossianic poems more interesting than the more cheerful castles of genuine ballads.

Not only the poetry but the prose of the middle part of the eighteenth century furnished good examples of architectural setting. Walpole was by no means the first author to employ architecture in the novel, although he used it in a different way than his predecessors did. Richardson's Pamela is confined in a mansion which, if less pretentious, is quite as forbidding as the dwellings which were later to terrify the heroines of the Gothic romances:

> About Eight at Night, we enter'd the Court-yard of this handsome, large, old, and lonely Mansion, that looks made for Solitude and Mischief, as I thought, by its Appearance, with all its brown nodding Horrors of lofty Elms and Pines about it: And here, said I to myself, I fear, is to be the Scene of my Ruin, unless God protect me, who is all-sufficient![113]

Clarissa Harlowe is threatened with imprisonment in her Uncle Antony's moated house, which is furnished with a chapel.[114] She fears that the chapel will be the scene of a forced marriage with the detested Mr. Solmes, and evidently her aversion to the moated house proceeds from this fear, rather than from any dislike of the house itself. Indeed she writes:

> And, upon my expressing my averseness to go, [the maid] had the confidence to say, That having heard me often praise the *romantic-ness* of the place, she was *astonish'd* (her hands and eyes lifted up) that I should set myself against going to a house so much in *my taste*.[115]

[113] *Pamela*, 1741, I, 138.
[114] *Clarissa*, 1748, II, 24, 39, 100.
[115] II, 36.

Further evidence of Clarissa's romantic taste is furnished in a foot-note:

> A piece of ruins upon it, the remains of an old chapel, now standing in the midst of the coppice; here and there an overgrown oak, surrounded with ivy and mistletoe, starting up, to sanctify, as it were, the awful solemnness of the place: A spot, too, where a man having been found hanging some years ago, it used to be thought of by us when children, and by the maid-servants, with a degree of terror; as the habitation of owls, ravens, and other ominous birds; and as haunted by ghosts, goblins, spectres. . . . [116]

In *Sir Charles Grandison,* Richardson's architecture is less alarming and more fashionable, since Grandison Hall is apparently a product of the Renaissance. The Lady's Drawing-room, for instance, is hung with green velvet, and the chairs are of the same material, with gilt frames. The house is shaped like an H, and it contains a hall, dining-parlor, two drawing-rooms, study, "oratory" (really a library), and music-parlor. The best bed-chamber is hung with tapestry, which, however, seems to conceal no secret passages.

These architectural references, like most of those which we have encountered so far, are few and meager, but they may have had some effect upon the Gothic romances. The imprisoned heroine is a character often encountered in these romances, and it may well be that the "handsome, large, old, and lonely Mansion" where Pamela was confined, gave suggestions to the novelists for their castles and abbeys. Certainly, resemblances to Pamela's prison can be seen in such novels as *The History of Joshua Trueman and Miss Peggy Williams* (1755), in which the heroine is carried off to a "house, which appeared to her the most desolate she had

[116] II, 273.

ever beheld." Her feelings upon entering it are not more cheerful: "She was in the dark, in a wild and lonesome house, and indeed scarcely any thing seemed capable of adding to the horror of her situation. . ." It appears later that the house is partly in ruins. When Peggy makes her escape, she finds that the environment of the house is suitably terrifying: "The stillness of the night, the shadow of tall trees, and the screaming of owls, gave a romantic horror to all about this distressed wanderer." The resemblance of this place to Pamela's prison, its loneliness, and the surrounding trees, all seem to show that the author of *Joshua Trueman* had *Pamela* in mind when he confined the abducted Peggy in the "wild and lonesome house."

Mrs. Sarah Scott, in *Cornelia* (1750), provides a more interesting place of detention for her heroine:

> She was put into one of those rooms, not uncommonly found in old castles, where the owner may lie concealed, in case intestine feuds and commotions, or other occasions, made it necessary. She soon found herself out of the hearing of any one; the little light she had, came in by the top of the room, which had so much the air of a prison, as would have raised terrors in a mind much less occupied by its own anticipating imagination.

The rescuers of an abducted girl in *The History of Miss Pamela Howard* (1773), find that she has been carried to a house which differs from its predecessors in being both Gothic and ruinous:

> ... when accidentally casting up my eyes down a narrow turning, I saw a large old-fashioned building, which seem'd greatly out of repair, and uninhabited. In the Gothic windows of this ruinous Mansion we beheld what we were in search of.[117]

[117] "By the author of Indiana Danby," II, 131.

The debt of this author to Richardson is made probable by the fact that the names of some of the characters in *Pamela Howard* are borrowed from Richardson's novels. Indeed the novelists of the eighteenth century showed a strange lack of inventiveness in naming their characters; Mrs. Sleath, for instance, in *The Orphan of the Rhine,* names her heroine after the heroine of Mackenzie's *Julia de Roubigné.* There are Louisas and Emmas without number. Even in naming buildings, is this same lack of originality shown; there are at least half a dozen Mowbray Castles, situated anywhere from England to Switzerland, in the novels of the last two decades of the century.

In *The Mutability of Human Life; or Memoirs of Adelaide, Marchioness of Melville* (1777), the heroine's place of confinement is definitely a castle:

> . . . we arrived at a small castle, whose very looks denounced the miseries of despair:—they assisted me out of the chaise, and we entered a hall of immense height and proportionate gloom, which conveyed an additional horror to the soul. We were received in a parlour not more calculated to chear the spirits, by a woman who seemed to officiate as housekeeper. . . .[118]

Not only is this prison a castle, but it has a subterranean passage, showing that the theme of *Pamela* is now being used with the setting of a typical Gothic romance. The "hall of immense height and proportionate gloom" is a feature which occurs in almost every castle of Mrs. Radcliffe and her contemporaries.

The theme of the imprisoned heroine is frequently encountered in later novels. Adeline, in Mrs. Radcliffe's *Romance*

[118] II, 230.

of the Forest, is carried off by the wicked Marquis to his castle. Emily is virtually a prisoner at Udolpho. Ellena is confined in the convent of San Stefano, and later in Spalatro's lonely house by the Adriatic. Mrs. Charlotte Smith's heroines are equally unfortunate: Rosalie is imprisoned in her mother-in-law's castle; Mrs. Glenmorris is confined in the abbey of Kilbrodie, and her daughter is abducted by Darnell, and taken to "an old mansion house of gloomy and gothic appearance."

These abducted heroines are often provided with unpleasant duennas, who seem to be descended from Mrs. Jewkes in *Pamela* and Mrs. Sinclair in *Clarissa.* Like Pamela, they are usually struck with dismal forebodings at the sight of their future prisons; Pamela's remark that her captor's house "looks made for solitude and mischief" is echoed through all the Gothic romances in such sentences as this:

> "Surely, thought I again, this castle was built for deeds of darkness; murder has been familiar with these walls."[119]

In *Disobedience* (1797), the heroine finds to her horror on her arrival at "a large and venerable pile, long neglected by its owners, and now fallen into decay,"[120] that there is a chapel in the garden. This, she fears, will be the scene of a forced wedding to the suitor whom her family are pressing upon her. Such a situation, needless to say, seems to be based upon Clarissa's fear of the chapel in her Uncle Antony's moated house. The heroine of *Disobedience* is later confined in Stanwick Castle, under the charge of the usual elderly duenna, but she succeeds in making her escape through a providentially discovered secret passage.

[119] Mrs. Eliza Parsons: *The Mysterious Warning* (1796), II, 55.
[120] "By the author of Plain Sense," II, 186.

To some extent, the prevalence of the imprisoned heroine can be traced to the romances of chivalry, where damsels are carried off by knights, and confined in castles, only to be liberated by other knights. There is an incident in Mrs. Griffith's *History of Lady Barton* (1771) which seems to be a burlesque upon such a theme.[121] Back to legendary times, castles have been the traditional strongholds in which hapless heroines are confined. Nevertheless, the theme of the imprisoned heroine, as used in the Gothic romances, seems to be derived from Richardson rather than from the romances of chivalry. Richardson was certainly much more familiar than the romances of chivalry to women of the class which produced most of the novelists of the eighteenth century. Even Spenser seems not to have been too popular with them, and Tasso and Ariosto were known to comparatively few. (There are five quotations from Tasso and nine from Ariosto at the chapter headings of the nineteen romances which have been enumerated.) To Pamela's "handsome, large, old, and lonely Mansion" must be traced most of the similar structures where eighteenth-century novelists confined their heroines.

Smollett's novels are little concerned with architecture, except *Humphry Clinker*, which will be discussed later. In *Ferdinand Count Fathom*, the episode where Monimia in the guise of a ghost appears to her lover in church at night is slightly reminiscent of the style of the Gothic romances, but no descriptions are given of the church. Fielding's novels contain little architectural description, although Mr. Allworthy's house is in "the Gothic stile." In the grounds stands the remains of "an old ruined abbey, grown over with ivy."

Sarah Fielding has left a few slight architectural descriptions. In *The History of the Countess of Dellwyn*, she

---

[121] II, 210.

makes contemptuous remarks about the renovation in modern taste of an old castle:

> And thus was this noble ancient Castle, which, in its old Form, struck the Imagination both with Dignity and Simplicity, filled with such trifling Gew-gaws, that it was dangerous to move, lest some of the Clock-work Trumpery should be thrown down, and put out of Joint. . . . [122]

In *The History of Ophelia*, the heroine is imprisoned in the Marchioness's castle, where she arrives "a little before it was dark." (Mrs. Radcliffe would here have inserted a sunset.) The castle is more carefully described than Pamela's lonely mansion:

> We first passed a moat, over which was a bridge so impaired by time and damp, that it threatened us with no small chance of visiting the frogs who inhabited underneath.
> The castle was then tottering with age; and may now perhaps, by the irresistible arm of old Time, be levelled to the ground: therefore I shall speak of the fabrick only in the past tense. The rooms were extremely large, wainscotted with oak, which was turned almost as black as ebony; and all the light that entered was from small casements, with a larger proportion of lead and iron than glass. The chimneys were as big as the arch of a large bridge.[123]

Dr. Johnson's *Rasselas* contains a surprisingly large amount of architectural description, although the author's primary interest is not with buildings:

> "My curiosity, said Rasselas, does not very strongly lead me to survey piles of stone, or mounds of earth; my business is with man. I came hither not to measure fragments of temples, or trace choked aqueducts, but to look upon the various scenes of the present world."

[122] 1759, I, 91.
[123] 1785, II, 74.

72   Sources of the Interest in Architecture

The palace in the Happy Valley is described in considerable detail, although Dr. Johnson does not attempt to give a real picture of it. Like the castle in Miss Fielding's *Ophelia*, his palace is lacking in landscape setting, ruins, or mantling vegetation, those essential features for the more graphically described castles of the Gothic romances. (Pamela's mansion was at least surrounded with lofty elms and pines.) One thing he does provide—secret passages—although he makes no use of them in the narrative, and leaves them quite devoid of the horror and mystery which usually accompany such architectural features. (In S. J. Arnold's *Creole*, a "Gothic" imitation of *Rasselas*, the secret passages are used to some effect.) Later in the story, Rasselas and his companions visit the Pyramids and the Catacombs. Pekuah is carried off by the Arabs, and is kept for a time in the Arab chief's castle, which is a stone structure with turrets overlooking the Nile valley. At the close of the story, she retires to the convent of St. Anthony, which is not described.

An important fore-runner of the Gothic romances is *Longsword, Earl of Salisbury, an Historical Romance* (1762), by Thomas Leland. The Gothic properties of this story are very slight, although the frontispiece to the first volume promises references to architecture. It shows a venerable monk raising from the ground a man in armor. In the background rises a strange medieval building, evidently intended for an abbey. The tracery of this structure is crude Perpendicular. An octagonal turret rises at one corner, crowned by a weather-cock, and partly concealed by a mysterious flight of steps which stand in the middle of the churchyard, leading nowhere. In the distance, over the crenellated gable, rises a square tower with corner pinnacles and a spire. The gable is crowned by a large cross, beneath which is a canopied figure of the Virgin and Child. This

Sources of the Interest in Architecture 73

peculiar, but undoubtedly Gothic building is thus described in the text:

> It's windows crowded with the foliage of their ornaments, and dimmed by the hand of the painter; it's numerous spires towering above the roof, and the christian ensign on it's front, declared it a residence of devotion and charity.[124]

The swooning knight is led through the "winding isles" of this abbey to a "retired chamber," where he is startled at midnight by an unexpected visitor:

> A rude knocking at the gates ecchoed through the arched Isles, and roused me from my gloomy dreams. Suddenly it ceased. Silence, still more alarming, and anxious expectation succeeded. I started up, and grasped my sword as it were instinctively.

In such a scene as this, architecture is put to an emotional use, a use which was developed to a much greater extent in the Gothic romances.

The frontispiece to the second volume also depicts a Gothic scene; this time it is a room in the interior of Longsword's castle. A traceried window and a large door in the background are provided with pointed arches, and the door is crowned with an elaborate coat-of-arms. A clustered column rises in the foreground, partly wrapped in the folds of a piece of drapery. At the foot of this, the Countess of Salisbury is swooning away. The descriptions of the castle are in mere references: it has a postern gate, through which the Countess escapes at midnight, and galleries, through

---

[124] I, 27.

which the baffled villain "ranged wildly." In the "dreary dungeon" is confined the faithful Oswald.

> 'Cursed castle, cried Raymond; 'cursed be the hour in which I first entered these fatal walls."[125]

Before 1765, and, indeed, before 1770, there is a great dearth of architectural description in the minor novels, even where there seem to be good opportunities for such description. For instance, *Memoirs of a Man of Honour* (1748) starts with the promising words:

> I come from a deep and horrid dungeon, where I have passed three weeks without seeing light; fastened to the wall by a huge chain . . .

On the next page we read:

> My situation is now more tollerable:—they have removed me to a chamber in the castle of *Inspruck* . . . .

After being provided with a castle and dungeon on the first two pages of the novel, it is disappointing to find the rest of the narrative distressingly unarchitectural. *Millenium Hall* (1762), by Mrs. Sarah R. Scott, starts with "A Description of Millenium Hall and the Country Adjacent," but the description includes almost everything but the architecture of the Hall, and we could wish a few details about "the magnificence of the ancient structure." The frontispiece depicts the Hall, but in a vague way which is hardly more informing than the text. In *The Life and Adventures of Indiana, The Virtuous Orphan* (1746), Mrs. Collyer describes the visit of the heroine to a church, where she pours forth her troubled soul. The church apparently has no Gothic horrors, however, and an illustration of it reveals the pilasters of a Georgian

---

[125] II, 149.

interior. Mrs. Charlotte Lennox frequently mentions castles in *The Life of Harriot Stuart* (1751) and *The Female Quixote* (1752), but she provides no descriptions. Hill's *Adventures of Mr. George Edwards, a Creole* (second edition, 1751), starts with a brief description of a house in Scotland Yard, but there are no further architectural developments. Similarly, *Each Sex in their Humour* (1764) starts with the words: "On the borders of Gloucestershire, in an antiquated mansion . . ." and provides no description of the mansion. Not until the 1780's did architecture become a common feature of the minor novel.

It is hard to draw specific conclusions from the large number of literary sources which have been discussed in the previous pages. Shakespeare apparently suggested the use of Gothic setting to intensify tragic scenes, but the Shakespearean influence upon the architecture of the Gothic romances is vague at best. Pope's *Eloisa to Abelard* made effective use of architectural setting for emotional purposes, and was quoted by Walpole and Charlotte Smith. Ossian probably suggested the lavish use of mantling vegetation in the architectural descriptions of the novels. Richardson's *Pamela* started a vogue for the imprisoned heroine which resulted in many important architectural developments in the Gothic romances. Such suggestions for such purposes might also have come from other sources, so that it is difficult to state definitely the precise amount of influence which exists. In the case of quotations, the novelists may well have sought passages to illustrate an already conceived idea, rather than to express an idea originating in the quotation itself. The impressive array of Ossianic quotations and imitations, however, suggests that this source, at any rate, exercised a real influence upon the Gothic romances.

The development of architectural setting in the novel was probably the outcome of a great number of coinciding factors, rather than of a definite literary evolution. The castles of Mrs. Radcliffe are not the logical result of enthusiasm for Shakespeare and Spenser, and none of the literary sources which have been discussed in this chapter can explain the origin of the Gothic romance without recourse to contemporary aesthetic factors. Reverence for ancestors associated itself with medieval castles at the same time that the growing appreciation of the "picturesque" made the castle interesting from another standpoint. The cult of the "sublime," sentimental interest in ruins, sentimental Catholicism, love of mystery, and desire for self-dramatization all converged from various quarters to encourage a taste for Gothic architecture. The growing interest in "romantic" literature was merely another manifestation of this trend, and it cannot be said that it was a more important manifestation than the others. Its particular interest for our subject lies in the fact that the literary sources of Gothic setting suggested ways of expressing the general architectural enthusiasm of the time in the form of descriptions in the novel.

This chapter cannot be closed without some reference to the German tales of terror, which began to be translated into English at the close of the century. Prominent examples are *Horrid Mysteries*, translated by P. Will from the German of Karl von Grosse, and *The Necromancer of the Black Forest*, supposedly translated from the German of 'Lawrence Flammenberg' (F. C. Kahlert) by Peter Teuthold. These tales have some architectural setting, but no more than that of contemporary English novels, and certainly of a far inferior quality to that of Mrs. Radcliffe and Mrs. Smith. There is little evidence that most of the minor English novelists read German at all. Schiller is the only German to be quoted at the chapter headings of the novels. German influence was only barely beginning to be felt in English literature by the close of the eighteenth century. The love of architecture shown in the English novel of that time was an indigenous development and not a foreign importation.

As further evidence of the lack of German influence upon the architecture of the English novel of the eighteenth century, there are few German castles in the novels before 1800. Mrs. Radcliffe's buildings are situated in Scotland, the Pyrenees, Italy, Sicily, and Switzerland. Mrs. Smith's castles are similarly located, although the castle of Rosenheim in *The Banished Man* and Ronlitz Castle in *The Solitary Wanderer* are Teutonic exceptions. Mrs. Roche's castles are in Scotland, Ireland, and France. Swiss castles figure in several tales, especially in *The Wanderer of the Alps*. Mrs. Sleath, in *The Orphan of the Rhine*, Mrs. Parsons in *The Castle of Wolfenbach*, and *The Mysterious Warning*, and Francis Lathom in *The Midnight Bell* are the principal early creators of German castles, and these novels all appeared after 1793. There are no German castles in the romances of Walpole, Miss Reeve, or Miss Sophia Lee, who were the chief Gothic writers before 1785. Charlotte Smith's two German castles appear in her later works. Consequently, the German influence upon the Gothic romances must be regarded as very slight in the eighteenth century. Had the novelists looked upon Germany as the land of romance, they would have located their castles in the Black Forest or on the Rhine, rather than in the Pyrenees and Apennines. Their preference for Italian situations was probably a result of the influence of Claude Lorrain and Salvator Rosa upon English taste, while the popularity of Scottish and Irish castles must be regarded as an example of Ossianic influence. It is needless to say that these buildings are foreign in name only; so far as their descriptions go, they are purely English.

The sources of the architectural setting of the English novel are widespread and complicated. It would be gratifying to be able to show the Gothic romance developing from Shakespearean and Spenserian influences through the medium of the poetry of Thomson, Gray, Collins, and the Wartons, but, unfortunately for the historian, such sources form only a small part of the numerous currents which converged to produce the Gothic setting of the novels. The ultimate source, of course, is the receptivity of the eighteenth century to impressions of the strangeness, mystery, and glamour of an environment which was more exciting than their own, that nostalgia for adventure and freedom and the out-of-doors that comes to civilizations which are too artificial and stifling. Without this receptivity, the paintings of the Italian Landscape school, the architecture of Walpole and his contemporaries, the poems of Ossian, and the novels of the Gothic school would have perished upon barren ground, and would have been immediately forgotten. The fact that such unpromising materials had such widespread results is a testimony to the impressionable quality of the age.

CHAPTER THREE

CASTLES, MANORS, AND ABBEYS

1

When Horace Walpole awoke from his famous dream about the gigantic hand, and wrote *The Castle of Otranto*, he brought architectural setting into a prominence which it had not hitherto enjoyed in the English novel. He introduced the Gothic romance. Gothic setting had, to be sure, been used before in the novel, and the bulk of architectural description in *Rasselas* is as large as that in *Otranto*, but nevertheless Walpole was really an innovator. He made his castle the background for the whole narrative, instead of using it for a mere episode; he made his architecture play a definite part in the plot by means of the subterranean passages and trap-door through which Isabella escapes; and he surrounded his characters with an atmosphere of horror which the castle itself does much to create.

The sources of his interest in castles are, of course, to be found in his dabblings with medievalism, and particularly in his own castle at Strawberry Hill. It is incorrect, however, to infer that the Castle of Otranto *is* Strawberry Hill. There are many things in Walpole's imaginary castle which do not appear in his real one, although both structures seem to have been modelled upon English manor-houses of the Tudor period. The Castle of Otranto is arranged around a courtyard, to which the main gate gives access. From the courtyard opens the chapel, as well as the great hall. The great hall is lighted by an oriel window, and at one end, apparently on a higher level, is a boarded gallery with latticed windows, leading to Hippolita's apartments; from this gallery, Matilda, unseen, watches her father's condemnation of Theodore. A council chamber is situated somewhere near the great hall, and the great staircase is in the same vicinity. Part-way up the stairs is a small chamber (in a tower) which had formerly been deserted because of its reputation for being haunted:

> "Nobody has dared to lie there, answered *Bianca*, since the great astrologer, that was your brother's tutor, drowned himself. For certain, Madam, his ghost and the young Prince's are now met in the chamber below..."

Near the top of the stairs is a gallery, with portraits. To the right of the gallery is the great chamber (ordinarily, in English houses, this room was over the great hall), and near the head of the stairs is Matilda's chamber, which is in the same tower with the haunted chamber, but on the floor above, the haunted chamber being apparently on a sort of mezzanine level. The tower is crowned with battlements, through which the wind whistles at night. To the right of the tower is the postern gate. Isabella, according to Bianca, "lies in the watchet-coloured chamber, on the right-hand, one pair of stairs." Hippolita's apartment is provided with an oratory. There is also a "black" tower where Theodore is confined, and an armory, where Manfred's arms are stored. The most interesting part of the building, however, is the secret passage to the church of St. Nicholas, leading from a trapdoor in the subterranean vaults of the castle, through which Isabella flees from her pursuers. Gusts of wind blow through these dismal regions, terrifying Isabella, and extinguishing her lamp. The vaults are inaccurately called "cloisters," and they constitute the most alarming feature of this sinister building.

Beside the horrors of Otranto, Strawberry Hill seems quite unpretentious. It has no enclosed court, no great hall with latticed gallery, no subterranean passage to a church. Walpole's literary creation, therefore, is more authentic in its details than his real castle, and certainly more formidable. Nevertheless, there is a vast difference between Otranto and the castles of the later Gothic novelists. The first Gothic

romance supplied plenty of architectural setting, but it left many gaps to be supplied by its successors.

In the first place, we are never given a picture of Otranto. The building is created in scattered references; we are not introduced to it by a long description, as we are in the romances of the 1790's. Nor is the building fitted to a landscape; it does not rise from a rocky crag, or a dense forest, or a beetling cliff by the sea. Its one haunted chamber is very modest in comparison with the vast suites which, in later novels, are exclusively inhabited by ghosts. Furthermore, until its catastrophic close, it is not ruined (although a stone has fallen through the roof of the subterranean vault) and it is apparently without any of that profuse vegetation with which later castles were to be so completely smothered. There are no secret passages within the castle itself, with exits behind the tapestry, or concealed in the panelling. Also Walpole is not, like some of his female successors, interested in the castle kitchen and its domestic appurtenances. In fact, as Scott remarks,[1] he is not interested in descriptions at all. His architectural setting is enough to support the narrative and no more.

Eight years after the publication of *The Castle of Otranto*, there appeared another tale with medieval setting: *Sir Bertrand*, a fragment appended as an illustration to an essay on the Gothic fancy in *Miscellaneous Pieces in Prose*, by J. and A. L. Aikin. According to Lucy Aikin's memoir of her father,[2] John Aikin was the author of *Sir Bertrand*, although it has been more frequently attributed to his sister, Mrs. Barbauld. In the tale, Sir Bertrand comes at night to a "large antique mansion, with turrets at the corners, and an ample porch in the centre."[3] The building is moated, and,

[1] Life of Walpole, in *Lives of the Novelists*.
[2] *Memoirs of John Aikin, M.D.*, by Lucy Aikin, Philadelphia, 1824, p. 19.
[3] J. and A. L. Aikin: *Miscellaneous Pieces in Prose*, 1773, 129.

unlike Otranto, is lavishly ruined: "The roof in various places was fallen in, the battlements were half demolished, and the windows broken and dismantled. A draw-bridge with a ruinous gate-way at each end, led to the court before the building."

The interior arrangement of the house is clearly shown. Sir Bertrand, after opening the creaking door, ascends a large staircase from the hall to a wide gallery whence another stair, "narrow and winding, and interrupted by frequent breaches, and loose fragments of stone," leads upwards to an iron grate giving access to an "intricate winding passage, just large enough to admit a person upon his hands and knees." This leads to a lofty gallery, at the end of which are ample folding doors opening into a large room, adorned with black marble statues. In the middle of the room is a coffin.

This building is much more clearly described than Otranto, so far as its arrangement is concerned. Also there is some attempt at a general description of the exterior at the beginning of the narrative. The addition of ruins is interesting, although there is no vegetation to give them an Ossianic aspect. Nevertheless, the descriptions of the building are very brief and colorless, quite lacking in detail. There is no landscape setting. Furthermore, Aikin's creation is not equipped with chapel, dungeons, or secret passages, those customary requisites for a good Gothic romance. The fragmentary nature of the tale, and the fact that the action takes place at night probably prevented any lavish use of description.

Still less architectural setting is found in the tale of *Sir Reginald du Bray*, which forms the second volume of *The Rival Friends, or the Noble Recluse* (1776). It was separately reprinted at Dublin in 1779, and a notice on the back of the title-page of this edition says that it "appears to be a literary offspring of Longsword, Earl of Salisbury." Sir Reginald lives in a castle which has a lofty hall, a chapel, and a dry moat. His enemy, Ardulph, lives in a nearby castle with moat, drawbridge, port-cullises, and courtyard. There is no description of either of these buildings.

In the following year appeared *The Champion of Virtue*, by Clara Reeve (the title was altered to *The Old English Baron* in subsequent editions). In her preface, Miss Reeve says that her tale is a "Gothic story, being a picture of Gothic times and manners," and that it is "the literary offspring of the Castle of Otranto." She does not hesitate, however, to criticize this literary progenitor. The frontispiece to her romance depicts a Gothic chamber, with arched doorways, and a ceiling supported by brackets of strange design.

Like Walpole, Clara Reeve indulges in almost no architectural descriptions. When the characters first come in sight of the castle of Lovel, she presents no terrifying pictures of frowning towers silhouetted against a lurid sunset, but merely remarks that some youths are shooting with crossbows in a nearby field. "There," said the servant, "are our young gentlemen at their exercises." The castle itself is a rather vague structure, but it appears that the main gates open into a courtyard, opposite to the great folding doors of the hall, from which room the great stairs lead to the gallery. There is a chapel somewhere. The east wing is deserted and haunted, and a west wing is under construction. The deserted wing is described with some care: a bedroom, a dining-room, and a large closet occupy the upper floor, besides a passage from which stairs lead to the rooms below. These rooms consist of two parlors and a closet; the door of the closet being concealed by tapestry. The only communication between this wing and the rest of the house seems to be through the bedroom upstairs, surely an awkward arrangement, so that to reach the fatal closet where the body lies, one has to go upstairs, through the bedchamber and passage, down the other stairs, and through the parlor.

As in *Sir Bertrand*, the arrangement of rooms is clearer than at Otranto, but there are no detailed descriptions, no landscape, no secret passages, and even no ruins, although the ceiling leaks in the haunted wing. In one respect, the architectural setting is even vaguer than in Otranto, because the castle of Lovel has a suspiciously modern air. The new wing is being built of brick, a material quite out of place in the orthodox romantic castle, which must always be constructed with stone walls, thick enough to contain secret passages at strategic points. The very mention of east and west wings recalls the formal mansions of the Elizabethan period rather than the medieval castle. In fact, the meager descriptions of the castle of Lovel suggest such a house as the Christ-church mansion at Ipswich, a building with which Clara Reeve, who lived much of her life at Ipswich, must have been familiar. Her castle even contains a "breakfast-parlor," a room which certainly does not have a medieval sound.

The contribution of all four romances are, therefore, very slight so far as the quantity of architectural material is concerned. One has subterranean vaults, another is ruined, and a third has a deserted wing and a door concealed with tapestry; but not one of them gives a connected description more than a couple of sentences in length of any building. It was not till 1785 that a romance appeared which made up for this deficiency: *The Recess*, by Sophia Lee.

Miss Lee had great imagination. Her story is a semi-historical novel, but she indulges in liberties with history which no modern novelist would dream of taking. She provides Mary, Queen of Scots, with twin daughters by the Duke of Norfolk; one twin becomes the secret wife of Leicester, while the other engages the affections of Essex. After such an astounding plot, one would expect Miss Lee to show considerable ingenuity in her architectural setting, and indeed she does. The twins spend their whole childhood in a most remarkable underground structure called the Recess, which gives the book its title.

> This Recess could not be called a cave, because it was composed of various rooms; and the stones were

obviously united by labor; yet every room was distinct, and divided from the rest by a vaulted passage with many stairs, while our light proceeded from small casements of painted glass, so infinitely above our reach that we could never seek a world beyond; and so dim, that the beams of the sun were almost a new object to us when we quitted this retirement.

This underground labyrinth was in the ruined convent of St. Winifred, which was connected by a secret underground passage with St. Vincent's Abbey. Upon the destruction of the Abbey, the secret passage was disclosed, and it was made to terminate in the new building which rose upon the site of the Abbey. The other end of the passage opened into the Recess by a door made of a portrait, which could be moved by a spring. Catholic refugees who lived in the Recess made other passages, one terminating in a hermit's cave, while a shorter one went to a secret door in a tomb, opening upon the ruins of the convent. These ruins are described in a passage which is nearer to the style of Mrs. Radcliffe than any description which had so far appeared:

> For a long way beyond, the prospect was wild and awful to excess; sometimes vast heaps of stones were fallen from the building, among which, trees and bushes had sprung up, and half involved the dropping pillars. Tall fragments of it sometimes remained, which seemed to sway about with every blast, and from whose mouldering top hung clusters and spires of ivy. In other parts, ruined cloisters yet lent a refuge from the weather, and sullenly shut out the day; while long echoes wandered through the whole at the touch of the lightest foot; the intricacies of the wood beyond, added to the magnificence of art the variety of nature.[4]

Here is that union of architecture with landscape which was to be so characteristic of the novels of the 1790's; here also is that element of terror which was to render Mrs. Radcliffe's

[4] Dublin, 1786, I, 55.

castles so exciting. Further material is provided in references to Kenilworth Castle in England, and Dornock Castle in Scotland, which both appear in the course of the narrative. In Kenilworth, for instance, there is a secret cabinet concealed behind tapestry. Miss Lee, in fact, provides all the materials for a highly developed Gothic setting: abbey, convent, and castle; subterranean passages, secret cabinets, concealed doors, ruins with vegetation, and landscape setting, all portrayed with considerable detail. Her architecture plays in the narrative a part which is at once decorative, structural, and emotional. She leaves very little to be added by her successors, and that little consists more in the scope than in the quality of description. Ann Radcliffe is said[5] to have attended the Misses Lee's school, and to have been a great admirer of Sophia's novel.

Warbeck: a Pathetic Tale (1786) is a semi-historical novel advertised to be in the manner of the *Recess*, but really far inferior to that work. (Sophia Lee translated it in 1774 from the French of d'Arnaud.) It contains almost no architectural descriptions, although some of the scenes take place in the Tower of London, and Warbeck (the Perkin Warbeck who tried to oust Henry VII) takes refuge at one time in a subterranean retreat.

While architectural setting was making this progress in the medieval or historical romances, it was by no means absent from the ordinary social novels dealing with contemporary life. Walpole's use of architecture, to be sure, does not seem to have been imitated immediately by contemporary novelists. *The History of Miss Indiana Danby* (1765) introduces both a convent and a castle without making any use of them. *The Convent, or the History of Julia* (1767) despite its title, contains no architectural descriptions. *Barford Abbey* (1768), by Mrs. Susannah Gunning, is equally disappointing. Mrs.

[5] *Annual Register*, (1824), 66, 217.

Gunning, who was evidently of a chilly disposition, informs us that, "the first thing in a house which attracts my notice is the fire." Evidently there was little else which could attract her, for her references to buildings are very meager. She does indeed tell us that "the very walls seem'd to speak," and that the "noble old structure" fires the beholder with wonder and delight, but details are lacking. In the *Cottage* (1769), there is also a complete dearth of architectural description, although Mrs. Gunning in one place becomes interested in the interior decoration:

> My little room, as I call it, to be hung with India paper, a chints window curtain, chairs and sopha covered with the same.—the new apartments, both above and below, furnished with blue lustring;—the old man's kitchen, and the furniture in it, to remain as it now is—the present apartments, above, to be hung with plain blue paper,—beds, window curtains and chairs, white callico.[6]

The Country Cousins (1767) contains a heroine who has been properly trained in the romantic school:

> Charlotte, having never been at Mead-field before, was still more struck than her father on her arrival at it, and could not, at the first wandering of her eye over the whole building, hinder herself from breaking out into exclamations of satisfaction; for as her father had brought her up with a predilection for gothic architecture, the antique air of it, which would have pained the optics of a meer [*sic*] modern, gave her a great deal of pleasure....[7]

Henry Mackenzie, introducing *The Man of Feeling* (1771), mentions a "venerable-looking pile," and proceeds to say that, "an air of melancholy hung about it," and that an old crow

[6] III, 65.
[7] I, 140.

sat croaking on a tree near-by. Here the description ends. In the *Man of the World* (1773), he brings us to a ruined chapel with "narrow gothic door," "vault," and "moss-grown altar." *Julia de Roubigné* (1777), by the same author, contains several good examples of architectural setting of the emotional type:

> We entered between two rows of lime-trees, at the end of which is the gate of the house, wide and rudely magnificent .... There was a presaging gloom about this mansion which filled my approach with terror.[8]

Emma, or the Unfortunate Attachment (1773) contains Gothic buildings of some importance, although the part that they play in the story is very slight. The heroine is apparently relieved to find, when she visits the castle of the Noel family, that the building is modern, and therefore has "no muddled moats about it, no draw-bridges to defend its entrance, nor do you find within it winding stair-cases leading to dark towers."[9] She also approves of her home at Spring-Park, but alas, "did the high-raised roof, the gilded cornices, the painted pannels, or inlaid floors, give me the smallest consolation, when I found myself deserted here?" Her husband takes her to another home at Rose-Court, and here we are provided with descriptions which we sought in vain in the romance by Emma's namesake (for her name too is Walpole):

> After traversing barren moors, and unfrequented paths, we at length stopped at a little gate, which closed up the entrance to a house encompassed by a high wall, which did not admit the least view of it. . . . on going in I saw the mouldering ruins of an once superb dwelling, lying in neglected heaps about it—here windows, which gaped for the glazier's assistance; there doors,

[8] I, 192-3.
[9] II, 77.

whose rusted hinges echoed through the passages when moved; worm-eaten tables and chairs; and chasms in the walls, through which the hooting of the owl, and the cry of the bat, entered every moment.[10]

The interior is no less forbidding:

> When we had scrambled through several dark rooms, we came to one wing, where time had not made quite so much devastation; a large room, wainscoted with oak, and lighted by one huge window, which the painted glass served to dim, and render gloomy at midday: the lowness of the ceiling, and the brownness of the floor, completed the emblem of a dungeon. Out of this I went into a smaller, which I call my parlour, and from whence I can see nothing but an immense grove of firs, whose darksome shade seems for contemplation made. The bed-chambers are not much more numerous or agreable.

This description is unusually detailed for its early date; it provides a bit of landscape (the barren moors, and the grove of firs); there are ruins; and there are such specific details as the oak wainscot, the large window with stained glass, and the brown floor. There is also a certain emotional effect from the house; indeed Emma says that "the house, even from its resemblance to the *colour of my fate*, has some charms for me; it gives me subject 'for meditation even to madness,' and I indulge myself in it to the full."

It is interesting to compare these passages from *Emma* with Mr. Dennison's description of a similar house in Smollett's *Humphry Clinker*. Smollett emphasizes the physical discomforts of his ruined house, while the author of *Emma* stresses the depressing atmosphere of Rose-Court; where Smollett provides nettles and docks, *Emma* has "an immense grove of firs, whose darksome shade seems for contemplation made." Smollett mentions dusty pictures, worm-eaten fur-

[10] III, 85.

niture, and leaky roofs; while the other gives us the large room with its oak wainscot and its great gloomy window of stained glass. *Emma*, which is the later of the two, is therefore a step nearer the Gothic romances in its architectural descriptions than is *Humphry Clinker*. There are, of course, other buildings mentioned in *Humphry Clinker*, but they are existing ones, visited by Mr. Bramble on his tour. Mr. Bramble disapproves of Gothic architecture because it makes the churches damp and cold; apparently he would have sympathized with Mrs. Gunning's fondness for fires. In Miss Blower's *Maria* (1785), the heroine wanders about an old castle at night; there is also a castle in William Hutchinson's *A Week at a Cottage* (1775).

From 1770 to 1785, the novels make increasing use of Gothic buildings. The romantic heroines are usually enthusiastic over them (or else are imprisoned in them, in which case they are not so enthusiastic), while people of fashion, who have not, like Charlotte in *The Country Cousins*, had the advantages of a romantic training, express their contempt of such rude and barbarous structures. Gothic buildings are also in great demand for hermits, and other recluses. Consequently one finds all kinds of references to medieval architecture. An example of the enthusiastic variety is provided by a character in *Masquerades*: "Your antique buildings always fill my soul with a pleasing kind of awe."[11] *Juliana* contains similar sentiments: "I felt myself impressed with respectful awe, when I entered these venerable walls."[12] Lady O'Shaughnessy in *The Story of Lady Juliana Harley* (1776) writes that "I love the grandeur of an ancient family-mansion."[13] A correspondent in *The History of Lord Belford and Miss Sophia Woodley* (1784) writes of "the Elms, the old romantic mansion you formerly so much admired."[14]

[11] "By the author of Eliza Warwick," 1780, I, 3.
[12] "By the author of Francis the Philanthropist," 1786, II, 149.
[13] By Mrs. Elizabeth Griffith, II, 102.
[14] II, 1.

A description of the enthusiastic kind is to be found in *Anna* (1785), by Mrs. Agnes Maria Bennett:

> The view of this ancient building, which had been for ages dignified with the name of castle, and the grandeur as well as the beauty of the surrounding woods, reaching from the front down to the edge of the river, over which a regular row of large white stones formed a convenient causeway, and from the back up to the top of the mountain, was an enchanting addition to the pleasant prospect from the parsonage.[15]

In opposition to these favorable comments stand the remarks of those Philistines who have not learned to prefer romance to elegant comfort, and whose sentiments resemble those of American tourists panting for modern shower-baths amid the more picturesque plumbing of Europe. A lady of fashion thus describes her arrival at Belford Hall (in *The History of Lord Belford and Miss Sophia Woodley*):

> At length . . . are poor Kitty and I arrived at this frightful old mansion. Never, I thank my stars, did I see such an antiquated, odious, structure! it wants nothing but a surrounding moat, and a draw-bridge, to make it pass for the ancient abode of some giant of old.[16]

Needless to say, this unromantic lady did not succeed in wedding the young Lord Belford. In Fanny Burney's *Cecilia*, Lady Honoria is equally disrespectful to the venerable charms of Delvile Castle, where she is visiting; indeed she horrifies Mr. Delvile by suggesting that his ancestral castle would need very few alterations to become an ideal county jail. A character in *Belmont Grove* (1785) says of Drayton Abbey: "I know a Lady, who would laugh exceedingly at the antique rusticity of the building."[17] The Professor in Bage's *Bar-*

---

[15] I, 211.
[16] 1784, II, 29.
[17] II, 18.

ham *Downs* (1784) criticizes Canterbury Cathedral, mentioning with scorn "the fine brown antiques, which I suppose you dignify with the name of statues."[18] The very worst Philistine is Matthew Bramble in *Humphry Clinker* (1771):

> The external appearance of an old cathedral cannot be but displeasing to the eye of every man, who has any idea of propriety or proportion, even though he may be ignorant of architecture as a science; and the long slender spire puts one in mind of a criminal impaled, with a sharp stake rising up through his shoulder.[19]

Similarly unfavorable opinions are expressed by those unhappy heroines who have the misfortune to be imprisoned in Gothic buildings by jealous husbands or wicked seducers. Pamela's confinement in the old and lonely house probably furnished a hint for these settings; although castles have always been the traditional place for abducted ladies. Thus the heroine of Mrs. Griffith's *History of Lady Barton* (1771) says that:

> More dead than alive, my duenna and I arrived at my destined prison—The house was old, large, and gloomy, extremely out of repair; the furniture as antique as the building, which was situated on a bleak and barren shore, opposite the Irish coast.[20]

Lady Manchester in *The Husband's Resentment* (1776) writes that,

> ... I returned to the Castle, or rather to my late Prison, for so horrid a Place deserves no other Name. Lady *Barbara* exclaimed, at the Sight of it, "What a shocking, gloomy Abode is here!"[21]

[18] II, 319.
[19] II, 140.
[20] III, 110.
[21] II, 52.

The heroine of *Emma, or the Child of Sorrow* (1776) thus describes Bellman Castle in Wales, where she has been entrusted to an old aunt of her husband's:

> Figure to yourself an old ruinated castle, over which time has triumphed, moated all around, with a horrid draw-bridge; I hear no sounds but the screaming of rooks, and whistling of the winds; all chearful sounds are wholly banished. The inside of this tremendous castle presents misery in another point of view; the furniture old and crazy; the hangings once rich, torn and defaced.[22]

Lady Melville, the heroine of *The Mutability of Human Life* (1777), describes the castle to which she was carried by the amorous Count de Lou:

> ... we arrived at a small castle, whose very looks denounced the miseries of despair:—they assisted me out of the chaise, and we entered a hall of immense height and proportionate gloom, which conveyed an additional horror to the soul.[23]

All these writers seem to agree that Gothic architecture arouses feelings of melancholy and awe; it is merely a question whether one happens to enjoy such sensations or not; the romantic ladies do, and the Philistines do not. One class of people, however, is peculiarly fitted to enjoy these contributions of Gothic art—the recluses. What could be more ideal for their purposes than a castle or abbey, preferably ruined! Accordingly the novelists provide them abundantly

[22] II, 105.
[23] II, 230.

with retreats of this sort. In *The Rival Friends; or, the Noble Recluse* (1776), Somers writes:

> I shun the haunts of folly and dissipation, and enjoy that solitude that is so requisite to me, on the sea shore. There, and where the majestic ruins of Netley Abbey shew the instability of human works, I bend my melancholy steps, and find an indulgence in those mouldering walls, that soothes the disorder of my mind.[24]

In *Masquerades* (1780), a character writes:

> I got into his carriage, and he drove me to the castle.— I have been here before, and well knew what a romantic place he had made choice of to indulge his melancholy in. The habitation is built in a Gothic style, very awful, very magnificent.[25]

Sir Howell Henneth, in Bage's *Mount Henneth*, shuts himself up in his ancestral castle ("a most noble Gothic structure, with an intolerable appearance of gloom."), and even arranges special coal closets, opening both into his room and into the passage, so that the servants need not disturb him when they bring fuel for his fire. The castle is also equipped with speaking tubes.

It can easily be seen, therefore, that when Charlotte Smith and Ann Radcliffe began to produce their castles at the end of the 1780's, they had many precedents. The medieval tales of Mrs. Radcliffe had the tradition of Walpole, Aikin, Reeve, and Lee behind them, while the social novels of Charlotte Smith enlarged upon architectural features which had been appearing in similar novels for the last two decades. It should also be apparent that during these decades, Gothic architecture was gaining in importance as a setting for the novel. The castles in *Sir Bertrand* and *The Old English*

[24] III, 169.
[25] IV, 79.

Baron are more clearly defined than Otranto, while *The Recess* contains Gothic setting which is more highly developed than any that had hitherto appeared. Similarly, in the social novel, there was very little Gothic setting until after 1770, and most of it did not come until after 1775, but from 1775 onwards there is a constant stream of castles and abbeys, figuring only in minor episodes, to be sure, but described more and more at length. It was now time for Charlotte Smith and others to write social novels in which buildings figure in more than minor episodes, eventually becoming the chief background of the novel; while Ann Radcliffe and her followers were to fill the Gothic romance to the saturation point with a peculiarly idealized form of architectural setting.

2

Mrs. Charlotte Smith was a very prolific woman. In a lifetime of fifty-seven years, she produced eleven novels and twelve children, to say nothing of poetry, essays, translations, history, and a book on birds. Her numerous literary productions were made necessary by her numerous offspring, whom she was obliged to support largely from her own earnings. Her novels, therefore, were primarily pot-boilers, but they were at least better than most of the novels of her day, and they were highly praised by Scott.[26] All but one of them contain important architectural descriptions.

Mrs. Smith's early life had given her some advantages for such descriptions. As a girl, she studied drawing under George Smith of Chichester, the landscape painter, and she admired the landscapes of the Italian school. In 1783, when her ne'er-do-well husband fled from his creditors, she took refuge with him in a desolate old château in Normandy, a building which probably provided suggestions for similar

---

[26] *Lives of the Novelists.*

structures in her novels. She also travelled a little in England; in 1788, for instance, she visited Penshurst, which she hails in her *Elegiac Sonnets*:

> Ye towers sublime, deserted now and drear,
> Ye woods, deep sighing to the hollow blast,

Later, she wrote "A Descriptive Ode supposed to have been written under the Ruins of Rufus's Castle among the Remains of an ancient Church on the Isle of Portland." The ruins of Netley Abbey are mentioned in one of her *Rural Walks*. One of her elegiac sonnets mentions the ruined church at Middleton. In a foot-note to *The Banished Man*, she refers to the "oubliettes" of Hurstmonceaux Castle in Sussex. Her reading, which was more extensive than her travels, probably had some influence on her architectural descriptions, and her quotations from Pope, Gray, Ossian, Percy, and Gilpin have been mentioned in the previous chapter.

Mrs. Smith's first literary efforts were her *Elegiac Sonnets* and two translations from the French. Her first novel, *Emmeline, the Orphan of the Castle*, appeared in 1788, and by the following year it was in its third edition, while the *Elegiac Sonnets* were in their fifth edition, showing that even her earliest compositions were popular. As the title implies, Emmeline is an orphan who lives in a castle (although she remains there during only the first ninety pages of the story), and the opening paragraphs inform us that the castle is so thoroughly ruined that only two of the bedrooms are habitable. Emmeline lives in a remote turret, a favorite location for such heroines, where "the stillness of the night, interrupted only by the cries of the owls which haunted the ruins, added to the gloomy and mournful sensations of her mind."[27] The castle contains the usual galleries, secret passages, and "arched and obscure apartments," with "windows dim with

---

[27] 3rd ed., I, 16.

painted glass." To these customary features, Mrs. Smith adds two rooms which her predecessors had omitted: one is the huge kitchen, blackened with the smoke of ages, and the other is the library, where the heroine tries to repair her neglected education. The libraries of Mrs. Smith's castles are usually full of tattered tapestry and black-letter books; this one is further equipped with nests among the shelves, where "the swallow, the sparrow, and the daw, had found habitations for many years." (One hopes that the lovely Emmeline found the black-letter books more intelligible than the sparrows did.) The exterior of Mowbray Castle (for so it is called) is described with a distinctness which shows the results of Mrs. Smith's pictorial training:

> It's venerable towers rising above the wood in which it was almost embosomed, made one of the most magnificent features of a landscape, which now appeared in sight.
> The road lay along the side of what would in England be called a mountain; at it's feet rolled the rapid stream that washed the castle walls, foaming over fragments of rock; and bounded by a wood of oak and pine; among which the ruins of the monastery, once an appendage to the castle, reared it's broken arches; and marked by grey and mouldering walls, and mounds covered with slight vegetation, it was traced to it's connection with the castle itself, still frowning in gothic magnificence; and stretching over several acres of ground: the citadel, which was totally in ruins and covered with ivy, crowning the whole.[28]

This picture is even clearer than Miss Lee's portrayal of the ruined convent, although it lacks the contrast and the color which are to be found in the best of Mrs. Radcliffe's descriptions. There is an attempt here to arrange the parts of the landscape with respect to the castle; the features of

[28] 3rd ed., I, 90-91.

the view are not merely enumerated, they are set in order, ending with the dominant feature, which is the castle keep. It is significant that the ruins at Mowbray are covered with "slight vegetation"; in her later novels, Mrs. Smith is not so sparing in her use of this decoration, which becomes anything but slight. In *Ethelinde, the Recluse of the Lake*, she lays it on with a lavish hand:

> Sitting down on a rustic and half ruined tomb, she contemplated with mournful pleasure the picturesque appearance it made adjoining the church, which was very antique, and its narrow windows half hid by mantles of ivy; while from among the mouldering buttrasses young ash trees waved their light leaves, and the fern, and the wall flower, with variety of lichens and mosses, were scattered about the broken grey stone of the roof, and among the inequality of the arches and windows.[29]

In the same novel is Grasmere Abbey, which is similarly smothered in vegetation. It is surrounded by ancient elms, and its buttresses are covered with fruit trees. Lady Newenden, a typical Philistine, is displeased with this "comfortless and dreary place," but Ethelinde, the heroine, finds it more congenial. *Celestina* (1791), Mrs. Smith's third novel, contains the château of Roche Martre, situated in the Pyrenees. This castle has grass in the courtyards, alder and ash trees on the fortifications, moss and wallflowers on the walls, and birds' nests on the battlements.[30] Indeed Mrs. Smith's castles are amazingly fertile: moss, vines, flowers, and even trees sprout luxuriantly from their walls. They must have resembled the "rockeries" which adorned so many gardens of the Victorian period.

Roche Martre is described with considerable care. Beyond the moat rise ponderous walls, on which the depredations of war are visible. At each end, stand towers of gray stone,

[29] 1789, V, 217-8.
[30] IV, 220.

Castles, Manors, and Abbeys 99

pierced with loops instead of windows. The first court is approached by a drawbridge across the half-filled moat. This court has arches and colonnades, and it communicates with the second court by a terrace. Inside the building is the immense hall with oak beams and narrow Gothic windows of stained glass. It is furnished with standards of armor. A stone staircase in a turret leads to the gallery. From the windows of the north gallery, the ruins of a fort on a mountain top are visible above a wood of fir and cypress. *Desmond* (1792) is provided with another castle, that of Hauteville, but there is not much description of this building. It is in Mrs. Smith's fifth novel, *The Old Manor House* (1793), that her architectural setting reaches its climax.

The building which supplies the title to this book is Rayland Hall, the home of an old spinster whose young cousin and protégé, Orlando Somerive, is in love with the housekeeper's ward, Monimia. The clandestine meetings of this couple are facilitated by the architecture of the house, so that Rayland Hall itself plays a very important part in the story. No long or minute descriptions are given of its "chaste and silent solitudes," but the building is gradually developed, bit by bit, as necessity arises. The housekeeper gives the following account:

> ... you know very well that Rayland Hall, which belonged to such famous cavaliers in the great rebellion, has a great many secret stair-cases, and odd passages, and hiding-places in it; where, in those melancholy times, some of my late Lady's ancestors, who had been in arms for the blessed Martyr and King, Charles the Second [sic], were hid by others of the family after the fight at Edgehill.[31]

The gate of the house opens into the great hall, whence the main stairs lead to the north and south galleries with their casemented bow-windows. Monimia lives in the customary

[31] IV, 340.

turret, where a door, hid by hangings, leads to a secret stair giving access to a lumber-room—and to the enamored Orlando. A private passage connects this lumber-room with the dilapidated chapel, supposedly haunted, which needs no ghost to make it gruesome:

> ... the old banners which hung over her head, waving and rustling with the current of air, seemed to repeat the whispers of some terrific and invisible being, foretelling woe and destruction; while the same wind by which these fragments were agitated hummed sullenly among the helmets and gauntlets, trophies of the prowess of former Sir Orlandos and Sir Hildebrands, which were suspended from the pillars of the chapel.[32]

The chapel has two Gothic windows, blocked with stonework and stained glass, and it opens on a court. Nearby is the library, where Orlando and Monimia have their secret meetings, and from which opens Orlando's little tapestry room. Adjacent to the library is a wainscoted summer parlor, with a glass door leading to the park. There is a deserted suite of rooms, formerly used for guests; there is a kitchen of "old-fashioned English style," and there are subterranean vaults where wine is stored and smugglers lurk. A secret closet, concealed by leather hangings and a sliding board, contains Mrs. Rayland's will.

Rayland Hall, therefore, plays an important part in the plot of the novel (something which Mrs. Smith's previous castles had not done), and it is also used occasionally for emotional effect, especially at the end of the book, when Orlando comes back to find it deserted and ruinous, with the tapestry of the library hanging in tatters. Mrs. Smith's strongest emphasis, however, is always upon the decorative, rather than the structural, or emotional, aspects of architectural setting.

[32] I, 234.

Her next novel, *The Banished Man*, appeared in 1794 (second edition in 1795). This book is remarkable because of the preface to the second volume, labelled *Avis au Lecteur*, in which Mrs. Smith complains that her contemporaries have stolen her castles, and that after erecting so many herself (of which she gives a list), she is seeking material for more. This important preface will be discussed later; it is sufficient to say here that Mrs. Smith's annoyance at her contemporaries did not in the least impede her further production of castles.

The castle of Rosenheim, in the first part of *The Banished Man*, is soon destroyed by fire, and vanishes from the narrative. The castle of Vaudrecour in Brittany is more carefully portrayed. It is surrounded by a morass, formed by the choking of the river with fallen ruins. Like others of Mrs. Smith's castles, it has an important kitchen, "an immense vault-like room." It also has "oubliettes," which Mrs. Smith in a foot-note defends by mentioning those of Hurstmonceaux Castle. The first impressions of D'Alonville, the hero, after crossing the drawbridge and gate, are thus described:

> He crossed the second moat by another draw-bridge, and came into the area of the castle; of the strength and magnitude of which he had till then had no idea. The same marks of depredation appeared about this entrance, as he had remarked at the gate-way. A stone porch was closed towards the internal part of the building by a massy door, which had been covered with plates and spikes of iron. Some of these had been torn off lately, and the door broken by the force that had been used. The immense hall into which this led him, was so obscure from its great height, its oak beams blackened by time, and its high and narrow windows, that it was with difficulty he could make out the objects with which he was surrounded: in some places the broken brick floor was strewn with pieces of those gigantic statues, some of which still remained entire, on a kind of cornice half way up the sides of the hall; and these, which had been

thrown down and broken, seemed to have been removed for the sake of the brass and iron armour they had supported.[33]

An open door across the hall leads to a long cloister, the narrow windows of which look into a courtyard full of tombs. The great staircase leads to the gallery, with colonnades of which Mrs. Smith says that "something like them may yet be found in old houses in England, now converted into inns; an open gallery running across from one part of the building to another; on one side opening into other apartments, on the opposite side supported by pillars."[34] There is a chapel in the building.

The castle in *Montalbert* (1795), which is named Formiscusa, is situated on a hill in Sicily. Here Rosalie, the heroine, is imprisoned at the command of her mother-in-law. Its interior is distinguished by a profusion of marble, otherwise it might as well be one of Mrs. Smith's English or French castles. *Marchmont* (1796) contains a much more important structure, one which indeed vies with Rayland Hall in importance, though it forms the background for a smaller part of the narrative. Mrs. Smith makes actual use of the hiding-places in this mansion, which is named Eastwoodleigh.

Eastwoodleigh is a manor-house rather than a castle, although the heroine, when she is brought to be imprisoned in it, is under a different impression:

> "The house!" cried Althea—"Good Heavens! it seems like the ruins of an immense castle."
> "Yes," replied Mrs. Wansford—"it is altogether very large still; yet some parts of it are quite fallen, and others are grown over with grass and ivy, having never been rebuilt since they were battered down in the civil wars."[35]

[33] III, 122-3.
[34] III, 146.
[35] I, 251.

Althea finds that the kitchen wing of the house is the only inhabited portion. After crossing a gloomy court, she is led to the servants' hall, with its stone floor, immense fireplace, and black beams. From there, a passage leads to a wainscoted parlor, while a gallery leads to the stairs to her chamber. The kitchen itself is a high vaulted room, from which the great copper utensils have been torn; in its roof is a trap-door through which the mistress of the house could observe the conduct of her servants. The kitchen is now deserted, however, the servants' hall being the present living-room. Mrs. Mosely, a former dependent of the family, guides Althea through the uninhabited parts of the house. Through a long passage, made dark by the boarding at the window, they enter a court which they traverse to reach the great door of the house. This opens into a vast hall, with mossy pavement, and huge chimney. A council-room and other apartments are adjacent to the hall, and the huge staircase leads up to a great banqueting-hall, decorated with much carving and gilding, now defaced, and with an elaborately coffered ceiling. Bedchambers and a music-room lie beyond. At this point, we are told that two more wings of the house are yet to be seen; in one of them fugitive royalty had once been sheltered, while the other contains a haunted apartment.

Soon Althea becomes aware that there is a mysterious person in the deserted part of the house—Marchmont, a descendant of the original owners, who is utilizing his knowledge of the secret hiding-places to escape his creditors. He tells her that there are three recesses in the thickness of the walls, connected by very narrow passages, and he shows her some secret panels giving entrance to these retreats. Eastwoodleigh is evidently a manor-house of the Tudor period, but the fact that Mrs. Smith quotes from her own sonnet on Penshurst at the opening of one of her descriptive chapters does not necessarily imply that she had that particular mansion in mind for the scene of the story. Her descriptive ode on the ruined church in the Isle of Portland is quoted in this novel.

The Young Philosopher (1798) has quite a variety of Gothic structures, chief among which is Sandthwaite Castle, the home of the de Verdon family. Lady de Verdon, who belongs to the Philistine type, has made alterations in the family seat, introducing modern windows, and making their recesses into conservatories. Miss de Verdon's room is situated, of course, in the remotest part of the castle, so that it is comparatively easy for her to escape with her lover, Glenmorris, who climbs up some ruins to the window of a nearby room. He takes her to his own castle in Scotland, "built on an almost perpendicular rock, its base beaten by the waves of the German ocean." Later she is imprisoned in the ruined abbey of Kilbrodie, but she escapes to take refuge in Lord Macarden's castle. Her daughter is abducted and confined in "an old mansion house of gloomy and gothic appearance,"[36] the gate-posts of which exhibit one of those botanical displays of which Mrs. Smith is so fond:

> There were two great brick pillars, with heavy stone work over them, which time had eaten into excavations, and which chance and nature had sown with wall-flowers, valerian, rag-wort, and anti-rhinum; within they were mantled with ivy, or lined with holly.

The last of Mrs. Smith's novels, *The Letters of a Solitary Wanderer* (1800), is not really a novel at all, but a series of novelettes, held together by a slight framework. The first of these tales is a genuine Gothic romance, since the action takes place in the past, and the scene is a ruined structure called Palgrave Abbey. The narrator is led over the structure by a Mrs. Lenthwaite, from whom he learns the narrative which follows. The situation at the beginning of this

[36] IV, 248.

narrative is not unlike that which Catherine Morland imagines to prevail at Northanger Abbey: the owner of Palgrave Abbey is ostensibly a widower, with two sons and a daughter; his wife's apartments are closed, but lights are seen moving through them at night. (His wife, of course, is really a prisoner in a remote part of the abbey.) The abbey, like Northanger, is arranged around a quadrangular court, but this court bristles with "night-shade, nettle, and henbane," decorations which Northanger lacks. Sir Mordaunt Falconbridge, the lord of the abbey, lives in three rooms in the northeast corner of the building, and one of these rooms communicates with the chapel and the cloister which runs around the court. The apartments of Edouarda, his daughter, also look into the court. There is a large brick hall, from which a porch gives access to the park. From Edouarda's rooms opens a lumber-room, whence a passage leads to a gallery in the chapel, beneath which are the family vaults. Lady Falconbridge's prison cell is near the chapel. There is a deserted gallery running the length of the building from east to west.

Mrs. Smith's contributions to the development of architectural setting are important, although not strikingly so. Her pictures are clearer than those of her predecessors, and she is especially careful in defining the arrangement of buildings with respect to the landscape. Her buildings are more domestic than those of previous writers; she describes manor-houses as well as castles and abbeys; and she lays more stress upon the library, the servants' hall, and the kitchen than upon battlements and dungeons. Her castles are usually fairly accurate—Mowbray Castle, her earliest, has for instance a keep ("citadel" she calls it), a feature which had previously been neglected. Roche Martre has both an outer and an inner court, the arrangement of which is clearly shown. Vaudrecour is furnished with "oubliettes," and it apparently has what is technically called an "outer ballium," although

Mrs. Smith does not use this term. Her references to Hurstmonceaux Castle and to the galleries of English inns show that she made at least an attempt at verisimilitude in her descriptions. Finally, in one of the tales in *The Solitary Wanderer*, she uses for her scene an existing building, Mont St. Michel. Her most distinctive contribution, however, is in the extraordinary profusion of flora which adorn her ruins; she displays all the enthusiasm of an ardent botanist, and decks her buildings with vegetation of which perhaps the most amusing specimen is the bouquet of nightshade, nettle, and henbane at Palgrave Abbey.

Moreover, she was among the first of these novelists to realize to what ridiculous lengths the Gothic craze was leading contemporary fiction. As early as 1794, she makes satirical remarks about the profusion of castles in the novel, and further comments appear in *The Young Philosopher* and *The Solitary Wanderer*. Because she wrote to support her family, however, she was obliged to comply with the popular demand, and so she continued to fill her novels with castles. Altogether, her novels describe three manor-houses, one Grecian pavilion, two temples, two ruined chapels, five abbeys, and thirteen castles—a total of twenty-eight separate buildings, all definitely portrayed, not merely mentioned. Every building is more or less ruined, and every building is provided with some landscape setting. Obviously then, Mrs. Smith was more interested in the decorative effect of her architectural setting than in its other aspects, although she did not neglect the latter. Also, although she portrays so many buildings, only three of them play a really important part in the narratives where they occur.

Furthermore, her descriptions never quite reach the emotional level which those of Mrs. Radcliffe sometimes attain. In Mrs. Smith's pictures, there is less of that vertical feeling, resulting from a lavish use of precipices, towers, and turrets, which helps to make Mrs. Radcliffe's castles so awe-inspiring.

Also she lacks Mrs. Radcliffe's strong contrasts of light and shade, the glowing sunsets and blazing torches which etch deep shadows on the castle walls. Mrs. Smith is not so adept as Mrs. Radcliffe in imparting a sinister air to her buildings. On the other hand, she succeeds better than Mrs. Radcliffe in making her buildings domestic and realistic. Her manor-houses, at least, seem quite authentic. Her foliage is certainly described more carefully than that of Mrs. Radcliffe. To use the terminology of the eighteenth century, Mrs. Smith's descriptions are usually "picturesque," while Mrs. Radcliffe's are "sublime."

Mrs. Ann Radcliffe was a much less prolific writer than Mrs. Smith, probably because her incentive was not so great. Her life was certainly far easier than Mrs. Smith's harassed career; her husband was an estimable man who did not wreck the family fortunes; and she had no dependent children to require constant earnings from her pen. Consequently she wrote only six romances, in contrast to Mrs. Smith's eleven, and of these six, the last was not published until 1826, three years after the author's death. This tale, *Gaston de Blondeville*, need not be discussed here, because it appeared so late, and also because its setting is an actual building, Kenilworth Castle.

Mrs. Radcliffe, like Mrs. Smith, was an admirer of Italian landscape. She lacked, however, Mrs. Smith's botanical tastes. As a child, she often visited her aunt's husband, Thomas Bentley, a man of great cultivation, at whose house she met many noted persons, among them "Athenian" Stuart. Later, she may have attended the school of the Misses Harriet and Sophia Lee in Bath; since she is said to have known them, and to have admired Sophia's romance, *The Recess*.[37] Her travels after her marriage were frequent, though seldom extensive, and most of them did not take place until the end

---

[37] *Annual Register* (1824), 66, 217.

of her literary career. She visited Holland, the Rhine valley, and the English lakes in 1794, publishing her account of them in the following year. By that time, her first four novels had been finished. Later in life she travelled frequently in England, but not abroad.

Her descriptions of real buildings are interesting to compare with her imaginary ones. She seems to have seen everything through a highly colored and romantic haze. Hardwick, for instance, which is decidedly a Renaissance and not a Gothic building, is thus portrayed in her *Journey*:

> Three towers of hoary grey then rise with great majesty among old woods, and their summits appear to be covered with the lightly shivered fragments of battlements . . .

It is only on closer inspection that the "battlements" turn out to be initials carved in stone. Windsor and Warwick both remind her of the ghost scene in *Hamlet*. She mentions the secret passages of Furness Abbey, which she visited in 1794, but Warwick, Kenilworth, Penshurst, Knole, and Blenheim she does not appear to have visited until the beginning of the nineteenth century.

Her favorite author was Shakespeare. She knew Ossian, whom she quotes in describing the ruined abbey in *The Romance of the Forest*. Her acquaintance with the "romantic" poets of the eighteenth century is proclaimed by the abundant quotations which she takes from them for her chapter headings. Furthermore, Miss Lee's *Recess* may well have furnished her with some hints, and she probably learned much from the novels of Charlotte Smith.

Mrs. Radcliffe's initial work, *The Castles of Athlin and Dunbayne*, appeared in 1789, the year of the publication of Mrs. Smith's *Ethelinde*, and the year following the appearance of Mrs. Smith's first novel, *Emmeline*. Athlin and Dunbayne are situated in Scotland, although they might just as well have been anywhere else (Scottish castles, in these romances, are distinguished by being perched upon rocks;

otherwise they do not differ from ordinary castles). Dunbayne is the more important and awe-inspiring of the two; we are told that "its lofty towers still frowned in proud sublimity." It is moated, and it has two drawbridges, the north one leading to the main gate, and the east one to a watch tower. There is a wide vaulted hall, a chapel, a great staircase, a gallery, dungeons, and vaults. A loose stone in the pavement of Alleyn's cell, and a movable panel in the wainscot of Osbert's prison afford means of escape to these two captives, since the subterranean vaults of the castle lead to an underground passage beneath the moat, opening into the forest. In this novel there is also an abbey, "whose broken arches and lonely towers arose in gloomy grandeur through the obscurity of evening."

In the next year, Mrs. Radcliffe published *A Sicilian Romance*, the scene of which is laid at the castle of Mazzini in Sicily. There are no long descriptions of this castle, although an abundance of short explanations make its plan fairly clear. It has inner courts, the number of which is not specified; it has the usual deserted wing (the south one in this case); and there are the customary vaults. Mazzini seems to have been constructed on a scale even more magnificent than that of most castles: the inhabited portion, for instance, contains a north and an east hall, a great gallery and an east gallery, a breakfast hall, and an oak parlor; while the deserted wing seems to be full of halls. One of them is thus described:

> It was a spacious and desolate apartment, whose lofty roof rose into arches supported by pillars of black marble. The same substance inlaid the floor, and formed the stair-case. The windows were high and gothic. An air of proud sublimity, united with singular wildness, characterized the place, at the extremity of which arose several gothic arches, whose dark shade veiled in obscurity the extent beyond.[38]

[38] I, 104.

Near this extraordinary room is an inner hall (former castles were usually content with one hall, but Mazzini seems to possess at least four). The black marble pillars are evidently inserted to give the castle an Italian atmosphere. There are, of course, secret passages: one leads to the woods, while the other gives access to the underground cell where Mazzini's wife is imprisoned. St. Augustin's Abbey, where the heroine takes refuge, is also conspicuous for its air of "proud sublimity." Its towers are "majestic," and the heroine "loved to wander through the lonely cloisters, and high-arched aisles, whose long perspectives retired in simple grandeur, diffusing a holy calm around."

In *The Romance of the Forest* (1791), Mrs. Radcliffe surpasses her previous architectural triumphs. The scene of this romance is laid in southern France, a region which Mrs. Smith had already used for the setting of part of *Emmeline*. The principal building is a deserted abbey, "overshadowed by high and spreading trees, which seemed coeval with the building." (Mrs. Smith would have said what kind of trees they were.) The eastern tower is almost demolished, but a western tower and an ornate gateway remain intact. Over the gate is a large window. La Motte enters the chapel, and passes from there into the nave of the abbey church, the shattered pillars of which, "seemed to nod at every murmur of the blast over the fragments of those that had fallen a little before them." There are also a great hall, a court with cloisters, and suites of apartments. One room has a mosaic floor, which Adeline calls to La Motte's attention; he replies that the style of the room is not strictly Gothic. There is a hidden trap-door, leading to vaults below, and Adeline discovers a secret door behind the arras of her room.

It is in *The Mysteries of Udolpho* (1794) that Mrs. Radcliffe produces her architectural masterpiece, probably the most interesting building which the Gothic romances have to

Castles, Manors, and Abbeys   111

offer. A radiant picture of it is given at the point when it first becomes visible to the approaching travellers:

> The sun had just sunk below the top of the mountains she was descending, whose long shadow stretched athwart the valley, but his sloping rays, shooting through an opening of the cliffs, touched with a yellow gleam the summits of the forest, that hung upon the opposite steeps, and streamed in full splendour upon the towers and battlements of a castle, that spread its extensive ramparts along the brow of a precipice above.[39]

Soon the vision fades:

> As she gazed, the light died away on its walls, leaving a melancholy purple tint, which spread deeper and deeper, as the thin vapour crept up the mountain, while the battlements above were still tipped with splendour. From those, too, the rays soon faded, and the whole edifice was invested with the solemn duskiness of evening. Silent, lonely, and sublime, it seemed to stand the sovereign of the scene, and to frown defiance on all, who dared to invade its solitary reign. As the twilight deepened, its features became more awful in obscurity, and Emily continued to gaze, till its clustering towers were alone seen, rising over the tops of the woods, beneath whose thick shade the carriages soon after began to ascend.

After a short journey through the woods, the travellers emerge upon a heathy rock, and reach the castle gates. Here another description is given, less colorful but more detailed than the first:

> While they waited till the servant within should come to open the gates, she anxiously surveyed the edifice: but the gloom, that overspread it, allowed her to distinguish little more than a part of its outline, with the massy walls

[39] II, 169.

of the ramparts, and to know, that it was vast, ancient, and dreary. From the parts she saw, she judged of the heavy strength and extent of the whole. The gateway before her, leading into the courts, was of gigantic size, and was defended by two round towers, crowned by overhanging turrets, embattled, where, instead of banners, now waved long grass and wild plants, that had taken root among the mouldering stones, and which seemed to sigh, as the breeze rolled past, over the desolation around them. The towers were united by a curtain, pierced and embattled also, below which appeared the pointed arch of an huge portcullis, surmounting the gates: from these, the walls of the ramparts extended to other towers, overlooking the precipice, whose shattered outline, appearing on a gleam, that lingered in the west, told of the ravages of war.

The carriage rolls under the portcullis into a gloomy court, and thence, through another gate, into the second court, the walls of which are "overtopt with briony, moss, and nightshade." Then the travellers enter "an extensive gothic hall, obscured by the gloom of evening, which a light, glimmering at a distance through a long perspective of arches, only rendered more striking." The arches open at one point into a vault, where a marble staircase ascends to a corridor leading to the upper apartments. At this point there is a huge window, extending from the fretted ceiling nearly to the pavement. Instead of ascending the stair, the travellers (Emily, and her aunt and uncle) pass through an anteroom into a large apartment, wainscoted with black larch wood. The high windows overlook the ramparts.

While they wait in this room, the old servant tries to tell Emily's uncle, Montoni, of all the repairs that are needed. Some of the battlements have fallen from the north tower; part of the hall roof has fallen in; the rampart wall has collapsed in three places; and the stairs to the west gallery are in a dangerous condition. No wonder that Montoni exclaims, "Well, well, enough of this!"[40] When Emily retires

[40] II, 179.

for the night, she loses her way in the labyrinth of apartments above. Her chamber, which she finally finds, is lined with larch wood, and from it a mysterious stair leads downward. The next morning, she is able to view from her window "the fortifications of the castle spreading along a vast extent of rock, and now partly in decay, the grandeur of the ramparts below, and the towers and battlements and various features of the fabric above."[41] After breakfast, she takes a more careful view of the castle:

> When Madame Montoni retired to her dressing-room, Emily endeavoured to amuse herself by a view of the castle. Through a folding door, she passed from the great hall to the ramparts, which extended along the brow of the precipice, round three sides of the edifice; the fourth was guarded by the high walls of the courts, and by the gateway, through which she had passed, on the preceding evening. The grandeur of the broad ramparts, and the changing scenery they overlooked, excited her high admiration; for the extent of the terraces allowed the features of the country to be seen in such various points of view, that they appeared to form new landscapes. She often paused to examine the gothic magnificence of Udolpho, its proud irregularity, its lofty towers and battlements, its high-arched casements, and its slender watch-towers, perched upon the corners of turrets.[42]

During the following days, there is constant turmoil in the castle; soldiers arrive or depart, and Emily is frequently obliged to flee in terror along the corridors and galleries. From time to time, further glimpses of the castle are afforded. There is, for instance, the banqueting-hall, of which the middle compartment rises into a vaulted roof, "enriched with fret-work, and supported, on three sides, by pillars of marble; beyond these, long colonades retired in gloomy grandeur,

[41] II, 211.
[42] II, 219.

till their extent was lost in twilight."⁴³ The single large window and the folding doors of this room afford a view of the wild Apennines above the west rampart. The east turret comes into prominence in a subsequent chapter; Emily climbs it at night to seek her aunt, who, she thinks, is imprisoned there. Then comes her interview with Barnadine, the treacherous sentinel, who tells her that her aunt is confined in the chamber over the great gate. An expedition to this place is planned, and on the following night, Emily speeds along a vaulted gallery off the hall to a terrace where she meets Barnadine. He conducts her to the ruined chapel, and then to the vaults below, explaining that this is the quickest way to the outer court, since he does not choose to unlock the inner one. They reach this court, where the light reveals "the high black walls around them, fringed with long grass and dank weeds, that found a scanty soil among the mouldering stones; the heavy buttresses, with, here and there, between them, a narrow grate, that admitted a freer circulation of air to the court, the massy iron gates, that led to the castle, whose clustering turrets appeared above, and opposite, the huge towers and arch of the portal itself."⁴⁴ From this court, they ascend a stair in one of the entrance towers, and Emily is shut up in an oak-wainscoted room. Later, just as she is about to be abducted from the castle, Barnadine's treachery is discovered, and a contest ensues just outside the gate, during which we are given a momentary glimpse of the walls and tower lit by the ruddy gleam of the torch.

When the castle is about to be besieged, Emily is removed, and during her journeys from and to Udolpho, vivid little pictures are given of its exterior:

> Emily had now a full view of Udolpho, with its gray walls, towers and terraces, high over-topping the precipices and the dark woods, and glittering partially with

[43] II, 401.
[44] III, 14.

the arms of the *condottieri,* as the sun's rays, streaming through an autumnal cloud, glanced upon a part of the edifice, whose remaining features stood in darkened majesty.[45]

On her return, she finds that the castle has resisted an attack:

> They continued to wind along the valley, and, soon after, she saw again the old walls and moon-light towers, rising over the woods: the strong rays enabled her, also, to perceive the ravages, which the siege had made—with the broken walls, and shattered battlements, for they were now at the foot of the steep on which Udolpho stood.[46]

After many adventures, Emily and her friends succeed in escaping from the castle. It is not long, however, before they are shipwrecked in the neighborhood of another castle, Château-le-blanc, in the Pyrenees near the Mediterranean coast. This castle has just been inherited by the Count de Villefort. The Countess, who belongs to the Philistine class, dislikes the castle: "What a dismal place is this!"[47] she exclaims upon approaching the entrance. "How long have you lived in this desolate place?"[48] she asks of the housekeeper. On the other hand, her stepdaughter, Lady Blanche, "resigned herself to the sweet and gentle emotions, which the hour and the scenery awakened."[49] Part of the castle is modern, and much of the older portion is deserted. Smugglers infest the uninhabited wing, entering through a secret passage in the thickness of the wall. There is the usual romantic scenery visible from the great Gothic window of the hall, and nearby is the convent of St. Claire, "seated near the margin of the sea."

The only remaining building of importance in *The Mys-*

[45] III, 167.
[46] III, 228.
[47] III, 349.
[48] III, 351.
[49] III, 347.

teries of Udolpho is an ancient fortress in the Pyrenees, which the approaching travellers first see by moonlight. "It was built of grey stone, in the heavy Saxon-gothic style, with enormous round towers, buttresses of proportionable strength, and the arch of the large gate which seemed to open into the hall of the fabric was round, as was that of a window above."[50] Evidently Mrs. Radcliffe is trying to say that the fortress is in the Romanesque style; anything Saxon would surely be out of place in the Pyrenees. This fortress figures only in a minor incident of the story, and it is far less important than Udolpho.

Indeed none of Mrs Radcliffe's castles quite reaches the level of Udolpho, although her next novel, *The Italian* (1797), contains a magnificent abbey, which, like Udolpho, is situated in the Apennines, amid rugged scenery. It is named San Stefano, and within its walls Ellena is confined to prevent her marrying Vivaldi. She finds the convent sufficiently forbidding:

> Partial features of the vast edifice she was approaching, appeared now and then between the trees; the tall west window of the cathedral with the spires that overtopped it; the narrow pointed roofs of the cloisters; angles of the unsurmountable walls, which fenced the garden from the precipices below, and the dark portal leading into the chief court; each of these, seen at intervals beneath the gloom of cypress and spreading cedar, seemed as if menacing the unhappy Ellena with hints of future suffering.[51]

Vivaldi, when he comes to rescue her, is similarly impressed; especially by the convent church:

> Its highly vaulted aisles, extending in twilight perspective, where a monk, or a pilgrim only, now and then

[50] IV, 250.
[51] I, 159.

crossed, whose dark figures, passing without sound, vanished like shadows; the universal stillness of the place, the gleam of tapers from the high altar, and of lamps, which gave a gloomy pomp to every shrine in the church:—all these circumstances conspired to press a sacred awe upon his heart.[52]

The entrance leads to the main court:

> Three sides of this were enclosed by lofty buildings, lined with ranges of cloisters; the fourth opened to a garden, shaded with avenues of melancholy cypress, that extended to the cathedral, whose fretted windows and ornamented spires appeared to close the perspective.[53]

Ellena is led through "many solitary passages" to the Abbess's parlor, and thence through the refectory to a cell, where she is confined. From the short passage outside her door, a flight of stairs leads up to a turret, the windows of which command magnificent views of the surrounding mountains. A second courtyard opens from the church, being bounded by the choir of the church, and by the rock, except for a gap which admits a vista of the landscape below. From this court opens a cave, containing a shrine, and from the back of the cave Ellena and Vivaldi escape by a secret passage. The prisons of the Inquisition form the setting for another part of the narrative. The description of these buildings is comparatively vague, merely mentioning the massy walls, towers, and turret of the exterior, and the hall, corridors, interminable winding passages, and vaults of the interior. More graphic pictures than these are provided of Spalatro's lonely house on the shores of the Adriatic.

Mrs. Radcliffe's particular contribution to architectural setting is "sublimity"—a word, which, in various forms,

[52] I, 303.
[53] I, 164.

appears in nearly all her best descriptions. She stresses the emotional influences of her buildings, their capacity to arouse awe and horror, while their more picturesque features are merely a means towards this end. In every one of her five romances, her buildings play an important part in the plot; their function is decorative, structural, and emotional, but especially the last. It would be well-nigh impossible, in works which are primarily narrative, to stress architecture more than Mrs. Radcliffe does.

This strange absorption in buildings and landscapes may perhaps be explained in the light of a suggestion which Miss McIntyre[54] has made in her study of Mrs. Radcliffe— simply that Mrs. Radcliffe was more interested in things than in people. Her available journals are almost wholly concerned with scenery and buildings; she does not appear to have lived a very social life or to have had many intimate friends; while her vivid descriptions reveal that peculiar sensitiveness to environment, which is the source of the best architectural pictures.

Although she is interested, like Mrs. Smith, in the decorative aspect of buildings, she always subordinates the picturesque side of architecture to the emotional significance. She emphasizes the perpendicular aspect of her buildings: they bristle with towers and turrets, springing from the verge of precipices. Windows are usually tall and narrow. At Udolpho we see "its lofty towers and battlements, its high-arched casements, and its slender watch-towers, perched upon the corners of turrets," and at San Stefano "the tall west window of the cathedral with the spires that overtopped it; the narrow pointed roofs of the cloisters; angles of the unsurmountable walls." She describes not only the building itself, but its effect upon the beholder. While Mrs. Smith's pictures are usually calm and clear, Mrs. Radcliffe's are vio-

---

[54] *Op. cit.*, p. 97.

lent contrasts of light and shade. We see Udolpho with the sunset glowing on the upper towers, and fading in purplish dusk on the lower portions; or we behold it partly illuminated by the ruddy glow of a torch, the rest of the structure remaining in darkness. The ends of large halls are always lost in gloom, and arches retreat in perspective until they vanish in shadow. Thus Mrs. Radcliffe imparts to her buildings a sense of mystery which is often lacking in the creations of Mrs. Smith. Dealing, as she does, with light and shade, Mrs. Radcliffe is less interested than Mrs. Smith in details, although her descriptions are seldom completely vague. She is not concerned with archaeological facts; and so her castles are less realistic than those of Mrs. Smith—she gives no footnotes about "oubliettes." Indeed Mrs. Radcliffe's castles are really fit to adorn a fairy tale; their situations are so romantic, their grandeur so stupendous, and their shadows so full of mystery.

Nevertheless, much as Mrs. Radcliffe's buildings differ from those of Mrs. Smith, there is enough similarity between them to show that one writer must have influenced the other.[55] Mrs. Smith's first novel appeared a year before Mrs. Radcliffe started to publish. In this novel there is a castle, inhabited by an orphan girl in a lonely turret, and the castle with its landscape is pictured much in the manner of Mrs. Radcliffe's earlier descriptions. The close of *Emmeline* takes the characters to the south of France, a region which Mrs. Radcliffe was later to invade. The castle of Roche Martre in Mrs. Smith's *Celestina* (1791) is situated in the Pyrenees, like Mrs. Radcliffe's Château-le-blanc in *Udolpho* (1794). Each château has a partly ruined pavilion, and a ruined fort in the vicinity. The vaults of Rayland Hall in Mrs. Smith's

---

[55] See C. McIntyre: *op. cit.*, 95, and E. Manwaring, *op. cit.*, 212; James R. Foster (P. M. L. A., XLIII, 465) thinks that most of the borrowing was done by Mrs. Radcliffe.

Old Manor House (1793) are infested with "ghosts" who turn out to be smugglers, and so are the vaults beneath the deserted wing of Château-le-blanc in Udolpho. Furthermore, it is almost certain[56] that Mrs. Radcliffe used Mrs. Smith's translation of Gayot de Pitaval's *Causes Célèbres* for the plot of *The Romance of the Forest*. More convincing than any of these reasons, however, is Mrs. Smith's own statement in her preface to the second volume of *The Banished Man*. She evidently has no doubts whatever upon the nature and direction of the borrowing:

> But my ingenious cotemporaries have so fully possessed themselves of every bastion and buttress; of every tower and turret; of every gallery and gateway, together with all their furniture of ivy mantles, and mossy battlements; tapestry, and old pictures; owls, bats, and ravens; that I had some doubts whether, to avoid the charge of plagiarism, it would not have been better to have *earthed* my hero .... where I should have been in less danger of being *again* accused of borrowing, than I may, perhaps, be, while I only visit
>
> "The glympses of the moon."

This remark succeeds a catalogue of Mrs. Smith's former castles, and a lament that she has used all her materials yet must find more. In her later novels, however, one sees traces of Mrs. Radcliffe's influence especially in the first story of *The Solitary Wanderer*. Each writer ended her career with a book in which a real building forms the setting: Mrs. Radcliffe using Kenilworth for *Gaston de Blondeville*, and Mrs. Smith using Mont St. Michel for one of the stories of *The Solitary Wanderer*.

The architectural descriptions of Mrs. Smith and Mrs. Radcliffe are the best which the eighteenth-century novel has to offer. Mrs. Smith, writing novels of contemporary life,

---

[56] C. McIntyre, *op. cit.*, p. 57.

depicts buildings which are more realistic, more detailed, and more domestic; while Mrs. Radcliffe, writing Gothic romances, the scene of which is laid in the past, produces buildings which are more spectacular, more awe-inspiring, and more mysterious. Although Mrs. Radcliffe's buildings had apparently the greater influence upon contemporary writers, the later architectural descriptions of the nineteenth century usually reverted to the realistic type of architecture depicted by Mrs. Smith. Scott was familiar with the work of both writers, as he shows in his biographies of them in *Lives of the Novelists*, and it seems impossible that he should not have drawn from them some ideas for buildings in his own novels. The hiding-places of Rayland Hall and Eastwoodleigh, where cavaliers hid during the civil wars, suggest similar retreats in his novels. Mrs. Smith and Mrs. Radcliffe were also the leaders of a host of minor authors who eagerly imitated one another's castles in order to comply with the prevailing fashion. The work of these satellites was in most cases far inferior to that which they copied.

3

The example of Mrs. Smith and Mrs. Radcliffe was not lost upon contemporary novelists, though the deluge of Gothic novels did not become really overwhelming until after 1794. Many of these lurid tales were published at the Minerva Press for William Lane (later Lane and Newman, and finally A. K. Newman). For nearly three decades, the castle and the abbey played so prominent a part in English fiction that novels dealing with them have been generally called "Gothic romances." Innumerable chap-books, usually condensations of long novels, also used Gothic setting, and so did the historical novel, which was then starting to develop. A group of these historical novels, appearing around 1790, will be reserved for a later chapter, though there is really little to distinguish them from ordinary fiction.

While the group of historical romances was appearing, the ordinary social novels continued to employ Gothic setting in increasing quantities. The popular Gothic romances never really supplanted the ordinary novel of contemporary life, although these novels usually assumed Gothic trappings, as the historical novel almost invariably did, in order to be in style. Gothic titles were popular, even for novels which had very little to say about Gothic buildings, or any sort of buildings. In 1786, for instance, appeared Anne Fuller's *Convent*, and in 1789 *The Solitary Castle* and *Seymour Castle*, novels which, in spite of their titles, contain very little architectural setting, and which are not tales of terror. The frontispiece to *The Solitary Castle*, depicting a semi-Gothic turret at the left, keeps up the illusion produced by the title. The principal building in the novel is indeed a castle, but it does not play an important part in the story, and the descriptions of it are meager and strange. Over the front door, for instance, is a portico covered with horseshoes, "which had been placed there as infallible preventives against witchcraft." In the hall is a mosaic pavement representing the Israelites crossing the Red Sea, the waves of the sea being depicted in a checkerboard design of red brick and white stone. Seven niches are occupied by statues of English kings, and, "to render the appearance of these statues perfectly terrible," the owner (a recluse) has dressed them in rusty armor. Near the castle is a Gothic temple, at the door of which the guests are showered by a "phantom" with manna from on high in the form of "biscuits, fruit, and confectionaries."

Seymour Castle, or the *History of Julia and Cecelia*, contains even less Gothic setting; the heroine merely remarks that the castle is "a fine Gothic building," and that the gardens defy her powers of description. (The descriptive powers of these heroines are seldom so easily daunted!) *Delia* and *Julia*, both published in 1790, and *The Woodland Cottage* (1796) all mention sight-seeing expeditions to nearby ruins.

The excursion in *Julia* (by Helen Maria Williams) comes to a disastrous end when an avalanche of stones rolls down from the ruined abbey and injures the heroine's ankle. The ruins in *The Woodland Cottage* are pronounced "prodigiously fine" by a lady, who is overcome with "awful astonishment."[57] In 1790, Mrs. Eliza Parsons, who later was to write full-fledged Gothic romances, published *The History of Miss Meredith*, to which Horace Walpole and Mrs. Bonhote are listed as subscribers. There is practically no architectural setting here, an old house being described merely as "a fine old romantic building." *The Errors of Education* (1792), by the same author, is equally disappointing; castles are mentioned but not described. It was not until 1793 that Mrs. Parsons complied with the popular fashion, and produced in *The Castle of Wolfenbach* a real Gothic romance. In *Lidora* (1791) the first chapter, supposed to contain a description of the castle, is omitted "because the manuscript was torn." Later novelists would take care that this chapter, above all others, should be preserved.

By the 1790's, even Mrs. Gunning, who in an earlier novel remarked that the first thing which she noticed in a house was the fire, allowed her attention to wander to other objects. In *The Anecdotes of the Delborough Family* (1792), she describes a priory with hall, chapel, and massy walls. Her *Memoirs of Mary* (1793) introduces an octagonal temple with secret gallery, while in *Delves*, she portrays Castle Talbot, the residence of a crazy old recluse:

> The profoundest gloom enveloped the without, as well as the within, of this vast heavy and stupendous building, which from the thickness of its walls, and the antiquity of its architecture, seemed to have been coeval with the creation.[58]

[57] I, 77.
[58] 2nd ed. I, 270.

Clara Reeve, whose *Old English Baron* so feebly described a castle, by this time improved her architectural technique. In *Sir Roger de Clarendon*, an historical romance, she depicts several castles. In *The School for Widows* (1791), she gives detailed descriptions of an old mansion, which the heroine, who is compelled to live in it, is not sufficiently romantic to appreciate:

> When I first saw the house, my heart sunk within me: I thought of all the haunted houses I had ever heard or read of—An old brick mansion, with Gothic windows, with square panes diamond-wise, and plaister divisions in the windows, a large porch in the center, with a seat on each side, and an iron balcony over it.[59]

Inside is a "large, gloomy hall, paved with black and white marble in squares," and wainscoted in oak. The chimney, which is large, is adorned with grotesque carvings. At the top of the customary "great stair-case" is the usual gallery leading to the chambers. There are four parlors downstairs, "large, dark, and gloomy; old wainscot, in small pannels; with old high-backed chairs and tables to match the rest of the furniture." One room is said to be haunted. The heroine has so little respect for antiquity that she turns one of the wainscoted parlors into a greenhouse.

Thus, most minor authors of the time introduced a little Gothic spice into their novels when they found such seasoning popular. Mrs. Agnes Maria Bennett, for instance, whose earlier novels (*Anna*, and *Juvenile Indiscretions*) had very little architectural setting, launched into full descriptions in *Ellen, Countess of Castle Howel* (1794). This is not a Gothic romance, but it includes long descriptions of a Gothic mansion called Code Gwyn, and of an abbey. Code Gwyn apparently has a square keep with corner turrets, like that of the Tower of London or Rochester Castle. The abbey has been spurned by its present possessors, who have erected a

---

[59] II, 109.

Castles, Manors, and Abbeys 125

new building beside it, preserving the old abbey merely as a relic of family pride. Mrs. Bennett's *Beggar Girl and her Benefactors* (1797) has more Gothic setting than any of her previous works had possessed.

The reactions of the various types of characters to Gothic architecture continue to be the same after 1788 as in the preceding decades. There are the usual exclamations of delight from romantic ladies, and of horror from the unromantic, while castles and ancient mansions are still the favored residences for imprisoned heroines and melancholy recluses. Lady Boyne, in Mrs. Parson's *Lucy*, says, "I doat on ruins; there is something sublime and awful in the sight of decayed grandeur, and large edifices tumbling to pieces."[60] A character in Mrs. Roche's *Vicar of Lansdowne* remarks that, "The fine old ruin impresses the mind with the most pleasing, the most awful, the most soothing sensations."[61] The heroine of *Caroline Merton* (1794) is unusually enthusiastic, even for one of her generation:

> How widely different are my sensations in this charming retirement! The venerable antiquity of the fabric; the pleasing gloom that reigns around; the portraits of gallant knights in their warlike accoutrements; and the several pieces of rusty armour which adorn the lofty hall, fill my mind with new and delightful Ideas. Often in imagination am I carried back to the ages [of] chivalry. I fancy myself presiding at the tournament, and adjudging the prize of victory. I am charmed with the scene and elated with my own consequence; till awakened from my dream by the sudden entrance of some intruder on my reveries, I find and for a moment regret, that it is not a reality.[62]

Quite different are the comments of Lady Powerscourt and her family, in Mrs. Jane West's *Tale of the Times* (1799). These ladies "joined in protesting, that, unless the dark

[60] I, 223.
[61] 2nd ed., 1800, II, 27.
[62] I, 67-8.

Gothic windows and hideous tapestry hangings were removed from the drawing-room, and light sashes and India paper substituted in their stead, they should fall into hysterics every time they went into the room . . . ."[63] Melissa, in *Melissa and Marcia* (1788), is delighted because:

> ". . . . instead of our heavy oak doors, low cielings, old fashioned chairs, gloomy tapestry, and our large rambling Hall stuck round with the prim figures of old Aunt Nell, and Cousin Bridget, with nosegays in their hands, and our tye-wigged beaux, and our ancestors screwed up in armour:—We have here the finest mahogany doors, lofty cielings, ..."[64]

Although imprisoned heroines are to be found in greatest abundance in the Gothic romances, they also flourish in the contemporary social novels. *Plain Sense* and *Disobedience*, both by the same author, include these unhappy women. The heroine of *Disobedience* has the good fortune to discover that a bookcase in the library of Stanwick Castle swings back, affording her an easy exit. The situation in William Godwin's *St. Leon* is somewhat different; here it is the hero who is imprisoned, but he is liberated from Bethlem Gabor's castle by a fortunate fire. In *The Castle of Eridan* (which, in spite of its imposing title, is not really a Gothic romance at all) the Duchess is confined in a room paved with stone and delightfully situated next to the castle drain, "which receives all the filth of the different parts of the castle, which caused an intolerable stench."[65]

The recluses who inhabit the castles of these novels are even more numerous than those who flourished in similar novels before 1788. The owner of "the solitary castle," in the novel of that name, is one of this number. In *The*

---

[63] I, 39.
[64] I, 34-35.
[65] By G. A. Graglia, 1800, p. 123.

Orphan Sisters (1793) there is an old miser who lives in a ruined mansion, most of which he leaves to decay, while he inhabits the servants' hall. The owner of Castle Talbot, in Mrs. Gunning's *Delves*, is referred to as "the crazy lord," and is an eccentric recluse. In *The Castle of St. Donats* (1798), by Charles Lucas, a recluse disguises himself as a bleeding corpse, and walks the castle grounds by night as a spectre—surely an ingenious and effective method for insuring seclusion!

When even the average social novel of the day contained so much Gothic setting, the amount in the full-grown Gothic romances may well be expected to be overwhelming—and it certainly is! It would be both tedious and useless to describe all the innumerable castles and abbeys which flourish in these tales; the most that can be done is to discuss briefly the architectural creations of the more prominent writers.

One of the best known of these writers is Mrs. Regina Maria Roche. Her *Vicar of Lansdowne* is not a Gothic romance, but in *The Children of the Abbey* and *Clermont* she produces excellent specimens of this type of fiction. Both these romances show strong Ossianic influence, and, in *Clermont*, Ossian is quoted in direct reference to a ruined castle. Mrs. Roche specializes in Scottish and Irish castles, though she occasionally strays across the Channel for her architectural setting. The principal building in *The Children of the Abbey* is Dunreath Abbey in Scotland, which is furnished with a ruined chapel and a deserted wing where the supposedly dead Countess dwells in seclusion. The walls of the chapel seem to be unusually fragile. The heroine, unable to obtain entrance, has sat down beside the chapel, and leaned her head against the wall, when "the stones gave way with a noise that terrified her, and she would have fallen backward had she not caught at some projecting wood."[66] Through the

---

[66] Exeter, 1826, III, 31.

chasm thus created by her head she enters the chapel, beyond which is a hall with stairs ascending to a gallery. In the middle of the book the scene shifts to Castle Carberry in Ireland, near which is St. Catherine's Abbey with the customary mouldering arches. In *The Nocturnal Visit*, there is a Scottish castle beside a lake, and later a more important one in the Pyrenees; the latter has flanking towers, bastions, a keep, and a hall with vaulted roof and marble columns. Then we cross the Channel again to Ireland, to visit the castles of Carrie-owen and Longhlean, of which the former is a home for virtuous old people. The castles of *Clermont* are situated in France; that of Montmorenci is especially important. Its effect upon the heroine is thus described:

> The vast magnitude and decaying grandeur of the château impressed Madeline with surprise and melancholy, which were almost heightened to awe and veneration on entering a gloomy-vaulted hall of immense size, with small arched windows, and supported by stone arches, ornamented with rude sculpture, and hung with rusty coats of armour; while against the walls the ancient implements of war were placed in curious devices of suns, moons, and stars.[67]

Mrs. Roche's pictures are often detailed, but they are never as spectacular as those of Mrs. Radcliffe.

The earlier novels of Mrs. Eliza Parsons were not Gothic romances. *Lucy* (1794) begins to assume Gothic characteristics. An old Irish castle by the sea affords refuge to a man and woman, together with a child whom they have rescued. There is a lurid description of storms battering the castle, but comparatively little description of the building itself, underground passages being its principal feature of interest. *The Castle of Wolfenbach, a German Story* (1793), also lacks details, although the castle has an un-

[67] 1798, I, 104.

inhabited wing, and there is a subterranean passage. *The Mysterious Warning, a German Tale* (1796), has a more imposing castle, with two courts, a hall with gallery on pillars, a vaulted passage, and a dungeon where the former owners of the castle are confined.

Mrs. Anne Ker seems to have been strongly influenced by Mrs. Radcliffe. The name of the heroine in *Adeline de St. Julian, or the Midnight Hour* suggests that of the leading lady in *The Romance of the Forest*. A monastery with vaults forms the setting for this novel. *The Heiresse di Montalde; or, the Castle of Bezanto* (1799) opens in the Pyrenees, a favorite location for so many Gothic romances. The first view of Bezanto is strongly reminiscent of Emily's first glimpse of Udolpho:

> When we first saw the Castle of Bezanto from the summit of a hill, the sun was glancing his departing rays on the turrets of its towers.

The driver says, "Yonder is Bezanto, madam, you can see the battlements of the towers above the trees."[68] The west tower of the building is mantled with ivy and briony, one of Mrs. Radcliffe's favorite combinations. There are marble pillars in one of the rooms. The general plan of Bezanto is square, with "a grand and striking round tower" at each corner.

Mrs. Mary Robinson's *Vancenza* (1792) receives its title from a castle, situated in a beautiful forest near a lake. Its gilded vanes "glistened to the eye of the far-distant traveller." Vancenza was built in the twelfth century, and it possesses the usual courtyard and lofty towers. *Hubert de Sevrac, a Romance of the Eighteenth Century* (1796), by the same writer, describes the château of Montnoir, situated in a Lombard forest. The building is partly ruined, and the cloisters encircling the great court are over-run with ivy and weeds.

[68] I, 172.

There is a chapel, and a "vast and lofty library" where a sliding bookcase gives access to a tiny oratory. The Marquis de Sevrac passes "melancholy hours" in composing imitations of Ossian. Another castle appears later in the story, but this château, we are told, "was not correctly entitled to that name: it displayed no antique towers, no strong portcullis, no battlements over-screening the deep moat, or backing the encircling rampart."[69] *Angelina* (1796) and *The False Friend* (1799), although they are not Gothic romances, contain much Gothic setting.

More important than Mrs. Robinson's descriptions, however, are the foot-notes telling where she got them. In one foot-note, referring to landscape descriptions in *Hubert de Sevrac*, she quotes William Coxe's *Travels in Switzerland* "for those beautiful and romantic descriptions of which so many novelists have availed themselves."[70] Coxe's *Travels* contains several long descriptions of mountain scenery, which really are quite similar to some descriptions in the novels; the first edition appeared in 1789, and the second in 1791; Smith's *Views*, which is also mentioned in one of Mrs. Robinson's foot-notes, was published in 1792. These books of travels are, in general, more concerned with landscape than with architecture.

The principal architectural feature of Stephen Cullen's *Haunted Priory* (1794) is a ruined convent, connecting with a castle of Punalada by a secret underground passage. Two years later, Cullen published *The Castle of Inchvally: a Tale —alas! too true*. This castle was built in the reign of Henry II, but early in the eighteenth century it fell into the hands of a lady of unromantic disposition who tried to pull it down, but found it too massive. The descriptions of Inchvally are more detailed and realistic than those of *The*

[69] III, 163.
[70] I, 30.

Haunted Priory, one reason perhaps being that Cullen is here describing an English building. The castle is the home of a Catholic family, and when the heir shows signs of apostasy, the family priest tries to frighten him back into the fold by appearing in his room through a secret passage at night, and groaning "Horrid! Horrid! Horrid!" Even more amusing than this "tale—alas! too true" is *The Castle of Hardayne* (1795), by John Bird. Hardayne is described by one of the characters as being full of "devils, and robbers, and screech owls, and them sort of things."[71] The hero goes to sleep on the floor of a room in the castle; during the night he falls through the floor into the vaults below. He stretches out his hand only to encounter a bleeding corpse. Finally he has to escape from the vault by climbing up the castle drain.

The Abbey of St. Asaph (1795), by Mrs. Kelly, is furnished with the unique feature of elastic stairs; when the heroine sets foot on the top step, the whole staircase gently collapses, precipitating her into the dungeons. Catherine Selden's *Count de Santerre* (1797) contains a remarkable gallery which is "a singular medley of the Gothic and Grecian."[72] Extremely complicated castles are depicted by the anonymous author of *The Mystic Castle: or, Orphan Heir* and *The Wanderer of the Alps: or Alphonso.* St. Siffrid's Castle, in *The Church of St. Siffrid* (1798), is a "medley of Gothic, Saxon, and Grecian architecture,"[73] having been partly remodelled by one of its owners. This description is similar to the one just quoted from *The Count de Santerre,* where the medley is so great that Gothic vaults spring from a double row of white marble Corinthian columns. The device of a movable statue giving entrance to a secret vault is used both in M. G. Lewis's *Monk* (1795)

---

[71] I, 22.
[72] I, 198.
[73] Dublin, 1798, II, 290, "by the author of Ned Evans."

and in George Moore's *Grasville Abbey* (1798). Mrs. Eleanor Sleath's *Orphan of the Rhine* (1798) has a ruined abbey and several castles, Elfinbach being the principal one. An equestrian statue of black marble, perched on a Corinthian column, adorns one of the courts of Elfinbach, and is depicted in the frontispiece to the book.

There are innumerable other novels of the time with Gothic setting, but it would be impossible to describe them all—one writer, however, cannot be omitted—Dr. Nathan Drake, whose *Literary Hours* contain three short Gothic tales, together with some interesting criticism. His critical essays show his great erudition, and in particular his familiarity with the work of contemporary novelists, of whom he mentions Horace Walpole, Aikin, Clara Reeve, Ann Radcliffe, M. G. Lewis, Charlotte Smith, and Henry Mackenzie. Mrs. Radcliffe, indeed, he hails as "the Shakespeare of Romance Writers."[74]

In the first volume of *Literary Hours*, is the tale of *Henry Fitzowen*. This is a short story, much like Aikin's *Sir Bertrand*, on which it is obviously modelled. Dr. Drake's architecture, however, is more exact than that of Aikin. Fitzowen's paternal castle has a barbican, an outer and an inner ballium, and a keep—terms not often found in the romances of the eighteenth century. Furthermore, Drake, in a foot-note, quotes a long passage from Henry's *History of England* describing a typical Gothic castle. The story of the abbey of Clunedale, which appears in the second volume of *Literary Hours*, is likewise furnished with a foot-note, this time describing the architecture of abbeys. The third volume contains the tale of *Sir Egbert*, in which the setting is Rochester Castle, and quotations are made from Thorpe's *History and Antiquities of Rochester*. Obviously, then, Dr. Drake was making an attempt to be realistic and archaeo-

---

[74] 3rd ed., 1804, I, 361.

logically accurate, an attempt which other eighteenth-century novelists had not so seriously made, although Charlotte Smith shows some tendency in that direction.

A nineteenth-century tendency is exemplified in Maria Edgeworth's *Castle Rackrent*, in which the successive owners of a building are seen through the eyes of an old family retainer. There are no architectural descriptions in *Castle Rackrent*, but this device of using a building as the framework for a story of its various owners is one which later appears in such variations as *Wuthering Heights*. Gothic setting plays an important part in several of Harriet and Sophia Lee's *Canterbury Tales* (1797-1805), notably in the tale of *Kruitzner*, by Harriet Lee, in which a lonely palace in Silesia, and a castle in Bohemia figure prominently. A secret passage in the Silesian palace permits the discovery of the murder upon which the plot hinges. Byron used this tale for his tragedy, *Werner*, and retained all the Gothic setting.

There are various methods of introducing castles in the novel of the eighteenth century. Sometimes the story opens with a description of a castle upon the very first pages, showing that the author wishes to lose no time in providing the proper Gothic atmosphere. This is the case in Mrs. Radcliffe's *Castles of Athlin and Dunbayne* and *Sicilian Romance*, in Mrs. Smith's *Emmeline*, in Mrs. Robinson's *Vancenza* and *Hubert de Sevrac*, in Mrs. Bonhote's *Bungay Castle*, and in *Godfrey de Hastings*, *The Castle of Beeston*, *The Mystic Castle*, and many others. This method has its disadvantages, because, if castle-description be the author's principal aim, it exhausts most of her thunder at the very beginning, with the result that the rest of the novel appears comparatively tame. Mrs. Radcliffe, in her later romances, was wise in deferring her architectural descriptions until the middle of the story. Thus she was able to present the building as it first appeared to approaching travellers—an obvious advantage for pictorial effect. Most novels dealing with imprisoned heroines take the opportunity of the doomed lady's arrival to describe her impressions of the destined prison.

When the visitor to the castle is a man, he generally arrives to seek shelter from a storm or to spend the night. Such is the case in *The Castle of Hardayne* by John Bird, and in *Sir Bertrand* by John Aikin. Occasionally, as in Mrs. Radcliffe's *Romance of the Forest*, the building is also used as a hiding-place. A woman in search of shelter usually goes to a convent (inhabited), and only in the most desperate circumstances does she take refuge in a ruin. Ghosts and recluses are discovered when they are already established in their places of seclusion—their arrival is usually left undescribed. Sometimes, as in the case of Château-le-blanc in Mrs. Radcliffe's *Udolpho*, a castle is inherited, and it is first seen through the eyes of its new possessors. In the social novels, the castle is often described by a guest, while in the travel descriptions, the buildings are, of course, portrayed as they appear to the travellers.

For the further development of architectural descriptions, the author usually relies upon the strong curiosity of her characters. A picture of the building is given either at the outset of the story or at the arrival of the characters, but it is a rare heroine who is content with what first meets the eye. The most artfully concealed trap-doors and sliding panels cannot escape her powers of detection, and she never sees a mysterious door without being impelled by a strange impulse to open it and explore beyond. Rusty locks and stubborn bolts fly open at her gentle touch, because her creator is only too eager to lead her through as many perilous chambers as she is able to describe. There is always something irresistibly alluring about the castles and abbeys of these romances. In the face of the most alarming dangers, and at the most inconvenient hours of the night, the intrepid heroes and heroines obey the urge to explore, and with fluttering hearts and candles penetrate to secret passages and gloomy dungeons. Their searches are often assisted by the aged housekeeper, a stock character in the Gothic romances, who is well versed in ghostly lore and genealogical anecdotes.

The Philistines never explore. On arriving at an old castle, they call loudly for a fire and warming-pans, and settle down in the snuggest parlor that they can find. The exploring is done by their romantic nieces and daughters; the Philistines being more interested in learning if the beds have been properly aired, and the damp floors suitably carpeted. A sliding panel has no allurements for them, and they take their principal comfort in complaining about the discomforts to which they are subjected in their gloomy residences. The more wealthy ones give vent to their displeasure in a more practical way by trying to renovate the castle, an attempt which invariably arouses the author's scorn.

The emotions aroused by these Gothic structures are always the same—awe and horror, which in their various aspects and combinations appear everywhere. Only an exceptionally romantic heroine, such as Charlotte in *The Country Cousins*, or the heroine of *Caroline Merton*, can derive pleasure unmixed with apprehension from an ancient castle. Upon most of these females the castle has a pleasantly terrifying effect.

Towards the end of the century, the castles are provided with an increasingly large number of rooms. The great hall is always an essential, but in some later novels, such as those of Mrs. Radcliffe, there are several halls. The great staircase and the galleries are also indispensable. Otranto contained an armory and a great chamber. Mrs. Smith brought the library, the servants' hall, and the kitchen into prominence, and banqueting-rooms appear in some of her novels. Castles which have been renovated, or which are not properly medieval, sometimes have breakfast parlors, summer parlors, or saloons. The chapel is an essential feature, and sometimes an oratory is also to be found. In the vicinity is usually a pavilion of some sort. There are always towers, generally designated by the points of the compass; a favorite arrangement is to have a tower at each corner, or, as at Udolpho, to have towers flanking the entrance. A moat is customary, but is sometimes omitted if the castle is situated on a mountain. Vaults or dungeons always occupy the lower regions of the castle, frequently communicating by subterranean passages with a nearby church, convent, or cave, or else merely ending in the forest. Different novelists have different tastes in woodwork: Mrs. Radcliffe's parlors are usually done in black larch wood; Mrs. Smith prefers cedar; while other writers often select oak. Scottish and Swiss castles are usually perched upon rocks, and Italian castles are lavishly decorated with marble.

The features of the abbey are even more conventionalized than those of the castle. The church, chapel, or cathedral, as it is variously called, is an essential feature, and so is the cloister. There are usually cells for the inmates, a refectory and a hall. Dr. Drake provides Clunedale Abbey with a chapter house also. Manor-houses are described much like castles, and indeed many eighteenth-century novelists did not distinguish between the two.

The main features of these medieval buildings are generally sufficiently authentic; but the details brought the Gothic romances into disrepute—the trap-door, the sliding panel, the entrance concealed by tapestry, the movable statue or portrait, the secret stair, the subterranean passage, and all the other "stock" mechanisms of the tales of terror. Genuine castles often possessed such features, to be sure, but hardly in such overwhelming profusion. Furthermore, these conventional devices soon become tiresome, as did the mantling ivy, the owls, bats, ghosts, and all the other furnishings of the typical castle. The reaction against this typical castle will be discussed in a later chapter.

It would take a long and cumbersome chart to show exactly how much the use of architectural setting increased in the period between 1788 and 1800; not only did the number of novels with important Gothic buildings multiply, but the number of buildings and the amount of description in each novel greatly increased. When one remembers that Charlotte Smith alone described twenty-eight buildings in her novels, and that *The Italian* mentions or describes fourteen separate structures, and that the year 1798 witnessed the publication of at least fourteen novels with architectural setting, one can form some idea of the vast increase in production which took place in these twelve years. Authors like Mrs. Parsons and Mrs. Bennett, whose earlier novels contained very little architectural setting, launched into full Gothic style by the close of the 1790's, while a horde of new Gothic writers appeared in print. Such a superabundance of castles inevitably produced a reaction, and it will be seen that even in the decade when architectural setting was reaching its climax, derisive comments about it were already appearing in the novel itself.

4

At the beginning of the nineteenth century, the Gothic romance entered a new phase. Mrs. Radcliffe had ceased writing, Mrs. Smith's career was ended by illness and death, and a fresh group of writers assumed leadership, though old favorites like Lathom, Lewis, Mrs. Roche, Mrs. Parsons, Mrs. Hedgeland, and Mrs. Meeke continued to produce novels. The trend towards historical background and archaeological research became increasingly apparent in the architecture of many novelists—this tendency, leading up to the castles of Scott and Ainsworth, will be discussed later. Some writers toned down their architectural descriptions, realizing, perhaps, the absurdity of overdoing such things; while others continued to produce castles that were even more incredible than those of their predecessors.

Of this last group, T. J. Horsley Curties is probably the best example. Even the castles of Mrs. Radcliffe seem almost insignificant beside his stupendous buildings. A concealed passage, in one of his castles, "descending into the vaults, winds for miles under the country";[75] the same castle is said "to rival even the Alps themselves in altitude and greatness";[76] the halls of another castle "might well conjure up ten thousand fearful fantasies and awfully solemn sensations."[77] No wonder that the heroine can hardly believe her eyes: "she would indeed have fancied the whole was rather a superstructure of fancy, and the huge Castle the work of magic, than the palace of a Scottish chieftain."[78] Curties is not too accurate in his terms, and it is surprising to read that "now no longer frowned the nodding capital of a once Saxon battlement, deeply overhanging the little painted embrasures of the stained casements."[79]

In contrast to Horsley Curties' castles and abbeys, those of Sarah Wilkinson are quite commonplace. A marchioness, in *The Convent of Grey Penitents*, takes refuge in that very unromantic place, Finchley Common, in a *cottage ornée*. The convent itself is given very little description. *The Fugitive Countess* is more interesting, architecturally, since its castle and convent both contain secret rooms, described in detail.

Louisa Sidney Stanhope is more lavish with her architecture than Mrs. Wilkinson, although there are hints, in her *Striking Likenesses*, of satire upon Gothic castles. The heroine, however, springs to their defence. When Lord Carberry asks: "Can you like to ramble among the time-beaten ruins

[75] *Scottish Legend*, 1802, I, 11.
[76] *Ibid.*, I, 98.
[77] *Ibid.*, I, 106.
[78] *Ibid.*, I, 135.
[79] *Saint Botolph's Priory*, 1806, I, 130-131.

of former magnificence?" she replies: "To me, my lord, though melancholy, they wear a pleasing aspect; for they reprove the existence of false pride, by holding up a mirror, in which the reflective mind may trace the fall of empires, and the destruction of earthly splendour."[80]

Her actual architecture is very much like that of Mrs. Radcliffe, although she speaks of castle towers as "grotesque"[81]—an adjective which Mrs. Radcliffe would have spurned. The appearance of the grotesque in architectural description, is indeed a sign of increasing realism. Louisa Stanhope has an eye for the picturesque, and, like Mrs. Radcliffe, she is fond of Apennine castles, sunset descriptions, and inquisition scenes. This similarity is most strongly marked in *Di Montranzo* (1810). The growing vogue of the historical novel influenced her romances, so that *The Crusaders* (1820), *The Festival of Mora* (1821), and *The Siege of Kenilworth* (1824), all have the sub-title "an historical romance." It is significant that these are among her latest novels, and that foot-notes upon architecture appear in *The Crusaders* and in *The Corsair's Bride* (1830), showing how the influence of the historical school of fiction extended even to so unhistorical a novelist as Louisa Stanhope. The same effect is noticeable in the novels of Mrs. Helme, whose *Magdalen* bears the sub-title "an historical novel," succeeding many novels which made no pretense of anything historical. Mrs. Helme's heroine, however, behaves like all the heroines of the Gothic school, and when she exclaims "my heart sunk within me," we know that she is entering the typical ruined castle. Louisa Stanhope's architecture also remains impossibly romantic to the very end: "Perched like an eagle's nest upon a giant pinnacle of flinty rock, the walls of St. Salvador bulged o'er the bed of the Baltic: so wild,

[80] 1808, II, 252-253.
[81] *Siege of Kenilworth*, 1824, I, 61.

so lone, so sublimely picturesque, so wrapped in the misty ether of awful grandeur, that its belfry, its coigns, and its towers, nodding o'er the feathery wave, seemed to sleep twice-fold upon its bosom. . . ."[82]

Anne of Swansea, like Louisa, was influenced by Mrs. Radcliffe, and the plot of the former's *Cesario Rosalba* bears suspicious resemblances to that of the latter's *Italian*. *Sicilian Mysteries*, like *Udolpho*, includes a visit to Venice. Anne does not confine herself to Italy, however; she is equally at home in Scotland, Ireland, and Germany; and her castles seem to travel from one country to another without any noticeable change. All these ladies are fond of the adjective "spiral": they produce "spiral" turrets, "spiral" stairs, and, in at least one instance, "spiral" windows.[83]

C. R. Maturin's descriptions of buildings are more realistic than those of most of his feminine colleagues, and he uses foot-notes in both *Melmoth* and *The Milesian Chief*, referring to travel books. In one place he speaks of turrets, "grotesquely perched." With this tendency towards realism, however, he combines an enthusiasm for castles which even the most enraptured female novelist could not surpass: a Sicilian castle, in *Fatal Revenge*, is said to "fill the mind with melancholy awe, and wild solemnity."[84]

Recluses continue to enjoy Gothic architecture, even after 1800. In G. D. Hernon's *Louisa* (1805), a gloomy forest is chosen by "a gentleman . . . . whose peculiarities and melancholy cast of mind, induced him to erect his mansion in this solitary retirement, the better to indulge the corroding grief that seemed to be preying on his vitals." This dwelling "was, by his particular direction, made to resemble a fortified castle or tower." The only habitable part of one of Horsley

---

[82] *Festival of Mora*, 1821, I, 138.
[83] Lady Morgan: *Novice of St. Dominick*, 3rd ed., 1808, I, 256.
[84] *Fatal Revenge*, New York, 1808, I, 301, 72.

Curties' ruins (in *St. Botolph's Priory*) "was in general denominated the Solitary Hermitage of the Recluse Saint Aubespine." At a ruined castle by the sea, one of David Carey's characters enjoys "the sublimest of reveries." Every day, he encircles the castle three times, places one of the wall flowers in his buttonhole, and returns home.[85]

The Philistines also still persist. One of Anne of Swansea's characters longs to return to London because "these dismal old castles vapour me to death."[86] A similar character in Mrs. Roche's *Contrast* refuses to look at "old stones and ricketty old walls" and says that "whenever I voluntarily incur fatigue, it is to see something worth seeing—something elegantly, new and fashionable."[87]

As for the romantic heroes and heroines, their rhapsodies reach even greater heights of ecstasy: ' "Ah, that romantic-looking tower!" cried De Montville; "how many hours have I passed in the contemplation of it. . ." '[88] Elizabeth, in Mrs. Roche's *Discarded Son*, enjoys walking through a ruined abbey, where the echoes of her footsteps "gave rise to sensations pleasingly awful."[89] Eugenia, in Mrs. C. Mathews' *Griffith Abbey*, is "enthusiastically fond of those mouldering records of antiquity."[90] A desolate tower, in Mrs. Golland's *Augustus and Adelina*, "inspired the mind of our hero with a solemn awe."[91] Mrs. Golland's descriptions, in fact, are apt to be incredibly naive. One of her castles "arose in a romantic spot 'midst Scotia's glens" where the waves "dashed in majestic currency."[92] A secret door is "concealed in a

[85] *Frederick Morland*, 1824, I, 59.
[86] *Secrets in Every Mansion*, 1818, II, 101.
[87] New York, 1828, I, 220.
[88] *Ibid.*, II, 98.
[89] 1807, I, 47-48.
[90] 1807, I, 206.
[91] 1819, II, 6.
[92] *Eleanor*, 1821, I, 3.

large terrific painting."[93] The moon, in *The Witch of Aysgarth*, is "shedding her chaste beams through a gothic arch."[94]

Perhaps the absurdity of the novelists' castles was accentuated by the fact that most Gothic romances were written by women. Literature has always been concerned with people, but it was under a petticoat régime that it became even more concerned with the dwellings in which people live. The contributions of men, such as Walpole, Aikin, and Dr. Drake, are not to be ignored, but the real development of architectural setting was brought about by women.

None of these writers was an authority upon architecture, or even a well-informed amateur. Horace Walpole probably was better acquainted than any of them with medieval construction, but Strawberry Hill stands to show how limited even his knowledge was. Few of his female successors had travelled very far: the Rhine valley marked the limit of Mrs. Radcliffe's excursions, while Charlotte Smith went no further than Normandy. Moreover, most of the travelling which these ladies did accomplish was done after their works were finished, when for the first time they had sufficient money and leisure. Most of them were members of the middle class, and they did not have the influential friends who could get them letters of introduction to places ordinarily closed to the public.

Probably their very ignorance of Gothic architecture heightened their appreciation of it; cathedrals and castles lose some of their glamour after one has examined the tracery, vaulting, and ornament of hundreds of them with an eye that can distinguish where Late Decorated leaves off and Early Perpendicular begins. Familiarity sometimes breeds contempt, in the case of buildings as well as of people. The best architectural descriptions which the century affords are

[93] *Ibid.*, V, 237.
[94] 1841, I, 34.

those of Mrs. Radcliffe, who had very little technical knowledge of Gothic construction, and whose pictures depict effects of light and shade rather than architectural details. Furthermore, it may be suggested that perhaps Mrs. Radcliffe was a little near-sighted (her description of Hardwick would imply that she was), and that the impression of grandeur which she found in castles was partly produced by ignorance of architecture and partly by inability to see it clearly. Buildings always appear more majestic through a mist, or at sunset, or by moonlight than in the glare of the mid-day sun, and Mrs. Radcliffe seems perpetually to be looking through a soft luminous haze. Had she lived a hundred years later, she surely would have quoted at her chapter headings:

> The splendor falls on castle walls
> And snowy summits old in story—

Another significant feature is the tendency of the novelists to use Perpendicular or Tudor architecture rather than the earlier and more strictly medieval variety. The Perpendicular style, which was the last of the genuine Gothic styles to be discarded and the first to be resumed after the interval of the Renaissance, was the most favorably regarded of medieval styles during the eighteenth century. Even Dr. Johnson, for instance, calls York Cathedral "an edifice of loftiness and elegance, equal to the highest hopes of architecture."[95] Moreover, the richness of Perpendicular ornament, the elaboration of fan vaulting, and the almost classical regularity and symmetry of the style were more in tune with the architectural ideals of the eighteenth century than were the plainer and more massive forms of earlier styles.

The prevalence of the "great stair-case" is an indication that the novelists favored the Tudor period in their architectural descriptions. The staircase in a medieval castle was usually a winding stone affair, cramped into a turret;

[95] *Letters* ed. G. B. Hill, i, 224.

it was not until the dawn of the Renaissance that broad flights of oak or marble appeared. Another tell-tale sign is the oriel window, or, as Mrs. Smith calls it, the "bow-window," a late architectural development, not found in the earliest castles. Also the great windows over the entrances to Mrs. Radcliffe's abbeys are more characteristic of Perpendicular churches than of earlier ones, and the "fret-work" which is so frequently mentioned in connection with vaulting seems to refer to the fan vaulting of the late Gothic period. Warwick, Penshurst, and Kenilworth, which are all frequently mentioned, are largely Perpendicular buildings. Indeed, Dr. Drake's description of Rochester Castle (which was not published until after 1800), and Mrs. Radcliffe's "Saxon-Gothic" fortress seem to be the only early attempts to describe Norman or Romanesque buildings.

Such emphasis upon architecture could not occur until literature had become the expression of a highly civilized people. To earlier generations, ruins had suggested ghosts, banditti, and wild animals too poignantly for comfort; it was not until the comparative security of the eighteenth century that such places could become resorts for people of romantic and contemplative dispositions. Earlier generations usually had too many real reasons for melancholy, to waste their time sighing over the relics of fallen grandeur. A building to them was a place in which to live; a ruin was desirable only as a quarry for stones; an abducted girl had too many other worries to spend much time shuddering at the grandeur of the turrets or the dreariness of the wainscoting.

Interest in inanimate objects is itself a sign of civilized literature; it implies leisure for contemplation, and a high cultivation of the perceptions on the part of the reader. Only when action and passion have sufficiently abated, can we appreciate the subtler aspects of our external surroundings. The leisure and the boredom of the English upper classes were probably important factors in the popularity of the Gothic romance with its accompanying castles and abbeys.

CHAPTER FOUR

TEMPLES, VILLAS, AND PAVILIONS

In contrast to the conventional Gothic setting, the novelists often introduced a baroque element—baroque in a very wide sense, since the term must be extended to include certain aspects of Greek, Roman, Egyptian, and Oriental architecture, as well as that of the late Renaissance. Perhaps the adjective "pagan" is most inclusive of these various styles of construction, suggesting as it does the ideas of voluptuousness, worldliness, and elegance in contrast to the more solemn and spiritual qualities of medieval architecture. There is seldom anything inspiring in the classical architecture of the novelists, except when it is in ruins, in which case it evokes the moral sentiments which all ruins conveyed to the eighteenth-century mind.

This very contrast between the two styles made them useful as foils to each other. Mrs. Radcliffe's castles and abbeys are often accompanied by great villas of the Renaissance, opposing the luxuriant order of classical magnificence to the luxuriant wildness of medieval splendor. Udolpho represents natural grandeur; the villas on the Brenta typify the grandeur of art. Fontanville Abbey is Christian and sublime, but the villa of the Marquis is pagan and luxurious. The convent of San Stefano impresses a "sacred awe" upon its visitors, but the Marchesa's villa on the bay of Naples resembles "the palace of a fairy."

In general, it may be said that the novelists reserved their baroque architecture for worldlings, and their Gothic architecture for heroines and villains. The main tragedies, of course, were laid in the castle; the villa was used only for contrast. Some novelists openly expressed their opinions about this opposition of styles. A character in Mary Ann

Hanway's *Falconbridge Abbey* (1809) says, "how much he preferred the solemn grandeur of their castles, with their appropriate decorations, to the light and airy habitations of their frivolous descendants!"[1] A lady in William Child Green's *Algerines* (1832) has never felt "the slightest inclination to exchange, for the gaudier corridors of a modern palazzo, the antique, but spacious chambers and galleries of that venerable residence."[2] Maturin goes so far as to say that "any man who withdraws his eye from a Gothic ruin to fix it on a Grecian palace will find the transition unfavorable. He will find in its very symmetry, and grace, and milder majesty, something mean and minute."[3] Eaton Stannard Barrett satirizes this attitude when he makes his heroine condemn "the villa mere lath and plaster; with its pretty little stucco-work, and its pretty little paintings, and its pretty little bronzes." She says that "nice, new, sweet, and charming, are the only epithets that one can apply to it; while antique, sublime, terrible, picturesque, and Gothic, are the adjectives appropriate to my castello."[4]

It was soon recognized that each style expressed a corresponding quality. John Galt describes a house which is "a splendid compilation of whatever had been deemed elegant in antique, curious in Gothic, or gorgeous in Oriental architecture."[5] Disraeli says that "however there may be a standard of taste, there is no standard of style."[6] To him, the Alhambra, the Parthenon, the Pantheon, and the Cathedral of Seville are merely different combinations of the same principles of taste. The young duke, in Disraeli's novel of that

[1] II, 132.
[2] I, 14.
[3] *Wild Irish Boy*, 1808, II, 11.
[4] *The Heroine*, 1813, III, 134-5.
[5] *Last of the Lairds*, Edinburgh, 1826, p. 137.
[6] *Contarini Fleming*, Part V, Chap. I.

name, makes a town house into an imitation of the Louvre, but is horrified to find that his ancestral castle is not pure Gothic. A character in *Vivian Grey* has a plan for making "every elevation of an order consonant with the purpose of the building"[7] the Corinthian order expresses pomp and elegance; the Tuscan, severe simplicity. Architectural eclecticism was certainly appearing in literature as well as in construction. Lady Morgan remarks that an Ionic temple is characterized by elegance, but that Corinthian pillars denote strength and magnificence.[8]

Important as the pagan element was in architectural setting, it rarely succeeded in supplanting the prevailing Gothic mood. Temples and villas are seldom provided with those secret passages, sliding panels, lonely turrets, and subterranean dungeons which had proved so serviceable in the novel; and they also lack the sublimity, mystery, and terror which the castles of the Gothic romances inspired. During the eighteenth century, the use of pagan architecture in the novel was largely decorative, seldom emotional, and almost never structural.

Roman ruins served the same purpose in the novel that Gothic ruins, or any ruins, could perform: their appearance was "picturesque," satisfying the reader's aesthetic tastes, while their strength and massiveness were "sublime," arousing the reader's emotions. Like all ruins, they suggested reflections on the glories of antiquity and the transitory nature of human grandeur—contemplations which always seemed pleasant to the eighteenth-century mind (although a character in C. Johnstone's *Arsaces* remarks that "such reflections were too painful to be pursued"[9]). *Arsaces*

---

[7] Book VII, Chap. II.
[8] *Wild Irish Girl*, 4th ed., 1808, I, 42.
[9] Dublin, 1774, I, 48.

describes a ruined amphitheatre, now the residence of a recluse:

> It was a circular building of vast extent, the walls of which had been so high, that, though a great part of them was fallen in several places, that which remained standing was still sufficient to exclude every creature without wings: nor could I perceive a place of entrance, for any other, as he led me all around it.
> I was just going to express my surprize at this, when my conductor stopped; and taking a ladder, which lay concealed at a little distance, he applied it to a narrow aperture in the wall, at a considerable height from the ground, into which, when we had ascended, he drew the ladder after him.
> I found myself, now, in a large gallery, arched overhead, and supported by massive pillars of the most exquisite workmanship. It looked into an open space, in the centre of the building, part of which was planted with fruit-trees of various sorts, and the rest cultivated as a garden, and filled with various kinds of vegetables.[10]

The prevailing enthusiasm for Roman ruins is contemptuously mentioned in *The Sentimental Spy* (1773). *Fashionable Follies* (1781) refers to an English traveller's visit to Roman ruins. Lord Nicknackerton, in Shebbeare's *Lydia* (1755), goes to Balbec "to measure the Proportions of the various Remains of Architecture to be found in that City, and compare them with what is yet to be seen at *Rome* and *Athens*."[11] Lord Liberal refers to this expedition in scornful tones, saying that "Ruins of all Things in the same Architecture are the most alike, and the least worth running much Risque to visit."

After 1790, references to Roman ruins become more frequent and more respectful. Charlotte Smith's *Montalbert*

[10] *Ibid.*, I, 43.
[11] IV, 138, 141.

Temples, Villas, and Pavilions 149

describes a ruined temple in an Italian village, with "a marble capital, or an half-buried column" appearing from the shrubbery. A ruined amphitheatre is mentioned in Mrs. Robinson's *Hubert de Sevrac* (1796), and another is more fully described in Mrs. Parsons' *Mysterious Warning,* published in the same year:

> Many superb pillars supported different parts of the structure. Nearly half of the inside was in ruins; but in some places there were regular seats rising over one another to an immense height.
> The whole exhibited a sullen state of grandeur sinking to decay. Half broken pillars of marble, or granite lay scattered in large fragments on a kind of mosaic pavement.[12]

Mrs. Radcliffe's *Italian* mentions Roman ruins in several places: Vivaldi, on his visits to Ellena, is obliged to pass through the archway of an old Roman fort, and, later in the romance, when he is brought to Rome by the officers of the Inquisition, he sees "some of those mighty monuments of Rome's eternal name, those sacred ruins, those gigantic skeletons, which once enclosed a soul, whose energies governed a world!" Catherine Selden's *Count de Santerre* mentions "an ancient temple, whose broken and mouldering columns were lying in huge fragments, half overgrown with weeds and briars."[13] Lord Glenmore, in A. Kendall's *Castle on the Rock*, goes to see Roman ruins in the Pyrenees. In *The Count de Novini* (1799), the hero takes refuge in "the centum camera; horrid dungeons, where Nero immured the unhappy victims of his tyranny."[14]

Greek ruins, though not so popular as the Roman variety, were not entirely neglected. Charlotte Smith's *Celestina*

[12] III, 167.
[13] Bath, 1797, II, 216.
[14] I, 175.

mentions a ruined Grecian pavilion in the Pyrenees (strange place for anything Grecian!). Ellis Cornelia Knight's *Dinarbas* (1790), a sequel to Dr. Johnson's *Rasselas*, praises the ruins of Athens:

> "The effect which those buildings produced on me," said Dinarbas, "is far superior to my powers of description: the noble simplicity of the Grecian temples, the elegance of their proportion, the harmony of their parts, and the majesty of the whole, give an impression of awe and of satisfaction, which no modern building affords."[15]

The popularity of ancient architecture increased in the novels of the early nineteenth century, corresponding very roughly with the vogue of the Greek and Roman revivals. In several instances, classic architecture actually assumed the most important place in the novel, a place where, in the eighteenth century, Gothic construction had reigned supreme. Lady Morgan's *Woman; or, Ida of Athens* (1809) describes the Acropolis, and Frances Clifford's *Ruins of Tivoli* (1810) introduces Hadrian's villa. Lockhart's *Valerius* (1821) is full of descriptions of ancient Rome. In Edward Upham's *Rameses* (1824), Egyptian architecture is lavishly portrayed. Croly's *Salathiel* (1829) and Horace Smith's *Zillah* (1828) describe ancient Jerusalem, with side excursions into other lands, *Salathiel* touching upon Greece, and *Zillah* upon Rome. Thomas Moore's *Epicurean* has Egypt for its setting. *The Last Days of Pompeii* is Bulwer-Lytton's attempt to resurrect Roman architecture as it appeared in its prime, and he introduces Roman ruins even in so unlikely a place as *Harold, the Last of the Saxon Kings*.

In many of these later novels, ancient architecture borrowed Gothic thunder by the introduction of secret passages and subterranean vaults, and also by the assumption of an

---

[15] p. 221.

emotional element which it had not hitherto possessed. The temples in Upham's *Rameses* are honey-combed with subterranean labyrinths; secret doors and stairs play a prominent part in Lockhart's *Valerius*; Arbaces' house in *The Last Days of Pompeii* has entrances for the partakers of his secret revels; there are dungeons in the temple of Cybele in Horace Smith's *Zillah*. Furthermore, these later descriptions of classical architecture have many of the sinister qualities of the Gothic romances. Upham says, of Egyptian chambers, that "their gloom, their ponderous bulk, their air, and sounds, all impressively reminded Rameses of death."[16] A house in Horace Smith's *Zillah*, "immured as it was within high walls, and surrounded by cloisters of black Gopher wood, was calculated to inspire solemn, if no mournful feelings.[17] *Valerius* mentions the "solemn Doric columns," "proud pinnacles glittering," and the "sublimity of the princely towers"[18]—of ancient Rome!

All through the nineteenth century, novels with classical setting occasionally appeared—familiar examples are Kingsley's *Hypatia* and Pater's *Marius the Epicurean*. Seldom, however, is any one building made to play a dominant part in these classical narratives. It is quite possible (as demonstrated by Harrison Ainsworth) to make a single castle or cathedral the theme and setting for an entire novel, but such a feat is more difficult with the temple or the villa. The great medieval castles are towns in themselves, whereas classic buildings are more limited in size and scope. It is much easier to lose one's way in Windsor Castle or the Tower of London than in the Parthenon or the Colosseum.

Sobriety and restraint are usually lacking in the novelists' descriptions of classic architecture. With their glowing colors

[16] III, 48.
[17] New York, 1829, II, 168.
[18] II, 52, 54, 58.

and rich burden of precious metals and stones, these buildings have many qualities which are more often found in the Orient. This exuberance pervades all the pagan architecture of the novels. Gothic architecture might be impressive from its bulk, its gloom, and its rich design; but pagan architecture added to these attractions the charms of frescoes, rich hangings, mosaics, gilding, and inlaid gems. In *Valerius*, "the marble, the brass, the ivory, and the flaming gold, everywhere lavished on arch, metope, and architrave—all conspired for a moment to dazzle my sight."[19] Disraeli, in *Alroy*, rises to heights of visionary description: "Pillars of many-coloured marbles rose from a red and blue pavement of the same material, and supported a vaulted, circular, and highly embossed roof of purple, scarlet, and gold."[20] Other examples are "a most singular fountain which rose from a basin of gold encrusted with pearls,"[20] and "a door of tortoiseshell and mother of pearl,"[20] and a "ceiling encrusted with green fretwork, and studded with silver stars," which rests upon "clustered columns of white and green marble."[21] The popularity of the Alhambra in the novels must be attributed to a fondness for such lush descriptions.

The architecture of the Renaissance is, naturally, mentioned often in the novels of the eighteenth century, because it was then the prevailing architectural style. Descriptions of this type of architecture are usually concerned with country villas, or with garden pavilions, all of which are characterized by lavish magnificence. A typical description of a Renaissance building is given in *Seymour Castle* (1789). This building, which is called Bellview, is actually described much more carefully than the castle which gives its title to the novel:

[19] II, 54.
[20] Part V, Chap. V.
[21] Part V, Chap. III.

> When you come to the house, a vestibule leads to the hall, which is magnificent; it occupies two stories in height, and is lighted with windows from the upper.
> The grand staircase is highly embellished with some of the finest pieces of Varrio; in the saloon, which is almost past description beautiful, are stories elegantly painted, taken from Virgil and Ovid; the walls of it, and of the drawing-room, are of a rich rose colour, the cornice highly ornamented with festoons of flowers. . . . at the four corners of each room are palm trees modelled in stucco, painted and varnished with various tints of green, which spread and support the dome; represented as formed of reeds bound together with ribbands, the cove is supposed to be perforated, and a brilliant sunny sky appears, which has a fine effect.[22]

Mrs. Radcliffe, in *The Mysteries of Udolpho*, invests her Renaissance buildings with the same splendor which characterizes her castles and abbeys. She uses sunsets to spread a Claude-like glow over her architectural creations. An excellent example of her work is the famous account of Emily's arrival at Venice:

> Nothing could exceed Emily's admiration, on her first view of Venice, with its islets, palaces, and towers rising out of the sea, whose clear surface reflected the tremulous picture in all its colours. The sun, sinking in the west, tinted the waves and the lofty mountains of Friuli, which skirt the northern shores of the Adriatic, with a saffron glow, while on the marble porticos and colonnades of St. Mark were thrown the rich lights and shades of evening. As they glided on, the grander features of this city appeared more distinctly: its terraces, crowned with airy yet majestic fabrics, touched, as they now were, with the splendour of the setting sun, appeared as if they had been called up from the ocean by the wand of an enchanter, rather than reared by mortal hands.[23]

[22] I, 78.
[23] II, 35.

When Emily sails up the Brenta, she sees more Renaissance architecture, again illuminated by a sunset:

> The grandeur of the Palladian villas, that adorn these shores, was considerably heightened by the setting rays, which threw strong contrasts of light and shade upon the porticos and long arcades, and beamed a mellow lustre upon the orangeries and the tall groves of pine and cypress, that overhung the buildings.[24]

These descriptions, as Miss McIntyre has shown,[25] were probably based on Mrs. Piozzi's *Journey*, but the very fact that Mrs. Radcliffe chose to include them shows that the architecture of the Renaissance had some attractions for her. In *The Italian*, she includes several buildings of this period; the most notable of them being Signora Bianchi's house (the Villa Altieri), the ruined villa where Schedoni and Ellena take refuge, and the Marchesa's villa on the bay of Naples. The ruined villa has a "light colonnade" around its interior court, and a wrecked marble fountain. The Marchesa's villa is hung with purple and gold, and "the vaulted cieling was designed by one of the first painters of the Venetian school; the marble statues that adorned the recesses were not less exquisite, and the whole symmetry and architecture, airy, yet rich; gay, yet chastened; resembled the palace of a fairy."[26] Adeline, in *The Romance of the Forest*, is confined by the wicked Marquis in rooms of a Renaissance type. Mrs. Robinson, in *Hubert de Sevrac*, describes a Renaissance villa, "constructed entirely with white marble, and in the most finished style of Italian architecture."[27] It has a portico and colonnades, with steps of Siena marble. "The interior of

---

[24] II, 121-2.
[25] Op. cit., pp. 58-61.
[26] III, 94.
[27] III, 58.

this terrestrial paradise was no less voluptuous," being filled with paintings, mirrors, and sculpture.

The garden architecture of the eighteenth-century novels is usually Renaissance, although, after 1790, Gothic and Oriental pavilions begin to flourish. Such temples and pavilions are very numerous, but they never play an important part in the story, and but little description is lavished upon them. Mrs. Gunning, in *The Memoirs of Mary*, introduces a pavilion which is lined with a false partition of canvas painted to resemble stucco. Behind the canvas is a secret gallery.

Oriental architecture was never used by either Mrs. Smith or Mrs. Radcliffe, but their contemporaries often mention it, and in one romance, Beckford's *Vathek*, it occupies a very important place. Although its use was usually decorative, it is occasionally employed for emotional effect, as, for instance, in Dr. Langhorne's *Solyman and Almena* (1762), where the ruins of Persepolis "gave the travellers a mournful and magnificent idea of the pristine grandeur of this edifice."[28]

The Bonze, or Chinese Anchorite; an Oriental epic Novel by d'Alenson contains an interesting description:

> In the midst of the island, was a romantic palace, in the free taste of China, which tied by no partial rules, admitted all the beauties of architecture; whether magnificently sublime, elegantly light and fanciful, or delicately chaste; yet, bearing such a profound correspondency, as to form one entire whole. A style where all but a great genius is lost; rules and rigid methods being the directors of secondary souls! Various beautiful bridges, led to as many glorious porticos full of gaity, painted florid, and blazing gold.[29]

[28] p. 63.
[29] 1768, I, 22.

Elsewhere in this novel is a profusion of temples, obelisks, pyramids, and porticos, while the frontispiece depicts a distant pagoda. William Tooke, in *The Loves of Othniel and Achsah* (1769) presents one of those florid pictures which are typical of eighteenth-century descriptions of the Orient:

> —In the first apartment which they entered, were all the beauties of nature united into perfection—the golden columns, supporting the vaulted roof, might vie with the produce of OPHIR. —Inchantment itself could not, with all it's boasted power, have raised so superb a structure. —The walls were composed of chrysolite and emeralds, . . . The shining pavement was composed of porphyry. —The stately arches formed a kind of pleasing maze—which added majesty and splendour to the whole. —Towards the east was built an altar of attractive beauty. . . .[30]

Orlando and Seraphina: a Turkish Story (1787) contains a subterranean passage, "whose sides and roof were of polished marble, and illuminated by an immense number of lamps of various colours."[31] In the same novel, there is "the castle of the seven towers," where Orlando is confined, and also explanatory foot-notes, one of which quotes Lady Mary Wortley Montagu's description of a chiosk, while another gives a slight description of a mosque at Medina, and a third gives a long account of Santa Sophia in Constantinople.

James White introduces the Alhambra in his *John of Gaunt*, while in *King Richard Coeur-de-lion* he describes a fantastic subterranean city beneath the deserts of Tartary. Joseph Trapp's *Sprite of the Nunnery* (1796) confines one of the characters in "a half decayed monument of Moorish architecture,"[32] which is incongruously furnished with a ruin-

---

[30] I, 51.
[31] I, 62-3.
[32] II, 52.

ous underground passage to a churchyard. S. J. Arnold's *Creole, or the Haunted Island* (1796), which seems to be an imitation of Dr. Johnson's *Rasselas,* secludes the emperor of Morocco's son in a castle erected on an island in the middle of a lake. This building is described as "airy and majestic, lugubrious and fantastic," and it is provided with a concealed mosque, but otherwise it seems more like a typical castle of the Gothic romances than a Moorish creation, since it has turrets, a library, galleries, a wainscoted room with a secret panel, and subterranean vaults where a hermit dwells. Another castle in the same romance is moated and embattled, and possesses no Oriental characteristics whatever. *Dinarbas* (1790), which is avowedly a sequel to *Rasselas,* mentions the palace in the happy valley, but with no additional description. In his travels, Dinarbas sees the mosque of Santa Sophia at Constantinople, which he compares unfavorably with the Greek temples. A mosque is mentioned in *The Castle of Eridan.*

The most effective use of Oriental architecture in the eighteenth-century novel is to be found in William Beckford's *Vathek* (1786). Vathek, like his creator, is fond of constructing things on a magnificent scale, so that at the opening of the story we find him adding five wings to his ancestral palace, and building a tower which is mounted by eleven thousand steps. A subterranean passage gives Carathis access to the palace, while secret stairs lead to the recesses where her mummies are deposited. No detailed pictures are given of Vathek's palace, but there are numerous references to porticos, halls, galleries, kitchens, and chambers, to say nothing of that Oriental convenience, the harem. At the close of the narrative, Vathek reaches the moonlit ruins of Istakar, where gloomy watch-towers and lofty columns with strange capitals soar from a terrace of black marble. Four colossal figures in stone guard the sculptured façade of the palace. The rock yawns before Vathek, revealing the staircase of polished marble, which he and Nouronihar follow until they reach an ebony portal opening into the famous hall of Eblis, with its vaulted ceiling, and its columns and arcades retreating in the distance till they vanish in the point where the tabernacle of Eblis stands.

Garden architecture in the novel is occasionally Oriental. Thus *Wilmot; or the Pupil of Folly* (1782) and *The Orphan Sisters* (1793) both mention Chinese bridges; Thomas Stabback's *Maria* (1796) describes a Chinese pagoda in Earl Fermor's garden; an Oriental pavilion is mentioned in Mrs. Roche's *Nocturnal Visit*; and a Turkish pavilion graces the gardens of the Renaissance villa in Mrs. Robinson's *Hubert de Sevrac*. Mr. Nonsuch's garden in Richard Graves's *Columella* (1779) contains both a Chinese bridge and a pagoda.

Apparently the fashion for depicting Gothic architecture in the novel brought with it an interest in other styles of architecture. All architectural descriptions in the novel are more numerous, more striking, and more detailed after 1790 than they were in the previous decades; Mrs. Radcliffe and her followers were able to feel the lure of Roman ruins and Palladian villas, as well as the more customary attractions of medieval castles and abbeys.

CHAPTER FIVE

REALISM DISPLACING ROMANCE

1

By 1795, a reaction against the typical romantic castle became apparent even in the novel itself. Charlotte Smith was already tired of the Gothic setting which she had helped to popularize, and her annoyance was shared by other novelists. The stereotyped castle and abbey had become so ridiculous, after constant reappearance, that some writers were ready to satirize the whole Gothic school of fiction; it was inevitable that many people should lack the romantic instincts necessary for an appreciation of medieval architecture, and it was equally inevitable that these matter-of-fact people should express their opinions in print. Jane Austen's *Northanger Abbey*, which was written in 1798, languished unpublished for twenty years, but other writers, hardly less outspoken, succeeded in airing their ideas immediately.

Mrs. Hervey's *Melissa and Marcia* (1788), for instance, contains an episode which is really a burlesque of the "imprisoned heroine" theme of the romances. Melissa is confined, by her husband's orders, in an ancient castle, "a gothic pile of building," turretted, moated, and mournful. Here she is consigned to the care of a Mrs. Croaker, mentioned as "the austere Croaker." One morning, at breakfast, the heroine finds a crumpled letter enclosed in her boiled egg.

> "Gracious heaven!" cried Melissa softly, ... "Perhaps the Castle is haunted, and some horrid spectre may appear."
> While she was debating this point internally, she saw the tapestry move, and, terrified beyond measure, she screamed. . . .[1]

[1] I, 262-3.

That night, Melissa cannot sleep; the wind whistles through the castle, and she fancies that there is something "preternatural" in the sound of Mrs. Croaker's snoring. Her suspense is ended by the appearance from behind the tapestry of a certain Mr. Prattle, who is in love with Melissa, and has disguised himself as the gardener's boy to gain admittance to the castle. He has discovered a secret passage opening behind the tapestry in Melissa's room, and terminating in a vault beneath the village church. Although Melissa pretends to be willing to escape with him, she tells Mrs. Croaker about the affair, and Prattle is captured in an amusing scene, when "they drove him along with many taunting jests, and shut him up in one of the towers of the castle."

Another burlesque incident, directed more against the romances of chivalry than the real Gothic romances, is to be found in Mrs. Griffith's *History of Lady Barton* (1771), when two men find "a castle, defended by a deep moat, great iron gates, a draw-bridge, and immense high walls." This sight proves very alluring to one of the two travellers, who observes that:

> The appearance of this extraordinary mansion, roused my chivalry; I figured to myself a beauteous damsel confined there by some horrid enchanter, or giant, and determined that I would, if possible, set the fair captive free.[2]

Their curiosity is still further heightened when they are told that the castle is occupied by two maidens, who live in complete seclusion. Spurred on by this account, the two travellers climb through vast thickets of briars, and scale the castle walls, only to find that the inhabitants are two ugly old women.

The effects of Gothic romances upon timid females are

[2] II, 210.

satirized in *Caroline Merton* (1794). Lady Fairford, a character in this novel, is visiting at C— Castle, "a large gothic edifice, situated on the brow of a bold hill." The castle is too Gothic for this lady's comfort, and her visit is not a happy one:

> Lady Fairford shuddered as she crossed the drawbridge. —When the massive gate closed after her, she looked as if she fancied herself shut out from all the joys of human society; and haunted chambers and evil spirits took immediate possession of her imagination.—
> She scarcely now speaks above a whisper, being absolutely terrified at the sound of her own voice. She examines the tapestry hangings before she ventures into bed, lest some goblin should be concealed behind them; and dreams of nothing but enchanted helmets, with nodding plumes, and the ghastly spectres of murdered Knights.—[3]

Miss Elizabeth Gunning takes a slight fling at the fashion for describing castles, when she introduces a castle of her own in her novel, *The Packet* (1794):

> The castle presents itself before me. What food does it exhibit for architects—what a regale for amateurs—what a hash of description it is now in my power to serve up, supplied with so many rich ingredients, if in one only, I had not been deficient! The Attic salt is wanting, without which I may increase the mess of words, but can give them no relishing flavour. . . .[4]

Later, she says that she is not going to expose her ignorance by "talking of orders I do not understand."

Charlotte Smith, in her preface to the second volume of *The Banished Man* (that same *Avis au Lecteur* which has

[3] I, 66-7.
[4] I, 37.

been mentioned in preceding chapters), says, beginning with a quotation from *Tristram Shandy*:

> "There was, an please your Honour," said Corporal Trim; "there was a certain king of Bohemia, who had seven castles."
> A modern Novelist, who, to write "in the immediate taste," has so great a demand for these structures, cannot but regret, that not one of the seven castles was sketched by the light and forcible pencil of Sterne: for if it be true that books are made, as he asserts, only as apothecaries make medicines, how much might have been obtained, from the king of Bohemia's seven castles, towards the castles which frown in almost every modern novel!

Later in the same novel, she remarks:

> D'Alonville could only observe that night that the house was very large, and furnished with ancient magnificence; but be not alarmed, gentle reader, though seven castles have been talked of in a preface, thou shalt not be compelled to enter on another at this late period of the story; . . . . its outward walls shall not be roughened by former sieges, or its entrance guarded with portcullis; the wall flower and the fern shall not nod over the broken battlements, nor shall the eastern tower, or any tower, be enwreathed with the mantling ivy.[5]

In *The Young Philosopher*, Mrs. Smith makes another thrust at the Gothic romances. One of the characters says:

> It [the tapestry] was nailed down so that I could not move it, nor could the wind perform any of those operations upon it which constitute great part of the terror in some novels I had read at Upwood. . . .[6]

---
[5] 2nd ed., IV, 107-8.
[6] IV, 256.

At the beginning of *The Solitary Wanderer*, Mrs. Smith continues the attack:

> My hills will boldly swell, my woods wave over as many nightingales as I can collect, my castles frown, and my streams fall, or murmur, or glitter, as luxuriously, and as frequently, as if I were the wandering and persecuted heroine of a modern novel in the very newest taste.

Twenty pages farther, she promises to give a history of Palgrave Abbey,

> . . . if, on nearer inspection, it shall seem worthy to appear, though only in manuscript, among the castles, towers, abbeys, priories and caverns, caves, cliffs, subterraneous passages and rugged ruins, rocks, and rifted battlements, which have filled so many pages, and excited so much admiration, both in the closet and on the stage.

In *Modern Novel Writing* (1796), Beckford makes fun of the Gothic novel, and he repeats the attack in *Azemia* (1797). Charles Lucas refuses to describe the Castle of St. Donats, in the novel by that name (1798):

> Reader, shall I give thee a description of the situation of St. Donats? No—so many excellent ones thou mayst read in various other castles that have been described by ancient and modern writers, that I shall willingly spare myself the trouble.[7]

Later, he says that "to present the reader a castle without a ghost, is, to the man of taste, a dish without sauce," and that "a castle without a ghost is fit for nothing but—to live in."

In the same year, appeared *More Ghosts!* (by Mrs. F. C. Patrick), which is frankly a burlesque upon the Gothic

[7] I, 78.

romances. The scene of this tale is an abbey in Yorkshire,[8] which was formerly inhabited by barefooted friars and by "those vestals usually denominated nuns." It is described as being "as pretty a dismal pile as ever pen has dilineated." Of the rooms, "many were *un*-inhabited, some *in*-habited, but all of them *haunted*." The abbots and nuns who were buried in "the spacious and awful cymetery" walk about at night, "clad in the same shrouds that enwrapped their clay-cold bodies, and are seen as regular [*sic*] as the owners themselves." Miss Bolton, one of the modern inhabitants of the abbey, dreams that there is a door behind the tapestry in her room. On awakening, she communicates the dream, and the door is found; but difficulty is experienced by the two people who try to go through it, because the doorway is too narrow to admit them both together, and each of them is afraid to be the first to enter. One incident in the book is a direct thrust at Mrs. Radcliffe:

> "Yes, Sir," said the housekeeper, who had read the Castle of Adolphus, "and I said that smugglers, for aught we knew, might have come thro' a hole in your Honour's bed, and so have carried you off, and forced your Honour to turn smuggler in your old age, as such things have been."[9]

A conversation is overheard in the dark by one of the inhabitants of the house; apparently a bloody murder is about to be perpetrated by two assassins, who, however, turn out to be servants discussing the slaughter of a hind for dinner.

The greatest of these burlesques, Jane Austen's *Northanger Abbey*, was not published until 1818, but as it was written in 1798, it can well be mentioned here. Catherine Morland, a girl who has been steeped in Gothic romances, is invited to visit her friends, the Tilneys, at Northanger Abbey. She

[8] I, 15-20.
[9] III, 105.

has very romantic anticipations about this building, for "her passion for ancient edifices was next in degree to her passion for Henry Tilney—and castles and abbeys made usually the charm of those reveries which his image did not fill." Henry makes fun of her expectations, telling her that Dorothy the housekeeper will conduct her to a remote room, and that in the night she will discover a secret door behind the tapestry, through which she will enter a small vaulted room communicating by a subterranean passage with the chapel of St. Anthony, not two miles away. The real Northanger is disappointingly modern. Miss Austen gives fairly detailed descriptions of its arrangement: it is a quadrangle with a court in the center, one side of which is entirely modern, while the other parts have been greatly renovated. Northanger has a hall, an antechamber, a "common" drawing-room, a "real" drawing-room, a library, a billiard-room, a kitchen with offices, a private room used by General Tilney, a lumber-room used by Henry, a gallery, and numerous chambers. The windows retain their Gothic shape, but are filled with modern glass, while the great fireplace has been contracted to contain a Rumford. In the course of the novel, the names of many Gothic romances are mentioned. Nor is *Northanger Abbey* the only novel in which Jane Austen takes a fling at these romances: Fanny Price, in *Mansfield Park*, expresses disappointment at the chapel at Sotherton:

> "This is not my idea of a chapel. There is nothing awful here, nothing melancholy, nothing grand. Here are no aisles, no arches, no inscriptions, no banners. No banners, cousin, to be 'blown by the night wind of Heaven.' No signs that 'a Scottish monarch sleeps below.'"

By the time that *Mansfield Park* and *Northanger Abbey* were published, satire upon the Gothic romances was fairly frequent. The introductions to Scott's *Waverley* and Irving's

Bracebridge Hall contain amusing references to this sort of fiction. Mary Julia Young, in the *East Indian* (1799),[10] describes the false alarms occasioned by a visit to a Priory, where a white dog is mistaken for a spectre. A foolish servant gives a ludicrous account of ominous white ravens which inhabit the building. Mrs. Hanway likewise satirizes the fears of credulous serving-maids, and says that "the horrors of the chambers of Udolpho, nor the moving plumes of Otranto, could not have more astounded these Abigails than did the workings of their own creative imaginations."[11] An unfortunate governess, in Alicia Lefanu's *Strathallan*, is terrorized by "a few hints, respecting the antiquity of the manor-house at Woodlands, and the reports that several of the rooms were haunted."[12]

In many nineteenth-century novels, satire is expressed by the characters themselves. A duchess, in Louisa Stanhope's *Striking Likenesses* (1808) exclaims sardonically: ' "Did the bat shriek from the clustering ivy?" turning to Antonia, "or the owl flap her wings from the cloisters?" '[13] Eaton Barrett's *Heroine* is the most thorough and amusing burlesque on the Gothic romances, and in it the trembling lady is told that "the Baron has just returned, and is searching for you through chapel, armoury, gallery; and west tower, and east tower, and south tower; and cedar chamber, and oaken chamber, and black chamber; and grey, brown, yellow, bottle-green, sky-blue; and every shade, tinge, and tint of chamber in the whole castle!"[14] One of Mrs. Golland's

[10] II, 196-205.
[11] *Falconbridge Abbey*, 1809, IV, 231.
[12] 3rd ed., 1817, I, 196.
[13] II, 223.
[14] Ed. Michael Sadleir, 1927, p. 325. A similar catalogue is given in *Prodigious* !!! (1818) I, 129. *The Hero* (1817) seems also to have been inspired by Barrett's *Heroine*. See Winfield H. Rogers: P.M.L.A., XLIX, 98.

characters inquires, "with a smile," if there is no ghost "that holds its midnight perambulations about these walls? it would give an additional grandeur to these ruins, if goblins and spectres held their wonted walk."[15] A character in Mrs. Johnstone's *Clan-Albin* (1815) is equally derisive:

> "But you don't inquire after my adventures in the haunted chambers of yonder chateau," said Norman smiling, "though I assure you, it is a very fit theatre for the freaks of any ghost from *Caenbeg* downwards."[16]

Thomas Love Peacock ridicules the Gothic romance in several places. The very title of *Nightmare Abbey* is expressive of this attitude, and *Melincourt* contains a castle of which "a very spacious wing was left free to the settlement of a colony of ghosts." *The Misfortunes of Elphin* satirizes the sentimental tourist, whose soliloquies "of philosophical pathos, on the vicissitudes of empire and the mutability of all sublunary things" (aroused, of course, by the contemplation of ruins), may be recorded in "a dapper volume."

This reaction against romance was manifested, not only in ridicule of romantic buildings, but in cultivation of realistic architectural description. Books of history and travel were searched for authentic accounts of architecture; ruins were examined; real buildings (preferably extant ones) replaced the imaginary edifices of the cruder romances; foot-notes and appendices were multiplied; history and archaeology came to the aid of fiction. Buildings still continued to be romantic, in many instances, but the terminology of their descriptions became more and more technical. Castles might still lose their heads in the clouds, but their visible parts had to be described with some verisimilitude.

[15] *Ruins of Ruthvale Abbey*, 1827, II, 205.
[16] IV, 223.

This trend towards realism appears in three expressions: travel episodes, where journeying characters comment upon famous buildings; historical novels, where ancient buildings in their original state are used like "period" furniture; and topographical fiction, where buildings peculiar to a given locality are introduced for "local color." The last variety is a comparatively late development, of limited scope, which need not be discussed at length here. It is most evident in such localized fiction as the New England stories of Sarah Orne Jewett, or the Suffolk tales of Miss Matilda Betham Edwards; but bits of it can be found in more prominent novelists, including Scott, who has been said to have "irradiated British topography." Harrison Ainsworth gives a characteristic example in *Rookwood* when he says that "some such ancestral hall we have occasionally encountered in our native county of Lancaster, or in its smiling sister shire," and he continues with a description of a typical Lancashire hall, with references to specific examples.

Travel episodes also can be quickly dismissed, because their references to buildings are never essential to the narratives containing them. Emily, on her visit to Venice in *Udolpho*, was the forerunner of a deluge of literary visitors to that striking city. The excursion to Persepolis in *Solyman and Almena*, the references to Santa Sophia and Greek ruins in *Dinarbas*, the mention of Trèves cathedral in *Fashionable Follies*, and the dispute over Canterbury Cathedral in *Barham Downs* are other early examples of buildings discussed by travellers. There is an excursion to Knole in Fanny Burney's *Camilla*, and her *Wanderer* mentions Arundel, Salisbury, Milton Abbas, and Stonehenge. Bath is frequently described in the earlier novels; in fact it is a familiar scene from the time of Smollett to that of Jane Austen.

Among the novels with more extensive travel descriptions, Smollett's *Humphry Clinker* may be mentioned. Here are described the travels of the Bramble household through England and Scotland, with frequent references to buildings.

Mr. Bramble's comments undergo a sharp change when he crosses the Scottish border; buildings south of that line receiving nothing but abuse, and buildings to the north being lavishly praised by this eccentric critic. York Cathedral arouses a diatribe upon Gothic architecture from his pen, but Glasgow Cathedral evokes a veritable eulogy. Evidently Smollett as a critic of architecture was swayed by local patriotism. Mrs. Elizabeth Hervey's *Louisa, or the Reward of an Affectionate Daughter* (1790) describes the heroine's tour through Holland and Germany, with frequent mention of important buildings. There are also some travel descriptions in Graves's *Columella*, where Stourhead and Longleat are pictured.

In the early nineteenth century, travel episodes become more numerous and prolonged, partly due, perhaps, to the example set by Byron in *Childe Harold* and *Don Juan*. The Bastille occurs often, visits to this building being usually of a compulsory nature. Rome, Jerusalem, Constantinople, the Alhambra, and Egypt are also popular subjects for the comments of itinerant characters. Disraeli's novels are particularly rich in travel episodes—especially *Contarini Fleming*. As time went on, however, the great increase of travel and the flood of travel literature made travel episodes in fiction seem very trite, and consequently the characters in modern fiction usually keep their comments to themselves when they visit historic shrines.

2

The increasing accuracy of architectural descriptions corresponds with the increasing vogue of the historical novel. The line between historical fiction (in its earlier stages) and the Gothic romance is difficult to draw, but the former always tended towards realism both in narration and description. The presence of a few historical characters, a few actual events, and a few real buildings suffices to distinguish these early historical novels from pure fiction. Leland's *Long-*

sword and Sophia Lee's *Recess* were among the earliest examples, but their historical content was very slight; it was about 1790 that the first important group of historical novels appeared.

The Castle of Mowbray (1788) differs very little from an ordinary Gothic romance. The castle has the usual ruined towers and broken walls, and Elwina finds, of course, that "a lonely part of the castle was allotted for her residence." Warwick Castle appears in the story, and, with the mention of a few historic characters, gives a slight historical background to the narrative.

In the following year appeared *Earl Strongbow* by James White. *Conway Castle*, a long poem by the same author, had been published in 1787, so White perhaps obtained some architectural inspiration from that building. In his preface to the poem, the modest author says that "After all, it must be confessed, that, except the novelty of the metre, the following stanzas have but little to recommend them"—a statement only too true!

Earl Strongbow begins with a description of Chepstow Castle, an actual building. The author wanders through this venerable structure, and on one of the towers he meets the ghost of Strongbow, who communicates to him the ensuing story. *Earl Strongbow* was followed in 1790 by *The Adventures of John of Gaunt, Duke of Lancaster*, from the same pen. This romance is introduced by the following explanation (to Vol. III):

> I obtained the volume thus: Wandering one sultry day in the year 1737 (being then but youthful) amidst the ruins of an ancient castle, well known to have been the residence of Geoffrey Chaucer, I chanced to hit my elbow against a wall in one of the chambers; the wall returned a hollow sound, which excited my curiosity. By degrees I peeled off so much of the plaister, that I could easily perceive that the cavity within had been, in old times, a cupboard of the Chaucer family.

In the cupboard, amid "Gothic earthenware," appears a roll of vellum, containing the narrative that follows. Windsor, Woodstock, Shrewsbury Abbey, and Carnarvon are among the buildings which supply the setting for this tale. In one place, the scene shifts to the Alhambra in Spain.

In 1791, White published *The Adventures of King Richard Coeur-de-Lion*, in which the architectural setting is provided by "the Castle of the Lake" and "the Tower of the Rock." A princess is confined in the top story of the tower, and the castle is distinguished by a gallery which is modestly described as "somewhat dismal"—an expression that is refreshing after so many galleries which were completely dismal. In the last volume, the scene shifts to the deserts of Tartary, where there is a fantastic underground city, illuminated by lamps hung amid clusters of jewels, and ventilated by iron tubes.

In 1791 appeared *Lady Jane Grey, an Historical Tale*, the scene of which, of course, is the Tower of London. In 1793 Clara Reeve, the author of *The Old English Baron*, tried her hand at historical romance in *The Memoirs of Sir Roger de Clarendon*. There are several buildings in this story, perhaps the most interesting being a very symmetrical castle near Montreuil, which is a quadrangle with central court and corner turrets, each turret being crowned by a cupola and occupied by a staircase communicating with the galleries which encircle the court.

After the deluge of Gothic romances began, historical novels were generally disguised as romances of the popular kind, the only difference being that real people and occasionally real buildings are introduced. Examples of this type are *Bungay Castle* (1796), by Mrs. Bonhote, *The Castle of Beeston: or Randolph, Earl of Chester. An Historical Romance* (1798), and *Godfrey de Hastings. A Romance* (1798). Stephen Cullen's *The Haunted Priory: or, the Fortunes of the House of Rayo, a Romance founded partly on historical Facts* (1794) may also be said to belong to this group.

Bungay Castle describes an actual castle of that name, located at Bungay in Suffolk. Mrs. Elizabeth Bonhote, the author of the romance, had bought the land on which the castle ruins were situated, and had then proceeded to utilize her purchase by writing a romance about it. In her preface, she says that "it is now the prevailing taste to read wonderful tales of wonderful castles," but she makes it clear that the idea had occurred to her before the present fashion for Gothic romances:

> The thought of publishing a novel under the title given to these volumes, has long been her intention,—a thought which originated in her living within the distance of twenty yards from these venerable ruins, which still attract the attention of the stranger and the curious.

In her opening description of the castle, she does full justice to its former splendor:

> . . . then it was that *Bungay Castle* reared its proud towers and battlements aloft; while its massy walls stood in gloomy and majestic grandeur, as if they could bid defiance to every design formed against them by man, and to the more certain influence of all-conquering time; so perfectly stupendous and strong was this once-spacious edifice, it was not only an object of desire to the proud and aspiring barons, but, it has been said, even to contending kings.

This "object of desire" now belongs, not to aspiring barons and contending kings, but to Mrs. Bonhote herself, who (according to the preface) "has purchased the little spot of ground on which stands the principal part of all that now remains of Bungay Castle."

Her story owes more to imagination than to research in

the castle ruins. The historical background is very slight. A prisoner of state has been sent to the castle, and is confined in a secret chamber, where the young people who live in the castle discover him; since he is consumptive, they move him to a deserted wing, which is sunnier. There are subterranean passages from the castle to a nearby nunnery and to Mattingham Castle, which has an outer ballium, and a "macchiolated and embattled gate."

The Castle of Beeston also deals with an existing building, perched on a rock in the vale of Chester. The great hall of this building overlooks the turrets of the lower ward. In the same romance appear the nearby castle of Peckforton and the monastery of Bunbury. *Godfrey de Hastings* mentions numerous castles. There is a foot-note about Woolsey Castle in Cumberland; Westminster Abbey and Windsor Castle figure in minor episodes; while the end of the narrative takes place in Ravenglas Castle and the adjacent priory of St. Godwin. There is nothing unusual in the description of these buildings.

Towards the close of their careers, both Mrs. Radcliffe and Mrs. Smith turned to historical fiction, the former producing *Gaston de Blondeville*, the setting for which is Kenilworth, and the latter including in her *Solitary Wanderer* a miniature historical romance for which the setting is Mont St. Michel. Kenilworth, in fact, is one of the most popular castles in fiction; besides *Gaston de Blondeville* and Sophia Lee's *Recess*, it appears in Miss Prickett's *Warwick Castle*, Scott's *Kenilworth*, and Louisa Stanhope's *Siege of Kenilworth*. Windsor, Warwick, and the Tower of London are also favorite locations for historical fiction. Westminster Abbey and Westminster Hall are often mentioned, though they do not form the background of any extensive narration. Among the cathedrals, Durham and Winchester seem to be the novelists' favorites. Conway Castle in Wales, and Stirling Castle in Scotland occur frequently. Netley and

Beaulieu are popular ruined abbeys, and Lindisfarne occasionally appears.

Together with the tendency towards description of real buildings comes a tendency towards increased accuracy of description—what one may call the "foot-note" trend. Indeed, towards the end of the century, foot-notes explanatory of architecture become much more numerous: *Orlando and Seraphina* quotes, in foot-notes, three architectural descriptions; Charlotte Smith has a foot-note about Hurstmonceaux Castle; Mrs. Robinson mentions in foot-notes the travel books from which she drew her descriptions; *Godfrey de Hastings* has a foot-note about Woolsey Castle; *The Castle of Eridan* has a foot-note about the Duchess's prison; while all three of Dr. Drake's stories in *Literary Hours* are provided with long foot-notes explaining architectural features. Technical terms, such as "outer ballium," "inner ballium," "macchicolation," "oubliette," etc., are more frequently found in the later novels than in the earlier ones. Kitchens, and drains, and other humble appurtenances of the castle are more in evidence, showing a tendency towards realism. Even Mrs. Radcliffe, whose earlier descriptions are more poetic than realistic, becomes almost technical in *Gaston de Blondeville*, and at the beginning of that romance there is a discussion about the dates of various architectural features.

After 1800, foot-notes about architecture become more and more numerous. Horsley Curties includes a note upon Carisbrooke Castle in *St. Botolph's Priory*; T. P. Lathy's *Invisible Enemy* quotes Coxe's *Tour of Poland*; Henrietta Rouvière Mosse's *Peep at our Ancestors* has a foot-note on Arundel Castle, and one on Guilford Castle from Grose's *Antiquities*; Lady Morgan's *Wild Irish Girl* has several foot-notes on buildings, including one on Dunluce Castle, and her *O'Donnel* has foot-notes and an appendix on Irish ruins. Jane Porter's *Scottish Chiefs* has many notes on buildings.

The Scottish Chiefs is an important forerunner of Walter Scott's Waverley Novels, in its use of architecture as well as in its use of Scottish setting and history. Like Scott, Miss Porter tries to describe actual buildings, and to describe them accurately. When she makes use of a subterranean passage, she is careful to state in a note that "the remains of this curious subterraneous passage are yet to be seen."[17] She does not go into rhapsodies over her buildings, or allow her characters to spend sentimental hours in contemplating them; her architecture supports her narrative but does not lead to long digressions. She is definitely on the side of realism, though she is not unaware of the more romantic aspect of medieval architecture. Technical words, such as barbican and ballium, are to be found in her descriptions, although she does not use such terms as much as Scott does. Her sister, Anna Maria, was fond of picturesque views of architecture, but the more sober Jane avoided mantling ivy and jessamine, and adorned her buildings with foot-notes only.

George Walker, in *Theodore Cyphon,* illustrates the changed attitude of novelists towards architecture. Some of his characters visit a ruined castle:

> As was natural our discourse turned on the remains of the building around us, but no knight of legendary lore was straying from his paternal domain; the case simply was, that Oliver Cromwell had, in his usurpation, battered it down, and the present Lord preferred an elegant villa to old walls. . . .[18]

In this substitution of historic fact for romantic glamour, the whole trend from romance to realism in architectural description is foreshadowed. The culmination of the historic tendency in fiction comes in the novels of Scott and his followers.

[17] *Scottish Chiefs,* 2nd ed., 1811, IV, 378.
[18] Alexandria, 1803, II, 3.

3

To most people, the subject of architecture in the novel immediately suggests the name of Sir Walter Scott. Though the Gothic romances are now read only by a few students, the creator of Rotherwood and Torquilstone is universally known, and his influence upon the Gothic revival has probably been greater than that of Walpole himself—certainly it has been far more permanent. It would be interesting to know how many "baronial" mansions owe their origin to a lurking enthusiasm for *Kenilworth* or *Ivanhoe*.

The architecture in Scott's novels, strangely enough, is rather less lurid than that of his predecessors. In picturesque qualities and emotional effect, it is far inferior to the architecture of Mrs. Radcliffe. His descriptions are sometimes marred by pedantic and inaccurate archaeology; they are realistic rather than poetic. Nevertheless, they have survived the castles of the Gothic romances, simply because Scott's stories are better. A novel cannot live by its architecture alone, and Mrs. Radcliffe's sublime descriptions fail to compensate for her stilted characters and flimsy plots. Scott's architecture has survived by virtue of the good narration for which it forms a background.

Scott, however, did not escape the spell of the Gothic romances, and much as his architectural descriptions differ from preceding ones, they were probably influenced by his wide reading. In spite of his satiric thrusts at the Gothic romances in *Waverley*, it is impossible to believe that Scott did not have a secret fondness for that school of fiction. Certainly he had read most of the Gothic writers, from Walpole to Maturin. The general preface to the Waverley novels says that he once contemplated writing an historical romance in the style of the *Castle of Otranto*, and a fragment of this projected work is printed as an appendix to the preface. Furthermore, Scott wrote short but appreciative biographies of Horace Walpole, Clara Reeve, Ann Radcliffe, and Charlotte Smith, in which he gives to their romances praise which no modern critic would bestow. To be sure, these memoirs were written as prefaces to a novelists' library, and Scott probably did not feel able to damn the works which he was introducing, but his appreciation sounds far too genuine to come from tact alone.

Scott did not differ from the Gothic novelists in his regard for the typical castle of the romances, except that his innate common sense enabled him to see its ridiculous as well as its sublime aspect. His attitude is well expressed in his memoir of Walpole:

> He who, in early youth, has happened to pass a solitary night in one of the few ancient mansions which the fashion of more modern times has left undespoiled of their original furniture, has probably experienced, that the gigantic and preposterous figures dimly visible in the defaced tapestry,—the remote clang of the distant doors which divide him from living society,—the deep darkness which involves the high and fretted roof of the apartment,—the dimly-seen pictures of ancient knights, renowned for their valour, and perhaps for their crimes,—the varied and indistinct sounds which disturb the silent desolation of a half-deserted mansion,—and, to crown all, the feeling that carries us back to ages of feudal power and papal superstition, join together to excite a corresponding sensation of supernatural awe, if not of terror. It is in such situations, when superstition becomes contagious, that we listen with respect, and even with dread, to the legends which are our sport in the garish light of sunshine, and amid the dissipating sights and sounds of everyday life.

In the first chapter of *Waverley*, Scott is evidently dwelling in the "garish light of sunshine," making fun of the Gothic romance and all its machinery, but in another mood he can be quite reverent, as in *Quentin Durward*, where he says:

> The distant sound of the choir, the solemnity of the deep and dead hour which he had chosen for this act of devotion, the effect of the glimmering lamp with which the little Gothic building was illuminated—all contributed to throw Quentin's mind into the state when it most readily acknowledges its human frailty....[19]

One feels that, but for his restraining sense of humor, Scott might easily have launched into all the architectural enthusiasms of Mrs. Radcliffe.

In *The Lay of the Last Minstrel*, he comes very near to doing so. The description of Melrose Abbey by moonlight, complete with owls, graves, and broken arches, might almost have been written by Mrs. Radcliffe. It is quite different from a similar scene in *The Antiquary*, where the romantic qualities of a ruined and moonlit monastery are decidedly tempered by the ludicrous encounters of Douterswivel and Edie Ochiltree. Scott did not permit himself, in prose, the descriptive flights which occur in his earlier poetry.

Waverley sets the tone for the architecture of the whole series of novels. It shows a feeling for the picturesque, and an occasional hint of emotional effect, but nothing which approaches the rhapsodies of Mrs. Radcliffe. Realism prevails, and there is a decided attempt at archaeological exactness. In a foot-note, Scott explains that he has based his description of Tully-Veolan upon several similar houses, which he mentions. Tully-Veolan is described in great detail; we are told its date, and the reasons for its architectural style; the dove-cote, fountain, gargoyles, and turrets are all mentioned in turn; and there are such long words as architrave and bartizan to give the description a technical air.

"Bartizan," indeed, is a bit of false archaeology which has

---

[19] Chap. XVII.

injured Scott's reputation as an antiquarian. He applies the word to the battlemented parapets often found on castle walls, but modern lexicographers agree that Scott himself, misled by older authorities, coined the word.[20] It occurs in *The Lay of the Last Minstrel* (where the first edition has a footnote calling it "battlement"), and in many of the novels. In *Ivanhoe*, a bartizan adorns Rebecca's prison, from which she threatens to hurl herself. Scott is rather fond of pseudo-technical terms, and one often encounters in his works such words as barbican, donjon, stanchion, fortalice, knosp, etc. Like his predecessors, he is inclined to attribute Norman architecture to the Saxons, as in his reference to the "Saxon" pillars of Kirkwall cathedral in *The Pirate*.

His zeal for archaeology is carried, perhaps, too far. Many of his novels contain long and rather technical footnotes, in which he identifies his buildings, or compares them with existing ones. The "burgh" especially arouses his enthusiasm, and so Norna's dwelling in *The Pirate*, and the Castle of Coningsburgh in *Ivanhoe* are furnished with long notes upon the origin and construction of these primitive fortresses. The text itself contains many descriptions which are sometimes unnecessarily long and detailed, and which, unlike Mrs. Radcliffe's descriptions, add little to the atmosphere of the story.

Not all Scott's novels have architectural background, though there are few without some traces of it. Scott's reputation for castle-building is probably due to the fact that his best-known novels, such as *Ivanhoe, Quentin Durward, Waverley*, and *Kenilworth*, are particularly full of architectural descriptions. *Ivanhoe*, which is probably the best known of them all, has no less than four buildings of major importance, all described in great detail. Torquilstone

---

[20] See the *New English Dictionary*. This view has, however, been challenged by W. Mackay Mackenzie: *The Medieval Castle in Scotland*, 1927, pp. 85-6.

is the greatest of these castles, and it forms the background for several of the most exciting scenes of the novel, including the sufferings of Isaac in the torture-chamber, the assault upon the castle, and the exploits of old Ulrica, who brings the building to its lurid and dramatic downfall.

Scott's castles often are placed in unusual and romantic situations, like Avenel in *The Monastery*, and Lochleven in *The Abbot*, both perched upon islets in mountain lakes; or like Wolf's Crag in *The Bride of Lammermoor*, and Geierstein in *Anne of Geierstein* upon their inaccessible rocks. Unlike his predecessors, Scott is interested in the rough keeps of Saxon and Norman times even more than in the florid architecture of the Perpendicular period—another proof, perhaps, of his archaeological tastes. Nevertheless, *Kenilworth* shows that he fully appreciated the magnificent effects of the later Gothic styles. Renaissance buildings are hardly mentioned at all, though *Woodstock* contains a reference to "the cumbrous magnificence of Vanbrugh's style" at Blenheim, and Scott seems to have shared Walpole's distaste for the "bastard" style of the Jacobean period. Classical ruins are mentioned in *Count Robert of Paris*.

As an historical novelist, Scott seems to have been fairly conscientious in his zeal for accuracy. For the most part, he uses real buildings for his setting, and, when he resorts to imaginary ones, he usually tries to give them an air of verisimilitude by comparing them with existing structures of the same period. His researches were painstaking, though occasionally unfortunate, and the reference notes to his buildings contain quotations from such authorities as Waldron's *Description of the Isle of Man*, Gough's edition of Camden's *Britannia*, Gordon's *Itiner. Septentrionale*, and the letters of Mr. Morrison of Perth. Considering the rapidity with which Scott's novels were produced, more intensive architectural research could hardly be expected.

The most concentrated architectural background is to be

found in *Woodstock*, where the title and the entire setting of the novel are supplied by the principal building. References to the intricacies of Rosamond's Bower occur throughout the narrative, and, at its end, these secret passages play an important part in delaying the pursuit of the fugitive prince. The explosion of the tower forms a dramatic climax which is comparable to the catastrophic ruin of Torquilstone in *Ivanhoe*. *Woodstock* is not only one of the most architectural of Scott's novels, but also one of those which are most lavishly supported by documentary evidence.

Scott's buildings primarily serve a structural purpose in the narrative. Secret passages and private stairs are to be found in almost every one of them, and they are frequently besieged or assaulted by hostile forces. He stresses the importance of the castle as a military post—something which the Gothic romances had not done. Udolpho, to be sure, was assaulted, but the heroine was fortunately removed from the scene of action, and we are given no description of the engagement. Scott, on the other hand, leaves his heroines in the castle, to watch and even to participate in its defence. The siege of Torquilstone is described through the medium of Rebecca's observations, when she sits at the window of Ivanhoe's chamber to tell him the news of the attack. The assault is vividly portrayed, from the initial attack upon the barbican to the final entrance of the victors into the castle; and the architecture of the castle plays a prominent part throughout the description.

Scott's buildings are not without picturesque qualities, though this aspect is somewhat subordinated to their main function. He has a good eye for effects of light and shade, as, for instance, in *Quentin Durward*, where "the broad glare of the torches outfacing the pale moon, which was more obscured on this than on the former night, and the red smoky light which they dispersed around the ancient buildings, gave a darker shade to that huge donjon, called the Earl Herbert's

Tower."[21] In *Waverley*, after describing the effect of a sunlit door at the end of a dark avenue, he says that: "It was one of those effects which a painter loves to represent, and mingled well with the struggling light which found its way between the boughs of the shady arch that vaulted the broad green alley."[22] On the other hand, Scott's descriptions of old buildings do not show a keen sense of color.

The emotional effects of his buildings are negligible, and in this deficiency lies his principal break with the tradition of the Gothic romances. Scott was too wise to endow his characters with the shuddering sensibilities of Mrs. Radcliffe's heroines; also his zeal for archaeological accuracy makes his buildings too precise for the mysterious haze with which Udolpho and kindred castles are enveloped. There is little mystery in Scott's architecture. We can see all four walls of his rooms; their ends are not lost in the shadows of receding arches. His towers are often high and impressive, but they do not soar sublimely. His secret passages and deserted rooms are trod by escaping prisoners or impatient lovers, not by trembling females with lamps. His characters, in short, are not supremely sensitive to their environment; they accept their castles as a matter of course, regarding them with the casual calmness with which such buildings probably were regarded in the Middle Ages.

Scott was by no means blind to the emotional effects of buildings. In his memoir of Walpole, he explains the inadequacy of a modern Gothic building by saying that: "It may be grand, or it may be gloomy; it may excite magnificent or melancholy ideas; but it must fail in bringing forth the sensation of supernatural awe, connected with halls that have echoed to the sounds of remote generations, and have been pressed by the footsteps of those who have long

[21] Chap. XXVIII.
[22] Chap. VIII.

since passed away." Scott was quite able to appreciate the awe with which Mrs. Radcliffe regarded her castles, but he also realized the absurdity of her rhapsodies. Furthermore, his novels are tales of action rather than of emotion, and consequently his characters could hardly be made supersensitive to the buildings around them. He chose to ignore the emotional effects of his buildings, preferring realism to romance.

This choice was probably a deliberate one. In his memoir of Mrs. Radcliffe, he compares her descriptions with those of Charlotte Smith, praising both, but saying that Mrs. Smith's more precise pictures could be depicted by an artist, whereas Mrs. Radcliffe's vague but impressive sketches would give him nothing definite to work upon. He contrasts Mrs. Radcliffe's description of the imaginary Udolpho with her description of the existing Hardwick, concluding that "*Udolpho* is an exquisite effect-piece, *Hardwick* a striking and faithful portrait." Faithful portraiture seems to have been Scott's favorite mode of description, but it must not be inferred that he was blind to other methods.

The effect of his novels upon the Gothic revival was undoubtedly tremendous. Since Walpole's time, Gothic had been cultivated by a mere coterie, but after Scott, it became universal, especially for ecclesiastical and collegiate building. Countless churches, mansions, and schools would probably never have displayed a single pointed arch had it not been for the indirect influence of Sir Walter Scott. He himself set the style by erecting a pretentious Gothic mansion upon his estate at Abbotsford. His influence was felt not only in England but in America and upon the Continent.

His influence upon architectural setting in the novel is less important. Historical novels continued to employ his methods; his archaeological tastes are reflected in the novels of Bulwer-Lytton; his Gothic setting survived in hundreds of romances, such as those of Harrison Ainsworth. Nevertheless, the main trend of architectural description in the novel was in another direction, towards a more intimate and domestic sort of structure—the personified house was beginning to appear. Scott is the culmination of the foot-note trend in architectural description, a pedantic tendency which developed in the later historical romances of the eighteenth century, and which was intensified in such works as Jane Porter's *Scottish Chiefs*. His castles are somewhat more accurate than those of the Gothic romances, but their gain in accuracy is counterbalanced by a loss in sublimity; Mrs. Radcliffe is remembered only for her descriptions, but Scott's fame rests upon a broader base.

4

Under Scott's leadership, the historical romance (and, with it, realistic architectural description) grew steadily more popular. Innumerable writers of historical fiction began to publish long series of novels; among the most prolific were Horace Smith, Harrison Ainsworth, Mrs. Anna Eliza Bray, G. P. R. James, and Bulwer-Lytton. Local novelists, like John Galt and Thomas Dick Lauder in Scotland, and John Carne in Cornwall, produced historical novels. It is significant that many of these writers also published books of travel or history, showing that the increased realism of their architectural descriptions had some solid basis: James was actually made historiographer royal to William IV because of his historical publications; Mrs. Bray published a *Tour of Normandy, Brittany* &c., *The Borders of the Tamar and the Tavy*, and *The Mountains and Lakes of Switzerland*; James Norris Brewer made extensive contributions to the *Beauties of England and Wales*, and published a descriptive and historical account of English palaces; Lauder published a tour of the coast of Scotland; Carne wrote recollections of his eastern travels; and Bulwer-Lytton wrote a history of Athens.

Of these novelists, Harrison Ainsworth is architecturally the most important. He literally did what the Gothic novelists are merely said to have done: he made his buildings the heroes of his books. The Tower of London is far more important in the novel of that name than Otranto or Udolpho were to their narratives. Ainsworth deliberately and openly arranged the story so that all the important parts of the building might be illustrated—the Tower itself is the *raison d'être* of the whole book. Ainsworth had practical motives also; he wanted the Tower to be more thoroughly restored, and to be made more accessible to the public. The same motives are apparent in *Windsor Castle*. *Old Saint Paul's* describes a building no longer extant, but its part in the story is just as important as the rôles of Windsor and the Tower in their respective narratives. The setting of *Rookwood* is an imaginary mansion, but it is based upon a real manor-house which, indeed, inspired Ainsworth to write the novel.

In spite of his painstaking efforts for historical accuracy, Ainsworth's descriptions are not wholly realistic. His introduction acknowledges indebtedness to Mrs. Radcliffe, whose romantic attitude towards architecture is evident in many of his descriptions. There is far more mystery and sublimity in his architecture than in Scott's, and there are scenes which have all the exaggerated glamour of the typical Gothic romance. Churches at midnight are especially conducive to these rhapsodies: for instance, the scene in the Manchester church in *Guy Fawkes*, and that in St. John's chapel in the *Tower of London*. Unlike the Radcliffe school, however, Ainsworth modelled even his imaginary buildings on real structures, and placed most of his emphasis upon historic edifices, which he describes not only in their original but in their present condition, with parenthetical suggestions for the benefit of the visitor. Ainsworth often makes little side remarks about his buildings, much as Victorian novelists give to their readers little confidences about the hero.

His local patriotism is evident even in his architecture: *Rookwood* praises the old halls of Lancashire and Cheshire; *Old Saint Paul's* refers lovingly to the church at Manchester; and *Guy Fawkes* makes even greater use of that building. Such feeling for local architecture is to be found in many of the historical novelists, including Scott himself; it shows the great advance of realism from the time when novelists described castles from Scotland to Sicily with deadly similarity.

Much of this local color appears also in the novels of Mrs. Bray, whose first husband (son of Stothard the painter) had taken her on sketching tours in France and the Netherlands. Mrs. Bray was something of an antiquarian, and she made a slight pretense of doing research for the setting of her novels. In the general preface to her works, she says that she consulted medieval illuminated manuscripts for details of costume and interior decoration, and that Southey's *Letters from Portugal* gave her some suggestions for the scenes of the *Talba*. Her interest in tapestries was so great that she was accused of stealing part of the Bayeux tapestry, and was vindicated with difficulty. She is unusually conscious of the carved ornament in medieval architecture, probably because of the training in visual observation which she acquired on her husband's sketching trips. In the *White Hoods*, she describes the architecture of Ghent with great care.

The architecture of the Netherlands appears also in the novels of Horace Smith, who describes Rotterdam in *Brambletye House*, and Bruges in *Walter Colyton*. He was an avowed disciple of Scott, to whom he sent a copy of *Brambletye House*, with acknowledgments, and he was a close friend of William Heseltine, another historical novelist, to whom he dedicated *Walter Colyton*, and to whose house he referred in *Brambletye House*. Like Ainsworth's *Rookwood*, the house in Smith's first important novel (Brambletye) was inspired by a visit to a real mansion.

Heseltine's *Last of the Plantagenets* is written in pseudo-archaic language, and his architectural descriptions are worthy of the ridiculous phraseology in which they are presented. He says that the tomb of Edward IV "is wrought in wondrous wise of pierced church-work,"[23] and he refers to "many fair houses, curiously builded after a gorgeous and gallant sort."[24] His foot-notes on architecture are unusually numerous.

The architectural descriptions of G. P. R. James are more sober than those in most contemporary novels. Like Ainsworth, he is fond of statistics, and he describes a banquet hall as being "eighty feet in length, by fifty in breadth; and the roof, of plain dark oak, rose from walls nearly thirty feet high, and met in the form of a pointed arch in the centre."[25] He does not indulge much in foot-notes or long descriptions; his architecture is quite realistic and prosaic, though the courtyard of one of his castles is full of the usual "weeds, and grass, and tangled shrubs,"[26] and he mentions "black frowning battlements."[27] In his novels of contemporary life, like *Morley Ernstein*, his brief architectural descriptions become almost photographic, and he shows a feeling for the grotesque.

John Galt launched into historical fiction, apparently in emulation of Scott, whom he dared to take to task for an historical error in *Redgauntlet*. Galt's novels, historical or

[23] New York, 1829, II, 42.
[24] *Ibid.*, I, 130.
[25] *Philip Augustus*, 1831, I, 129.
[26] *Richelieu*, 1829, II, 65.
[27] *Philip Augustus*, II, 12.

otherwise, have even less architecture than Scott's, and that little is singularly uninteresting. He speaks of a castle as having "pepper-box corners"[28]—a description which no true romanticist would relish—and he refers to an abbey "with its lofty horned towers and spiky pinnacles."[29] This prosaic attitude is evident in Sir Thomas Dick Lauder's novels also. Lauder speaks of a church with "divers uncouth projections,"[30] and of castle towers with "their tall thin necks surmounted by curiously projected square tops of various architecture."[31] Nevertheless, Lauder has an eye for the picturesque (in fact he edited Uvedale Price's work on that subject); he was himself something of an artist; and he describes burning buildings with great gusto.

John Carne also likes conflagrations, and his description of a burning cathedral is comparable to Lauder's. Carne, however, is more enthusiastic and less accurate than Lauder in his architectural setting; in *Stratton Hill*, we find "obtuse Gothic arches,"[32] "a small arch, in the Saracenic style," and a "zig-zag Norman arch"—all in the same building! He is fond of ruins, mantling vegetation, and moonlight scenes.

Bulwer-Lytton's descriptions, especially in the *Last Days of Pompeii*, are elaborate and archaeological. His foot-notes are almost as numerous as those of Scott or Miss Porter, yet he philosophizes upon ruins in the manner of the eighteenth-century novelists, and occasionally (as in *Eugene Aram*) he anticipates the personified architecture of later writers. In fact he bridges the gap between the architecture of the Gothic school and that of the Victorians; he describes castles with

---

[28] *Rothelan*, Edinburgh, 1824, I, 280.
[29] *Ringan Gilhaize, Edinburgh*, 1823, I, 149.
[30] *Lochandhu*, Edinburgh, 1825, I, 83.
[31] *Ibid.*, I, 168.
[32] New York, 1829, I, 26.

all the gusto of Mrs. Radcliffe, but he can also describe cosy or grotesque structures with all the domesticity of Dickens. In referring to a castle, he speaks of "the frown of its time-worn towers,"[33] yet in *Lucretia* we find a room with a *"nooky appearance."*[34] To these contrasting qualities, he sometimes adds a florid touch worthy of Disraeli or Beckford; his buildings are often accompanied by luscious gardens, or adorned with such things as a "light roof, which, half Gothic, half classic, in its architecture, was inlaid with gilded and purple mosaics."[35] An American lady modelled her house upon descriptions of the Alhambra in Bulwer-Lytton's *Leila*, so that this florid architectural setting has not been without effect.

The historical novelists have shown many different attitudes towards architecture. Some are archaeologists, and devotees of the foot-note; some are romantic and inaccurate; some are fond of oriental lushness; some combine various qualities. The general effect of this historical trend, however, was to discredit the absurd castles of the Gothic romances, and to make descriptions more accurate and realistic. Historical fiction, after Scott, was apt to be a masculine rather than a feminine affair, and its architecture tended to substitute fact for imagination, and vividness for glamour.

Just as Gothic setting became fashionable in the 1790's, even among authors who had previously shown little interest in it, so historical accounts of actual buildings became popular during the time of Scott. Novelists like John Galt, whose real talent lay elsewhere, tried their hands at historical fiction; the adjective "historical" was more and more frequently inserted in the sub-title "a romance"; Louisa Stanhope and other survivors of the Gothic school made excursions into

[33] *Zanoni*, Book V, Chap. I.
[34] *Lucretia*, Chap. II.
[35] *Rienzi*, Book IV, Chap. I.

this new field. The resulting increase in realism, and the development of a more prosaic attitude towards architecture doubtless helped to prepare the way for the homely intimacy that distinguishes many buildings in Victorian fiction. The steady increase of specific detail in architectural descriptions was certainly a step in this direction, and so was the introduction of grotesque features into the hitherto elegant architecture of the novel.

CHAPTER SIX

LATER ARCHITECTURAL DEVELOPMENTS IN THE NOVEL

1
Architecture in Early American Fiction

The architectural setting of the early American novel may best be described as the fruit of a great national "inferiority complex." Many early American authors felt obliged to describe architecture simply because their English contemporaries were doing it. To be sure, there was practically no American architecture worth describing, but the novelists exaggerated what little there was; invented castles out of whole cloth; or despairingly fled to Europe for architectural refuge. Though the American colonies had declared their political independence of England in 1776, it was many years before they achieved literary freedom—if, indeed, they can ever be said to have achieved it. The books which were read in America in the years around 1800 were nearly all English books, so it is not surprising that the Gothic romances should have influenced the American novel, which was at that time in the most impressionable years of its infancy. In the year 1795 appeared two American editions of the *Romance of the Forest*, one edition of the *Mysteries of Udolpho*, and one of *A Sicilian Romance*, to say nothing of American editions of Lathom's *Castle of Ollada*, Charlotte Smith's *Montalbert*, Mrs. Fenwick's *Secrecy; or the Ruin of the Rock*, and two American editions of *Count Roderic's Castle*. From that year onwards, there was an increasing flood of American reprints of Gothic romances. The Gothic romance and architectural setting were, of course, inseparable companions, and it is interesting to see them on their transatlantic travels.

The American novelist with Gothic ambitions was certainly in a dilemma. He had the misfortune to live in a country which was utterly destitute of medieval architecture.

There was not a ruined abbey, a towering cathedral, or a frowning castle in the whole United States. Spanish missions, indeed, existed in Mexico and California, but to the New Yorker or Pennsylvanian of the 1790's, these regions were as unknown and remote as Siberia. A cathedral was soon to arise in Baltimore, but it was not to be a Gothic cathedral (though a Gothic plan was submitted), and it was never very awesome in architecture or dimensions. Certain Indian villages were known as "castles," but no architect would recognize them as such; they were merely miniature capitals of Indian tribes, fortified villages of huts and wigwams. Manor-houses, to be sure, existed in large numbers, especially in the Southern states and in New York, but the very best of them were no better than the second-rate or third-rate English country houses, and the oldest ones (which were usually the poorest) were not much over a century old. The Georgian mansions of tidewater Virginia and Maryland provided none of the gloomy halls, secret passages, and dizzy turrets which were so essential for a Gothic romance.

Bereft of abbeys, cathedrals, and castles, the novelist was left with only the humble manor-house and the yet humbler church. Substitutes were available, however. He could place the scene of his story in Europe, and wallow in medievalism to his heart's content; he could lay his narrative in the wilderness, and replace the sublimity of the castle by the grandeur of the forest; or he could cut the Gordian knot by boldly sprinkling his native land with entirely imaginary castles. All three courses had their disadvantages. Most American writers of the day knew too little about European architecture, or any architecture, to create a really convincing castle. Nature, of course, was indigenous, but cliffs and caves were never entirely satisfactory as substitutes for frowning battlements and gloomy dungeons. The American novelist was faced at every turn with obstacles when he tried to give his story a romantic setting. His efforts to overcome these obstacles are often amusing.

Some novelists, indeed, dodged the whole dilemma by refusing to have anything to do with architectural setting. Charles Brockden Brown openly expressed his contempt for Gothic trappings, though one of his earlier and obscurer works, the *History of the Carrils and the Ormes*, is full of architectural references, and Dunlap, who reprints it, says that it is an expression of the author's strong architectural tastes. In Brown's better known works, however, the most ambitious architectural creation is a garden temple in *Wieland*. Helena Wells is even more contemptuous of Gothic setting, though she mentions a castle in the *Step-Mother*.

The cave was one of the best substitutes for Gothic architecture that America could furnish. It was dark and mysterious; it possessed winding passages and great columned halls; and its associations with wild animals and ferocious savages made it sufficiently terrifying for even the most ardent lover of Gothic romance. In James French's *Elkswatawa* is a stupendous cavern, supported by columns of satin spar. The description of the interior is concluded with a significant comment:

> How tame and common are the most splendid palaces, with all their decorations of art, when compared with these secret dwelling places of nature. How tasteless are the most exquisite specimens of architecture, when compared with the rude gothic grandeur of these large subterranean abodes.[1]

Other caves occur in Brackenridge's *Modern Chivalry*, and in Flint's *Shoshonee Valley*, where "the roof was the arching vault of nature's masonry in everlasting stone."[2]

Other writers sought their castles in foreign lands. Mrs. Rowson describes a Welsh castle in *Reuben and Rachel*, a novel which has many of the characteristics of the Gothic

[1] New York, 1836, I, 214-215.
[2] Cincinnati, 1830, I, 114.

romance, as its sub-title, *A Tale of Old Times,* implies. An Irish structure, called O'Halloran Castle, appears in James McHenry's *O'Halloran.* The buildings in Poe's stories are almost all European.

Sometimes the novelist went, not to Europe, but to the more remote portions of his own continent for his architecture. John Neal's *Logan* mentions "the stupendous fortress of Quebec": "It arose in abrupt, castellated, rocky fragments, boldly out of the horizon and water, like the strong hold of some river divinity."[3] Timothy Flint, in *Francis Berrian,* describes the palaces and churches of Mexico: "Mrs. Radcliffe's castles, and priests, and ghosts, and winding-sheets, and spectres, figured in succession before my mind's eye."[4] Even the Aleutian Islands are used by Timothy Flint, in *Shoshonee Valley.* On one of the islands he places a Russian castle, called Ostroklotz, which forms the prison for the abducted heroine. (American heroines of the early novels were apparently just as unfortunate as their English sisters.) The Russian standard floats from the highest tower of Ostroklotz, which is certainly a striking edifice:

> It was evidently composed of the massive blocks of white stone from the singular hills, that arose in its vicinity. Covered on the roof, as it was, with the bark of the white birch, it shone in the morning sun with a dazzling whiteness, forming a strong contrast with the deep and funereal green of the larches, that surrounded the open space.[5]

Ostroklotz has a massive gate and a spacious dining-hall. A subterranean cavern extends beneath it. No wonder that "to persons, like the captives, who had never seen such works of

---

[3] Philadelphia, 1822, I, 246.
[4] Boston, 1826, I, 154. Robert M. Bird's *Calavar* and *Infidel* make lavish use of Aztec architecture.

art before, the fortification had an aspect of the most imposing grandeur"!⁵

Castles on the Pacific islands are sufficiently improbable, but such a structure on Long Island Sound is simply incredible—yet Isaac Mitchell's *Asylum* provides us with such a building. Melissa, the heroine, is imprisoned in it by her aunt, who claims that the castle was erected by her ancestors for defence against the Indians. The opening description is quite reminiscent of the style of the Gothic romances:

> The sun was low; they proceeded through fields in a foot path, over rough and uneven ways, directly towards the Sound; they walked about a mile, when they came in sight of a large, old-fashioned, castle-like building, surrounded with a moat, crossed by a drawbridge, and with high, thick, wooden walls. . . . After passing the bridge, Melissa's aunt raised it, unlocked the gate, and they entered the inclosure, which was overgrown with rank grass and rushes; the avenue which led to the house was almost in the same condition. The mansion was of real Gothic architecture, built of rude stone, with battlements . . . .⁶

The courtyard of the castle is surrounded by a wall of hewn timbers, crowned with spikes, and as smooth as glass. Nevertheless, the intrepid hero succeeds in scaling it—only to find that the lady has fled.

Another extraordinary American castle is to be found in the tale of *St. Herbert*, which appeared in 1796 in the columns of the *New York Weekly Magazine*. Two lovers, wandering not far from New York, are told that "there is not another building within ten miles unless it is an old stone castle that nobody will live in." The lovers decide to take refuge in this interesting building, and they are obliged to force their way through cobwebs "that hung in sheets across the hall." The apartments of the castle are said to be "very elegant," but the description of them is vague.

⁵ Timothy Flint: *op. cit.*, II, 136.
⁶ Poughkeepsie, 1811, II, 58-9.

John Neal, in *Brother Jonathan*,[7] depicts another American castle: "a sort of Dutch castle—with ponderous wooden battlements; heavy pine turrets; and sumptuous carved work, of great strength; remote antiquity, and illustrious fashion—for that part of the world." It is not surprising that "our hero stopped short, with a feeling of awe," and we are told that "the chill of the place—the grandeur of the old house—actually smote upon his weary heart." This structure is likewise in the vicinity of New York.

When the novelist was not content with mere cliffs and caves, yet was too conscientious to rear castles on Long Island Sound, his best American substitute for the castle was the block-house. This peculiarly American structure was a squat square tower of logs, with an overhanging second story, and its military function, massive walls, and gloomy interior made it slightly comparable to the watchtowers of Europe. John Neal, in *Brother Jonathan*, tries to give Gothic atmosphere to such a building:

> A part of the preacher's house was very old and "awful," for that portion of the world; having withstood, for nearly fourscore years, the revolution of empires, and of seasons. The older part of the pile; that, which the cattle now occupied, was built of solid square timber; and had been a "block house"; or fort,—in the early Indian wars, of that colony. The whole was overshadowed by great, overgrown trees; a part of the ancient wilderness of the country.[8]

Other American buildings are sometimes used to give the desired atmosphere. In John Neal's *Logan*, there are references to the mansion of a colonial governor, with stone vaulted stairway and a courtyard. A haunted Dutch church adorns *Brother Jonathan* by the same author. Neal's

[7] 1825, II, 406.
[8] I, 139-140.

Later Architectural Developments 197

Randolph contains an interesting commentary upon contemporary American architecture. He says that Baltimore cathedral is "the grandest building, of its dimensions, that I ever stood within."[9] He praises the beautiful churches of New Haven, "all in a cluster; and, if I may be allowed so to speak, of different orders; one, at any rate, seems really *Gothick*."[10] The city hall at New York and the capitol at Washington are criticized.

Neal's description of Annapolis, in the same novel, is a good example of his architectural exaggerations; for he transforms that pleasant Georgian city into a sinister relic of medievalism. He shudders at the "silent, old fashioned feudal grandeur" of the houses. Annapolis, he says, has "a strange, foreign air." "The venerable solidity, fashion and spaciousness, of the dwelling-houses—all standing apart and alone—surrounded by heavy, well built walls—with towers, wings, arches, and abutments—are of another age—another country—another race of men." His awe reaches really ludicrous proportions:

> Indeed, sir, you must feel it—every man must feel, standing as we are now, alone, at night, in a vast chamber like this, looking out upon the whole city of Annapolis, that here dwelt the ancient nobility of Maryland—haughty and lonely. It looks dark and sullen, as the retreat of decayed gentility—almost baronial gentility—should look. Mr. Omar, I was never more affected with the solemnity of the place, than on that night. I wandered, I know not how long, nor hardly in what direction, with my eyes upon the ground, continually asking myself what had become of the ancient people—whose dwelling places, about me, were no longer inhabited; or inhabited by strangers to their blood, who had bought *manors and castles*, literally, for a few hundreds of dollars.[11]

[9] Philadelphia, 1823, I, 65.
[10] I, 116.
[11] I, 336-7.

While the minor American writers were thus dabbling in architecture, the more important ones did not neglect it. There is architectural setting, for instance, in Irving's *Legend of Sleepy Hollow*, and in *Bracebridge Hall*. Irving's description of Westminster Abbey in the *Sketch Book* shows his susceptibility to the charms of Gothic architecture, and his acquaintance with the Gothic romances is attested by a reference to Mrs. Radcliffe in an early diary.[12] Irving also showed Gothic inclinations when he remodelled a Dutch cottage into the rambling mansion which he named "Sunnyside."

More noteworthy, though less well known, are the architectural references of James Fenimore Cooper. Cooper, who likewise possessed Gothic tastes, mentions both Mrs. Radcliffe and "Monk" Lewis in one of his novels. Like Irving, he preferred a Gothic air in his residence, and he remodelled the old family mansion at Cooperstown accordingly. In a letter headed "Hall, Cooperstown, April 22nd, 1840" he writes:

> I have just been revolutionizing Christ Church, Cooperstown, not turning out a vestry, but converting its pine interior into oak, *bona fide* oak, and erecting a screen that I trust, though it may have no influence on my soul, will carry my name down to posterity. It is really a pretty thing—pure Gothic, and is the wonder of the country round.[13]

This passage reads like a letter from Horace Walpole. Unfortunately, the rood screen, instead of carrying Cooper's name to posterity, was torn down forty years later, and survives now in only a few fragments. On the brick walls

---

[12] George S. Hellman: *Washington Irving Esquire*, New York, 1925, p. 28.

[13] Ralph Birdsall: *The Story of Cooperstown*, Cooperstown, 1917, p. 265.

of the church may still be seen the scars where Cooper changed round arches to pointed ones, and added ornamental buttresses.

The scene of Cooper's first novel, *Precaution*, is laid in England. It is purely a social novel, without Gothic tendencies, but it introduces a "princely mansion," of which "the lofty towers were tipt with the golden light of the sun." *The Spy* is an American tale, and it contains a slight description of a country house, called "the Locusts." In the *Pioneers*, Cooper describes with some irony the primitive but pretentious buildings of early Cooperstown. It is in his later novels that his architectural ingenuity is best displayed.

A group of European narratives are the most architectural of these novels, though they are less interesting than the American tales. *The Haidenmauer*, an historical romance, is very reminiscent of the style of Scott, but the description of a midnight mass, followed by the spectacular burning and sacking of an abbey, would do credit to Mrs. Radcliffe. *The Headsman* introduces a Gothic chalet on the banks of Lake Leman; *The Bravo* leads us through the intricacies of the Doge's palace in Venice; *Mercedes of Castile* brings us to the courts of the Alhambra (a building already described by Irving); *Wing-and-Wing* includes a ruined temple on a Mediterranean island; and *The Pilot* brings us back to that familiar building, the English manor-house.

Cooper's architectural ingenuity was more severely taxed by his American stories. The block-house is his favorite structure—but how changed it is! Real block-houses were of very small dimensions, but Cooper, in the *Wept of Wish-ton-Wish* rears a super-block-house, consisting of a stone basement, two upper stories, and a garret which forms the sanctum of a Puritan patriarch. A stone well-shaft penetrates the interior of the building, and, when the block-house is burned by the Indians, the inhabitants escape by hiding in the well. *The Pathfinder* describes the siege of a block-house on one of the Thousand Islands of the St. Lawrence. In *The Deerslayer*, there is a similar building, reared on piles above the surface of Lake Otsego, and ironically named "Muskrat Castle." It is accompanied by a small floating fortress called "the Ark." *Wyandotté* describes a remarkable frontier mansion perched on a rocky knoll in the center of a drained beaverpond. It is a rambling building, surrounding a central courtyard (a favorite arrangement of Cooper's) and protected by a stone wall and encircling palisades. *Satanstoe* introduces a similar fortress, also containing a central court. There is an extraordinary Dutch house, with twisted chimneys, in *The Water Witch*; and the old stone mill at Newport plays an important part in the beginning of *Red Rover*.

Needless to say, Cooper, like several of his contemporaries, exaggerated the importance of American frontier architecture. Stone masonry was almost never used in such primitive buildings, except sometimes in chimneys. Four-story block-houses, great manor-houses in the wilderness, and island castles are all exceedingly improbable. Cooper's very exaggeration of these buildings is proof of his romantic attitude towards architecture, and of his desire to provide his novels with a more interesting setting than the American frontier actually afforded.

Nathaniel Hawthorne also exaggerated the importance of early American architecture. In both the *Scarlet Letter* and *The House of the Seven Gables* he goes beyond the Georgian buildings of the eighteenth century to the semi-Gothic houses of seventeenth-century New England—a significant step, for it shows his Gothic tendencies. The principal building in the *Scarlet Letter* is Governor Bellingham's mansion, with its arched door, flanked by towers, its embowed hall window, and its Elizabethan furniture. The House of the Seven Gables is a humbler mansion of the same period, but it possesses Gothic details which must have been very unusual, to say the least, in the Jacobean houses of New England, and which prove the assertions of the author and his family that the house was not modelled upon an existing structure in Salem. Even the Old Manse has a few of the same features. The British soldier, in *Septimius Felton*, dreams of his home in England, and we are told that it has Elizabethan gables.

Hawthorne likes to stress the mossy qualities of these buildings, and particularly in the case of the House of the Seven Gables, he makes them seem as venerable as if they had stood for a millennium instead of a mere century and a half. He resembles Cooper in his unconscious effort to give to the buildings of the new world an importance which they did not merit; in Cooper's case the importance was one of physical size and romantic situation, while in Hawthorne's novels, the exaggeration is of age and spiritual qualities.

In the *Marble Faun*, however, Hawthorne reverts to the attitude of Mrs. Radcliffe; indeed the English title of the book (*Transformation: or, the Romance of Monte Beni*) suggests the titles of the Gothic romances. Hilda's lofty tower, and Donatello's ancestral seat in the Apennines, bathed in Claude-like sunsets, are obviously influenced by the spirit of the Gothic romances. When Kenyon tries to imagine ghosts in the Colosseum, Hilda replies:

> "You bring a Gothic horror into this peaceful moonlight scene."

The architecture in W. G. Simms' tales illustrates most aspects of American architectural setting. There are blockhouses (*Yemassee, The Scout*), ruins (Jamestown in *Southward Ho!* and Dorchester in *The Partisan*), "castles" (the swamp fortresses in *Eutaw*), "ancient" fortified manorhouses (Piney Grove in *Mellichampe*), ridiculous public buildings (*Guy Rivers*), and even some Spanish-American setting though without much architecture (*Vasconselos* and *The Damsel of Darien*). Nature's architecture is described even more abundantly than man's.

It would be useless to follow all the later ramifications of architectural setting in American fiction, ranging from the Virginia mansions of Thomas Nelson Page to the Maine cottages of Sarah Orne Jewett. By the 1890's, literary nostalgia had brought Georgian architecture back into favor, and Page, in *The Old Gentleman of the Black Stock*, defends the Colonial house against its Victorian successors. Of late years, however, even the Victorian house has crept into literary repute. Future novelists may be able to make something of the skyscraper, which, if left to go to ruin, should make the medieval castle quite tame by comparison. America has emerged from architectural poverty, and novelists no longer need to pretend that there are castles on Long Island Sound, or turreted baronial mansions in Annapolis.

2

The House Personified

In the novels of the nineteenth century, architecture came to life. The house awoke from its previous inanimate condition, and began to assume human characteristics. Chimneys yawned—and became throats. Windows peered— and became eyes. The whole façade lifted up the light of its countenance, and revealed, to the sensitive observer, a face that was startlingly lifelike. Hawthorne said that the aspect of an old house affected him like a human countenance;[14] Sarah Orne Jewett's cottages "face the sea apprehensively, like the women who live in them";[15] Dickens compares the Maypole Inn to an old man nodding in his sleep, whose little panes of glass are drowsy, whose bulging front projects over the pathway, whose bricks are "yellow and discoloured like an old man's skin," whose timbers have decayed like

[14] *The House of the Seven Gables*, Chap. I.
[15] *By the Morning Boat*.

teeth, and whose ivy is "a warm garment to comfort it in its age."[16]

Such comparisons are important merely as symbols of deeper things. The eye and the window had, indeed, been associated in metaphor since Biblical times, when *Ecclesiastes* warned of the days when "those that look out of the windows be darkened." Spenser, in the *Faerie Queene*, introduced that famous medieval allegory, the human body as a castle. Thomas Fuller aptly called Gothic columns the legs of a cathedral; those of Westminster Abbey were slender (*"greatest legs* argue not the *strongest Man"*), while those of old St. Paul's were obese ("little Legs would bowe under so big a body"). Innumerable castles, in the Gothic romances, had frowned defiantly upon their foes.

Between such early symbolism and real personification, there is nevertheless a wide gulf. Allegorical buildings, though sometimes personified, were never personalities; Spenser's house of Alma is the human body in abstract terms, not the body of one particular individual. Fuller, though providing his cathedrals with legs, never goes so far as to call Wells a beautiful lady, or Durham a stern warrior. The castles of the Gothic romances frown, but merely in the sense that a cliff or a crag may be said to frown; such buildings evoke emotions in those who look at them, while remaining inanimate themselves. To the novelist of the eighteenth century, the castle had seemed a sublime or picturesque adjunct of natural scenery, pleasing the eye like a moss-covered rock, or intimidating the spirit like a great mountain or a gloomy gorge. You feared the castle, but you never loved it. It could overawe, but it could not charm.

Charm, indeed, was the magic quality that quickened architecture into life. The house became a soul, warmed into existence by the tender intimacies of generations of inhabi-

[16] *Barnaby Rudge*, Chap. I.

tants, who of their collective personalities gave the house a personality of its own. If you were at all sensitive, you instantly felt the personality of such an "atmospheric" house whenever you crossed its threshold; just as you felt the magnetism of a charming woman when you came into her presence. This sensitivity has progressed so far that books are now written, telling us how to give personality to our houses, much as we are told how to educate our children.

The personified house made its debut into fiction at a time when the novel was becoming chiefly concerned with the middle classes. The reasons for this coincidence are obvious. In the first place, the novel of middle-class life enabled the writer, himself a member of the middle classes, to describe houses in which he was at home as he was never at home in the castle. To love a building, one must feel at home in it; and, to personify a building, one must be capable of loving it. The eighteenth-century novelist, preoccupied as he was with the nobility and the gentry, had little occasion to describe the type of house with which he himself had intimate associations—consequently his buildings are not personalities.

In the Gothic romances, the obvious architectural features are never taken for granted. We are told again and again that the windows are pointed, the walls battlemented, and the passages vaulted; while we are left totally ignorant of the local color, the intimate domesticities, the personal qualities of the castle. One reason for this dearth of personality is, obviously, that the author is out of his element when he enters the seats of the mighty. When Mrs. Radcliffe describes a castle, it is with the awe of a sightseer who is being conducted on a visitors' day through those rooms which are occasionally thrown open to the public. The aged housekeeper who guides the Gothic heroine through her castle is suspiciously like the women who conduct parties of tourists through the state rooms of such places as Knole and

Later Architectural Developments 205

Penshurst. One expects to hear the clink of a shilling at the end of the tour.

The very strangeness of the castle, was, of course, an advantage to the writers of the Gothic school, because it accentuated the terrifying qualities of the scene. The personified house, with its human qualities, is obviously unsuitable for evoking the emotions of horror and fear; therefore the castles were deliberately made inhuman. The castle's very antiquity was also a hindrance to personification, because the buildings of a too remote past are so incongruous with modern life that they lose their human aspect. Thomas Hardy remarks[17] upon a house "of no marked antiquity, yet of a well-advanced age; older than a stale novelty, but no canonized antique; faded, not hoary; looking at you from the still distinct middle-distance of the early Georgian time, and awakening on that account the instincts of reminiscence more decidedly than the remoter, and far grander, memorials which have to speak from the misty reaches of medievalism." He goes on to say that: "It was a house in whose reverberations queer old personal tales were yet audible if properly listened for; and not, as with those of the castle and cloister, silent beyond the possibility of echo."

Moreover, the castle was not only too unfamiliar to be personified—it was also too big. Personality develops most quickly in houses of moderate dimensions. The great house inevitably retains some of the impersonal characteristics of an institution; it is too vast to be filled with books that have really been read, pictures that are actually cherished, or those well-born household articles which are homely but beloved. It would take a powerful personality to fill the halls of Udolpho. On the other hand, personality requires some breathing-space. It is seldom found in the houses of the very poor, because the mere physical necessities of life occupy

---

[17] *The Woodlanders*, Chap. IV.

all the available space. When the cooking-stove, the dinner-table, and the bedstead, to say nothing of the plumbing, are crowded into one room, personality knocks in vain at the door. It is in the medium-sized house that individuality makes itself at home; the palace is too chilly, and the hovel too cramped.

Archaeology is likewise fatal to this humanizing process. The personified house is the product of sympathy, not of erudition; it is not to be found among foot-notes and appendices. The conscientious historical novelist, therefore, has rarely succeeded in bringing his buildings to life. He has captured their substance rather than their spirit; he has substituted archaeological foot-notes for the subtler notation of the soul; he has poked among the ruins and unearthed a museum rather than a home. Personality is not a matter of early English crenellation, or of Perpendicular tracery. The foot-notes to the *Last Days of Pompeii*, for instance, show that Bulwer-Lytton based his descriptions upon the actual discoveries of archaeology; yet his houses remain as empty and inanimate upon paper as they are in Pompeii today. On the other hand, Walter Pater, in describing the villa of Marius the Epicurean, has created, with much less effort than Bulwer-Lytton, a real personality. The traveller, we are told, "would pause by the way, to read the face, as it were, of so beautiful a dwelling-place." It is a "coy, retired place," where nothing could happen "without its full accompaniment of thought or reverie." The descriptions of "White-Nights," as it is called, are very slight—the tower with its pigeon-house, the family chapel, the encroaching farm, the worn mosaic pavement, the warm crumbling walls—yet, meager as these descriptions are, they succeed in giving the house a personality which no mere archaeologist could impart.

Furthermore, neither the blood-and-thunder fiction of the Gothic romances, nor the dry-as-dust archaeology of the historical novels was fit soil for the flowering of that delicate quality, so inadequately called "charm." This quality probably made its way into the novel by way of the essay; at least the personified house is certainly more closely related to the gentle family of Charles Lamb and Washington Irving than to the tribe of Walpole and Lewis. It is equally removed from the terrifying castles of the Gothic romances and the more realistic buildings of Scott and his followers. Therefore, the greatest contribution of the nineteenth century to architectural setting lay, not in the aftermath of the Gothic romance, a form of literature which has persisted under various guises to this day, nor in the archaeological exactitude of the rapidly developing historical novel, but in the personified houses of various Victorian novelists. The architecture of Scott and Stevenson is in the tradition of the Gothic romances, but there is no precedent in the novel of the eighteenth century for the architecture of Hawthorne and Dickens.

Among early examples of personification are Miss Mitford's bay window, "hanging over the water, as if to admire its own beauty in that clear mirror,"[18] and Harrison Ainsworth's house which even in the daytime "had a sombre and suspicious air, and seemed to slink back from the adjoining houses, as if afraid of their society."[19] Bulwer-Lytton says that "Some houses have an *expression*, as it were, in their outward aspect, that sinks unaccountably into the heart—a dim oppressive eloquence which dispirits and affects."[20] Mrs. Marsh in *Castle Avon* (1852) describes a house "seeming to look out through her closed, small-paned windows, with a most disconsolate air."[21]

The House of the Seven Gables is one of the best examples of the personified building. Throughout the narrative, the House itself is the dominating feature; it is at once an

---
[18] *Belford Regis*, Philadelphia, 1835, I, 11.
[19] *Jack Sheppard*, Epoch the Second, Chap. XVI.
[20] *Eugene Aram*, Book IV, XI.
[21] III, 73-4.

ever-present background and an ever-present character. It visits upon its inhabitants the curse incurred by their ancestor; in fact the whole story hinges upon the reactions of the Pyncheon family to this "dwelling of so much hereditary misfortune."

Hawthorne makes it quite evident that the House is a personality. His descriptions of it are clothed in human terms.[22] It withdraws itself from the street, "but in pride, not in modesty." The seven gables present the aspect "of a whole sisterhood of edifices breathing through the spiracles of one great chimney." The very timbers are "oozy, as with the moisture of a heart." The deep projection of the second story gives the House a "meditative look," and you instantly saw that "it had secrets to keep, and an eventful history to moralize upon." In a storm, the House makes "a vociferous but somewhat unintelligible bellowing in its sooty throat (the big flue, we mean, of its wide chimney)."[23] In fact, says the author, "It was itself like a great human heart, with a life of its own, and full of rich and somber reminiscences."[22]

The personality of the House, like human personalities, can be modified by circumstances. The coming of Phoebe produces an instant change:

> It really seemed as if the battered visage of the House of the Seven Gables, black and heavy-browed as it still certainly looked, must have shown a kind of cheerfulness glimmering through its dusky windows as Phoebe passed to and fro in the interior.

Phoebe succeeds in throwing a "kindly and hospitable smile" over her chamber, which, the night before, "had resembled nothing so much as the old maid's heart; for there was

[22] Chap. I.
[23] Chap. XVIII.

neither sunshine nor household fire in one nor the other."[24] She exerts a "purifying influence" upon the atmosphere of the household. The House, however, exerts an influence upon her in its turn, just as it influences all the characters of the story. Indeed the characters are mere phantoms when compared with the House itself, for the book is chiefly concerned with spiritual values, and in these the House seems richer than any of its inhabitants.

To follow the personified house through all its variations would be useless. It has remained in fiction to this day, and there are few novelists who have not at one time or another made at least a slight use of it. As a literary form it has certain disadvantages. Though it undoubtedly gives to architectural descriptions a vividness which could be obtained in no other way, and though it is an admirable conveyance for the emotional effect of unusual buildings, it may only too easily be carried to absurdity, degenerating into pure sentimentality. It is at best an exaggeration, and at worst a falsehood. The personification of the house is really an example of that sacramental feeling with which the human race likes to deify its surroundings—that imagination which saw dryads in trees, and tritons upon the waters. The Christian religion was perhaps a contributing factor, covering the land, as it did, with churches where one was supposed to feel that the Lord was in His holy temple; the advent of the personified house in literature coincided with the Oxford movement in England.

Whatever its origins, however, it is clearly a product of civilization—some would say, of decadence. The eighteenth century had become sensitive to the house as an object, but the nineteenth century began to feel it as a personality. This increased sensitiveness to environment is, perhaps, an

[24] Chap. V.

over-refinement. It certainly does not flourish in the literature of pure realism. Seen in the clear morning light, the house is, after all, mere wood and stones; personification visits it only with the dusk of evening and the mists of unreality. It is an intrusion of poetry into the realm of prose, a gigantic metaphor like the "conceits" of the seventeenth century. Metaphors have their value, however, and poetry is not to be despised because it crops up in fiction, and the twilight has a beauty of its own.

3

The Bizarre House

Architecture, like everything else, has its freaks. There is no community which does not blush for some fantastic and ridiculous structure that makes us rub our eyes in amazement. Some of these buildings are purely comic, while others exercise the repulsion of monstrous deformity, but, in any case, the reactions that they arouse are unusually strong. The novelist was quick to see the literary advantages of such houses. There is something in a grotesque building which adds a subtle horror to tragic scenes; crimes seem more sinister and terrors more terrible within its walls—on the other hand, a grotesque setting intensifies the comedy of lighter themes; obviously, eccentric people demand eccentric housing. To the eighteenth century, all medieval architecture seemed more or less bizarre, but, by 1830, the deluge of Gothic romances and historical novels had made the castle only too commonplace as a literary background. Frowning turrets and panelled halls no longer seemed fantastic; they had lost their novelty. Gothic architecture had become both fashionable and respectable, and the novelist, by thus "making an honest woman" of his mistress, found that he had robbed her of her greatest charm.

All architectural setting is, to some extent, a search for the bizarre; but it is only within the last century that the search has become a very noticeable one. Before that, it was sufficient for a building to be old-fashioned and ruined; but now the element of eccentricity came to be considered desirable. The bizarre house must be absurd and disreputable. It might be a product of some whimsical style (like the Gothic or Greek revivals); it might be a freak of individual caprice (in which case it was often called somebody's "folly"); it might be an exotic (like a Swiss chalet in Florida, or a summer hotel in mid-winter); it might be uncouth by its very function (like an insane asylum); it might even be a commonplace building with extraordinary repairs. In any case, it must owe its absurdity to human vagary. A genuine ruin may seem misshapen, but an artificial ruin is grotesque; Warwick Castle is not ridiculous (to most modern observers, at least), but Strawberry Hill is; a dilapidated abbey, however fantastic its shape, is authentic architecture chiselled by authentic decay, but the same abbey remodelled into a railroad station would be absurd and bizarre.

The grotesque house made its appearance at the same period with the personified house, and for the same general purpose of heightening the emotional effect of architectural setting. The two types were seldom combined, however, because a building which is meant to arouse terror or derision is not likely to possess those lovable qualities which brought the personified house to life. A *tour-de-force* is apt to be rather inhuman, and a house which looks like nothing on heaven or earth usually seems too strange to arouse the intimacy of human relationship.

The principal exceptions to this rule come from the pen of Dickens. It is only to be expected that a writer who excelled in grotesque characters should also excel in grotesque houses, and that he should treat both his human and his architectural freaks with the same touch of tender humor. Dickens' houses are queer personalities, with all the idiosyncracies of eccentric humanity. They are usually leaning somewhere to peer at something; they have absurd decorations and crazy excresences; and they belong to no particular style, being outcasts from architecture much as their inmates are outcasts from society. Dickens revels in "wildernesses of corner houses, with barbarous old porticoes and appurtenances; horrors that came into existence under some wrong-headed person in some wrong-headed time, still demanding the blind admiration of all ensuing generations and determined to do so until they tumbled down."[25]

All Dickens' buildings seem ready to tumble down at no distant date—their leaning propensities are really remarkable. Mrs. Clennam's house, in *Little Dorrit*, "had it in its mind to slide down side-ways; it had been propped up, however, and was leaning on some half-dozen gigantic crutches: which gymnasium for the neighboring cats, weather-stained, smoke-blackened, and over-grown with weeds, appeared in these latter days to be no very sure reliance."[26] (At the end of the book, the props give way, and the house collapses.) Other decrepit buildings are to be found in the same novel—"rickety dwellings. . . . where their little supplementary bows and balconies were supported on thin iron columns, seemed to be scrofulously resting upon crutches."[27] In *Great Expectations,* some distorted houses look "as if they had twisted themselves to peep down at me."[28] David Copperfield fancies that Mr. Wickfield's house "was leaning forward, trying to see who was passing on the narrow pavement below."[29] In *Our Mutual Friend,* the Six Jolly Fellowship-Porters ("a tavern of a dropsical appearance") is described as "a narrow lop-

[25] *Little Dorrit,* Chap. XXVII.
[26] Chap. III.
[27] Chap. XXVII.
[28] Chap. XX.
[29] Chap. XV.

sided wooden jumble of corpulent windows heaped one upon another as you might heap as many toppling oranges, with a crazy wooden verandah impending over the water; indeed the whole house, inclusive of the complaining flag-staff on the roof, impended over the water, but seemed to have got into the condition of a faint-hearted diver who has paused so long on the brink that he will never go in at all."[30] The Maypole Inn, in *Barnaby Rudge,* looks as if it were nodding in its sleep, and the typical house in Clerkenwell is "dozing on in its infirmity until in course of time it tumbles down, and is replaced by some extravagant young heir, flaunting in stucco and ornamental work, and all the vanities of modern days." Gabriel Varden's house is described as "a modest building, not very straight, not large, not tall; not bold-faced, with great staring windows, but a shy blinking house, with a conical roof going up into a peak over its garret window of four small panes of glass, like a cocked hat on the head of an elderly gentleman with one eye."[31]

Dickens, unlike many other novelists, is not interested in fantastic country seats, and the architectural aberrations of wealthy dilettantes. His houses, like his characters, are thoroughly plebeian, and whatever gentility they may have had in better days is very down-at-heel. For this very reason, his grotesque houses are often personalities; they are thoroughly naive and human, in contrast to more sophisticated dwellings which are conscious of styles and periods.

The wealthy amateur with eccentric architectural tastes has always been a favorite character in English fiction (and, it may be added, a character often found in real life). He appears in the social novels of the eighteenth century; glimpses of him are afforded by Scott and Miss Edgeworth; he cuts quite a figure in the stories of Thomas Love Peacock;

[30] Book I, Chap. VI.
[31] Chap. IV.

and he emerges fairly often in later novels. The earlier novels, as a rule, are more interested in the man, and the later ones are more concerned with his architecture; indeed in many of the later books the eccentric gentleman is already dead by the time that the story begins, and we know him chiefly through his constructions. This is the case, for instance, in Mallock's *New Republic*, where "Lawrence's Folly," the setting of the narrative, is the legacy of an eccentric uncle. It is also the case in Aldous Huxley's *Chrome Yellow*, the setting of which is a Tudor house with towers topt by privies, the work of an ingenious ancestor. Llanabba Castle, in Evelyn Waugh's *Decline and Fall*, is the extravaganza of a deceased Lancashire mill owner with Victorian Gothic tastes. The fantastic Gothic revival house in Michael Sadleir's *Privilege* was inherited from an imitator of Beckford.

The distinction between past and present "follies" is an important one. If you build a queer house for yourself, the house, being your own expression, exercises no great influence upon you, but if you acquire the queer house of a mad uncle, the psychological effect of the architecture is usually much greater. There is something doubly uncouth and disreputable about "follies" which are no longer new—follies, in architecture as well as in life, seem appropriate only for youth.

The grotesque house, therefore, is at its most grotesque when it has grown old, for age merely adds to its eccentricities. It is used most effectively when it bursts, full-blown, upon the reader, without any previous explanation of the motives for its construction. Much of the dramatic quality of Chesterton's settings in his Father Brown Stories comes from the suddenness with which these weird structures loom into view; we are abruptly confronted with Pendragon Hall, or the house of the Darnaways, or the bamboo retreat of

Prince Saradine. Explanations follow afterwards; but not until a moment of nightmare has elapsed.

The sinister qualities of Gothic architecture seem to have been inherited by the Gothic revival, which is used to impart a gloomy atmosphere to several tragic tales. "Bly," the setting of Henry James' *Turn of the Screw*, is a building of this style, and a murder, in Michael Sadleir's *Privilege*, is made more gruesome by being committed in a Gothic revival ruin nicknamed "Otranto." Sometimes, however, the houses of the Gothic revival are merely ridiculous, as in the case of Mr. Wemmick's house in Dickens' *Great Expectations*. The classic revivals lend themselves less easily to sinister effects, though O'Neill's *Mourning Becomes Electra*, to borrow an example from the drama, employs the Greek revival for sinister purposes. There is a slightly malevolent air to "Cadover," a Roman revival house which plays a prominent part in E. M. Forster's *Journey's End*. Hardy's *Two on a Tower* deals with a gigantic Roman column which has been remodelled into an astronomical observatory. The forbidding qualities of the principal building in De Morgan's *Old Mad House* are due less to its classical architecture than to its previous function. The grotesque effect of the Clennam house in Dickens' *Little Dorrit* is produced by its enormous props, although some eccentricity must also be ascribed to the canopy over the door "of festooned jack-towels and children's heads with water on the brain."

Summer-houses, pavilions, seaside resorts, and other temporary structures are favorite sources of the bizarre, because their flimsy gaiety is appropriate only when they are in good repair and in good weather—which they seldom are. Nothing seems quite so grotesque as a tawdry summer hotel in mid-winter. Chesterton realized this fact in making a deserted seaside pavilion the scene of a murder in *The God of the Gongs*, and, in another detective story, Eberhard's

Hunting's End, the setting is provided by a hunting-lodge, snowed in. A rickety summer-house, leaking rain on its inmates, and overhanging a filthy river, is the fitting scene of a tea party served by Miss Sally Brass in Dickens' *Old Curiosity Shop*. Conrad's novels are full of ephemeral tropical buildings which have fallen on evil days—for example, "Almayer's Folly" in the novel of the name, and the deserted mining camp in *Victory*.

There are all kinds of bizarre houses. It is hard to define a type of architecture whose only qualification is that it must be queer, but some indication has been given of the prevalence of such structures in recent novels. For tales of mystery or terror, and for extravaganzas of eccentricity, the advantages of a grotesque setting are obvious. Modern fiction seems to be employing this setting to an increasing extent, probably because modern writers have a greater knowledge of architecture and a keener eye for subtleties of effect. The ruined castle has long been outmoded as a source of horror, and writers who reintroduce it are usually careful to include startling variations on the original theme.

CHAPTER SEVEN

THE CONTRIBUTIONS OF ARCHITECTURAL FICTION

In summarizing a literary trend, one naturally pauses to ask what good it has done. In this case, appraisal is unusually complicated, because two arts are involved, and we must consider the effect of architectural setting, not only upon the literature which contains it, but upon architecture as well. Its ultimate value depends, of course, upon the influence which it has exerted through both these mediums upon human life.

Its effects upon architecture will probably be deplored by architects, because literature has certainly played havoc with architecture, and there seems to be no certain hope that it will cease to do so. The human race is incurably tainted with "make-believe," a weakness which fiction encourages, and which the architectural setting of fiction has communicated to architecture itself. Children read about the enchanted castles of fairy tales, and wish that they themselves could live in such castles; adults read about interesting buildings in romantic novels, and proceed to copy those buildings in their own constructions. Literature has made people demand that architecture satisfy their emotional and imaginative yearnings, and these yearnings are often aroused by the architectural setting of fiction.

The enchanted castle symbolizes what is most significant in the literary use of architecture. When we open a novel, we step into another person's life—and into another person's house. In realistic fiction, the house and the life are usually like those that we already know, but in romantic novels they are more glamorous. When literature is an escape from the monotony of every-day life, it is often an escape from everyday architecture as well. We cross the drawbridge of the enchanted castle, and, for the time being, bid farewell to the cramped living-rooms and dining-rooms of ordinary existence.

The architecture of escape exists not only in fiction but in reality, accounting for the popularity of Gothic cathedrals, Tudor colleges, and Georgian homes in modern America. It is useless for modern architects to preach modern architecture to people who want an imaginative escape from modernity, and there will always be such people, for electicism prevails in life as well as in architecture. All the past styles of building are (with modifications) available for present use, and so are all the past styles of living—thanks to literature. One may be a churchman and live in the Middle Ages; one may be a country gentleman and live in the eighteenth century; one may even be a Latin scholar and live in the Roman Empire. When so many kinds of spiritual allegiance exist, it is to be expected that corresponding varieties of architecture will also flourish, and it is useless to hope for any consistency or uniformity of design. It is idle to urge people to give up their Georgian doorways or their Tudor mullions when they have secret yearnings for colonial America or Elizabethan England.

The architecture of English fiction is both a record of such yearnings and a means of focusing them. The eighteenth century felt bored with its Georgian architecture, so the novelists stepped forward to paint the glamour of Gothic castles, thereby fostering the revived medievalism of which the Gothic romance was itself an expression. Scott and Walpole posed as medieval barons, built medieval houses, popularized their medieval longings in fiction, and thus made countless readers yearn for medievalism too. The Greek and Roman revivals likewise had literary sponsors, just as the Renaissance, before them, had been ushered in by literary influences. America, at the dawn of the twentieth century, was growing bored with Victorian architecture, so novelists like Thomas Nelson Page, by romanticizing the classic mansions of the ante-bellum South, helped to revive the domestic architecture of colonial and early republican times.

Therefore, so long as fiction can produce a love for past styles of architecture, those styles will continue to flourish. The professional architects of the eighteenth century scorned the Gothic revival, but popular demand forced it upon them. When a man's imagination is captured by Tudor manor-houses, it is useless to tell him that he must not copy a dead thing of the past; the client already sees himself through the oriel window of a panelled hall, and Tudor architecture, for him, is not dead at all. Has he not been talking to Queen Elizabeth herself in the pages of his favorite novel; has he not groped through the secret passages by the light of a rush candle, and climbed the turret stairs? When literature thus brings the past to life, the architecture of the past can never be buried, for it is never dead. Bulwer-Lytton, in the preface to his *Last Days of Pompeii*, says that it is his intention "to people once more those deserted streets, to repair those graceful ruins, to reanimate the bones which were yet spared to his survey; to traverse the gulf of eighteen centuries, and to wake to a second existence—the City of the Dead!" When such people are engaged in the task of resurrection, it is difficult for the past to stay buried. By means of the printed page, we can live in any century we choose—with all the modern conveniences.

In the Gothic revival of the eighteenth century, England witnessed the perfect example of literary intrusion into architecture. Nobody was then interested in medieval construction for its own sake; the Gothic revival sprang from literary motives; it was fostered by literary architecture, and it was thrust by literary amateurs upon professional architects who did not want it. The same occurrence is likely to be repeated at any time. The very fact that a great style of the past seems hopelessly dead is an invitation for its revival. On the other hand, there is the consolation that a style revived is never quite the same as it was in its original form, and that a style discarded is seldom without some influence upon its successor.

Utility, durability, and beauty have always been the essentials of good building, but the novelists intensified a demand for sentiment also. A house which merely served its purpose and looked well was not enough for them; it must have "atmosphere" of some sort; it must appeal to the imagination; it must satisfy emotional needs as well as utilitarian and aesthetic ones. To them, a purely modern architecture, devoid of all reminiscence, would be as an arid desert. The house must, like popular painting of the Victorian era, "tell a story"; the shift in style depends upon the story it is expected to tell.

No doubt, this is all very bad. It subjects the art of building to the caprices of fashion, as Geoffrey Scott ably pointed out in his chapter on the Romantic Fallacy. The architectural setting of fiction has done much to discourage the plunge into new modes of design. By its hold on the popular imagination, it can swing architecture in almost any direction it chooses, and architects are powerless to stop it—unless they turn to novel-writing themselves. To those who regard architecture as a science as well as an art, this sentimentalizing process seems doubly deplorable; it leads to the "dressing up" of buildings with useless ornament that has no connection with their function.

Such criticism is perhaps valid, but, human nature being as it is, there seems to be nothing else to expect. People are incurably sentimental and romantic; they like to dramatize themselves against suitable backgrounds; they prefer new buildings that are flavored with reminiscence to new buildings that are merely beautiful and serviceable. It cannot be denied that a cow-stable which looks like a ruined abbey is more striking, whether you like it or not, than a cow-stable which merely looks like a cow-stable. To be sure, modern conditions and materials impose a certain uniformity upon contemporary buildings, regardless of style. It may be that style will come to resemble the optional flavors that may be added to certain kinds of desserts—one may choose peach, strawberry, or lemon architecture. It will be useless to protest that architecture is neither peach, strawberry, nor lemon, and it will be useless to urge people to eschew such flavors if popular fiction is making their mouths water for them.

The architectural setting of fiction is, then, a means of directing, intensifying, and recording popular architectural nostalgias. Its effect upon architecture, as we have seen, has been of doubtful value; its effect upon literature is not altogether fortunate. It is just as bad to make literature draw a floor-plan as it is to make architecture tell a story. To do in one medium something which is more appropriate to another is usually a mistake, and it is doubtful if narratives so preoccupied as the Gothic romances with architecture can ever belong to the highest order of literature. The concentration of a novelist's attention upon inanimate objects rather than upon human life, is usually unfortunate, and it seems futile to waste literary talent upon pictures which can be expressed much better, and comprehended much more easily, in the medium of paint rather than in that of words. On the other hand, it must not be forgotten that architectural setting heightened the emotional value of tragic literature by providing it with a suitable background, and that it furnished new devices for plots and new scenery for descriptions.

Furthermore, some examples of architectural setting are so well written that they are worth reading purely for their style. It would be absurd to condemn such bits of good prose merely because they are not essential to the narrative—and in many cases they are very essential. Architecture, after all, is a subject of interest to many people; buildings exert as great a psychological effect as any other form of environment; the crime of ignoring architecture in fiction is surely as great as the fault of overstressing it. Housing is an important factor in human existence, and architectural setting, though it first invaded the novel under an extravagant Gothic guise, remains to assume a legitimate place commensurate with the actual influence of architecture upon life.

The architecture of fiction, despite some bad effects upon architecture and literature as arts, has yet exerted through them an influence which is not without value to humanity. The glamorous buildings of the romantic novel awakened the public mind to the poetic qualities of architecture, and to a sense of the picturesque in building design. Architectural setting increased our enjoyment of the great edifices of the past by bringing them to life, and by peopling them with characters that were no less real for being alive only in the imagination; it opened magic portals to those who never saw the gates of a real castle. It is not unpleasant to be able to lay down one's novel, echoing the words of the old opera song: "I Dreamt that I Dwelt in Marble Halls."

By such means, it has given enjoyment to many readers, and, if it has sometimes encouraged architectural absurdities, it has encouraged them in people who would probably have perpetrated some sort of absurdity anyway. The enchanted castle, whether in literature or in architecture, is a harmless extravagance, and it should not be brutally demolished merely because it sometimes has towers of papier-maché or battlements of stucco. In the radiant mists of romance, even such flimsy materials as these can loom with impressive splendor.

INDEX

General Subject Index

American novels, 191-201, 207-9, 219.
Ancestral reverence for castles, 7-12.
Archaeology, 26-30, 167, 174, 179.
Catholicism, interest in, 22-3.
Garden architecture, 37, 155, 158.
German influence, 76-7.
Gothic revival, 31-50, 176, 183, 214-5.
Gothic romance, 79-86, 107-44.
Greek architecture, 149.
Greek revival, 27, 150, 215.
Historical novel, 73-4, 84-6, 121, 169-90.
Local color in the novel, 168.
Mystery in architecture, 18-9, 119.
Nature and architecture, 15, 193.
Oriental architecture, 37, 155-8.
Perpendicular Gothic, 33-41, 143-4.
Philistines, 91-2, 126, 141.
Picturesque, the, 12-5, 98-9.
Recluses, 93-4, 126-7, 140-1.
Renaissance architecture, 36, 152-5.
Ridicule of Gothic castles, 106, 159-67.
Roman architecture, 147-9.
Roman revival, 150, 215.
Romances of chivalry, 70.
Ruins, love of, 19-22, 31.
Self-dramatization in architecture, 23-5.
Sublime, the, 15-8, 118.
Travel descriptions, 30, 168-9.

Index of Novels and Authors

Abbey of Clunedale. (*See* Drake, N.)
Abbey of St. Asaph. (*See* Hedgeland.)
Abbot. (*See* Scott, Walter.)
Adam, Robert, 27, 34, 42.
Adelaide. (*See* Mrs. Edgeworth.)
Adeline de Courcy, 21.
Adeline St. Julian. (*See* Ker.)
Adventures of John of Gaunt. (*See* White, Jas.)
Adventures of King Richard Coeur-de-Lion. (*See* White, Jas.)
Adventures of Mr. Geo. Edwards. (*See* Hill, J.)
Aikin, John, *81-3*, 94, 132, 134, 142.
Aikin, Lucy, 81.
Ainsworth, Harrison, 3, 151, 168, *183-7*, 207.
d'Alenson, 155.
Algerines. (*See* Green, W. C.)
Almayer's Folly. (*See* Conrad, J.)
Alroy. (*See* Disraeli.)
Anecdotes of the Delborough Family. (*See* Gunning, S. M.)
Angelina. (*See* Robinson, M.)
Anna. (*See* Bennett, A. M.)
Anna St. Ives. (*See* Holcroft.)
Anne of Swansea, 140.
Ariosto, 70.
d'Arnaud, 86.
Arnold, S. J., 2, 72.
Arsaces. (*See* Johnstone, Chas.)
Asylum. (*See* Mitchell, I.)
Aubrey. (*See* Dallas, R. C.)
Augustus and Adelina. (*See* Golland.)
Austen, Jane, 24, 105, 159, *164-5*, 168.
Azemia. (*See* Beckford.)

Bage, Robert, 91, 94, 168.
Ball, Edward, 18, 21.
Banished Man. (*See* Smith, Mrs. C.)
Barbauld, Mrs. A. L., 81.
Barford Abbey. (*See* Gunning, S. M.)
Barham Downs. (*See* Bage.)
Barnaby Rudge. (*See* Dickens.)

224 Novels and Authors

Barrett, E. S., 146, 166.
Beckford, Wm., 3, 9, 18, 22-3, 28, 31, *42-7*, *157-8*, 163, 189, 214.
Beggar Girl. (*See* Bennett, A. M.)
Belmont Grove, 91.
Belmour. (*See* Damer.)
Bennett, Mrs. Agnes Maria, 10-1, 14, 91, *124-5*, 137.
Bentham, James, 28.
Bird, John, 14, 53, 63, 131, 134.
Bird, Robert M., 194.
Birdsall, Ralph, 198.
Black Robber. (*See* Ball.)
Blower, Miss, 90.
Bolton, Arthur T., 42.
Bonhote, Mrs. Elizabeth, 123, 133, *171-3*.
Bonze. (*See* D'Alenson.)
Boswell, Henry, 28, 49.
Bracebridge Hall. (*See* Irving, W.)
Brackenridge, Henry, 193.
Brambletye House. (*See* Smith, Horace.)
Bravo. (*See* Cooper, J. F.)
Bray, Mrs. Anna Eliza, 184, *186*.
Brewer, J. N., 18, 184.
Bride of Lammermoor. (*See* Scott, Walter.)
Brontë, Emily, 133.
Brother Jonathan. (*See* Neal, J.)
Brown, C. B., 193.
Buck, Nathanael, 28.
Bulwer-Lytton, E., 150-1, 183-5, *188-9*, 206-7, 219.
Bungay Castle. (*See* Bonhote.)
Burney, Fanny, 11, 91, 168.
Butler, Samuel, 56.
Byron, Lord, 25, 169.

Calavar. (*See* Bird, R. M.)
Camden, Wm., 180.
Camilla. (*See* Burney.)
Canterbury Tales. (*See* Lee, H. and S.)
Carbonières, Ramond de, 30.
Carey, David, 141.
Carne, John, 184, 188.
Caroline Merton, 24, *125*, 135, 161.
Carter, John, 28.
Castle Avon. (*See* Marsh.)
Castle Chapel. (*See* Roche.)
Castle of Beeston, 53, 57, 133, 171, 173.
Castle of Eridan. (*See* Graglia.)

Castle of Hardayne. (*See* Bird, J.)
Castle of Inchvally. (*See* Cullen.)
Castle of Mowbray, 170.
Castle of Ollada. (*See* Lathom, F.)
Castle of Otranto. (*See* Walpole.)
Castle of St. Donats. (*See* Lucas.)
Castle of Wolfenbach. (*See* Parsons.)
Castle on the Rock. (*See* Kendall, A.)
Castle Rackrent. (*See* Edgeworth, Maria.)
Castles of Athlin and Dunbayne. (*See* Radcliffe, A.)
Cecilia. (*See* Burney.)
Celestina. (*See* Smith, Mrs. C.)
Cesario Rosalba. (*See* Anne of Swansea.)
Chambers, Sir Wm., 8, 26, 32, 42.
Champion of Virtue. (*See* Reeve, C.)
Chesterton, G. K., 214-5.
Children of the Abbey. (*See* Roche.)
Chrome Yellow. (*See* Huxley, A.)
Church of St. Siffrid, 53, 131.
Clan-Albin. (*See* Johnstone, Mrs.)
Clarissa. (*See* Richardson.)
Clark, Kenneth, 23, 40, 43-4, 49.
Clermont. (*See* Roche.)
Clifford, Frances, 150.
Cobbett, Wm., 9.
Collins, Wm., 50, 58, 77.
Collyer, Mrs. S., 74.
Columella. (*See* Graves, R.)
Congreve, Wm., 55-6.
Conrad, Jos., 216.
Contarini Fleming. (*See* Disraeli.)
Contrast. (*See* Roche.)
Convent, 86.
Convent. (*See* Fuller, A.)
Convent of Grey Penitents. (*See* Wilkinson, S. S.)
Convict. (*See* Parsons.)
Cooper, J. F., 4, *198-201*.
Corsair's Bride. (*See* Stanhope, L. S.)
Cottage. (*See* Gunning, S. M.)
Count di Novini, 20, 53.
Count di Santerre. (*See* Selden, C.)
Count Robert of Paris. (*See* Scott, Walter.)
Count Roderic's Castle, 191.
Country Cousins, 87, 90, 135.
Coxe, Wm., 30, 130, 174.
Creole. (*See* Arnold, S. J.)
Croly, Geo., 150.

Crusaders. (*See* Stanhope, L. S.)
Cullen, Stephen, *130-1*, 171-2.
Cunningham, Allan, 21.
Curties, T. J. Horsley, 14, 18, *138*, 141, 174.

Dallas, R. C., 15.
Damer, Mrs. Anne, 15.
Damsel of Darien. (*See* Simms, W. G.)
David Copperfield. (*See* Dickens.)
Decline and Fall. (*See* Waugh, E.)
Deerslayer. (*See* Cooper, J. F.)
Delia, 122.
Delves. (*See* Gunning, S. M.)
De Morgan, Wm., 215.
Desmond. (*See* Smith, Mrs. C.)
De Sousa, 28.
Dickens, Charles, 189, 202-3, 211-3, 215-6.
Di Montranzo. (*See* Stanhope, L. S.)
Dinarbas. (*See* Knight, E. C.)
Discarded Son. (*See* Roche.)
Disobedience, 69, 126.
Disraeli, B., 146-7, 152, 169, 189.
Drake, Dr. N., 28, 55-6, *59*, 63-4, *132-3*, 136, 142, 144, 174.
Dryden, John, 56.
Dugdale, Sir Wm., 28.
Dyer, John, 58.

Each Sex in their Humour, 75.
Earl Strongbow. (*See* White, Jas.)
East Indian. (*See* Young, M. J.)
Eberhard, 215-6.
Edgeworth, Mrs., 21.
Edgeworth, Maria, 133, 213.
Edwards, Matilda Betham, 168.
Eleanor. (*See* Golland.)
Elkswatawa. (*See* French, J.)
Ellen. (*See* Bennett, A. M.)
Emily, 59.
Emma, or the Child of Sorrow, 93.
Emma, or the Unfortunate Attachment, 88-90.
Emmeline. (*See* Smith, Mrs. C.)
Epicurean. (*See* Moore, Thos.)
Errors of Education. (*See* Parsons.)
Errors of Innocence. (*See* Lee, H.)
Ethelinde. (*See* Smith, Mrs. C.)
Eugene Aram. (*See* Bulwer-Lytton.)
Eutaw. (*See* Simms, W. G.)
Evelina. (*See* Burney.)

Falconbridge Abbey. (*See* Hanway.)
False Friend. (*See* Robinson, M.)
Fashionable Follies. (*See* Vaughan.)
Fatal Revenge. (*See* Maturin.)
Female Quixote. (*See* Lennox.)
Fenwick, Mrs., 191.
Ferdinand Count Fathom. (*See* Smollett.)
Festival of Mora. (*See* Stanhope, L. S.)
Fielding, Henry, 70.
Fielding, Sarah, 70-1.
Flint, Timothy, 193-5.
Forster, E. M., 215.
Foster, James R., 119.
Francis Berrian. (*See* Flint, T.)
Frederick Morland. (*See* Carey, D.)
French, Jas., 193.
Fugitive Countess. (*See* Wilkinson, S. S.)
Fuller, Anne, 122.
Fuller, Thos., 203.

Galt, John, 146, 184, *187-9*.
Gaston de Blondeville. (*See* Radcliffe, A.)
Gilpin, Wm., 20, 30.
Godfrey de Hastings, 133, 171, 173, 174.
Godwin, Wm., 126.
Golland, Mrs. C. D., *141-2*, 166-7.
Gordon, Alex., 180.
Gough, Richard, 28, 180.
Graglia, G. A., 126, 157, 174.
Grasville Abbey. (*See* Moore, G.)
Graves, Richard, 158, 169.
Gray, Thos., 20, 32, 50, 58-9, 77.
Great Expectations. (*See* Dickens.)
Green, Wm. Child, 146.
Griffith Abbey. (*See* Mathews, C.)
Griffith, Mrs. Elizabeth, 10, 70, 90, 92, 160.
Grose, Francis, 28, 174.
von Grosse, Karl, 76.
Gunning, Miss Elizabeth, 161.
Gunning, Mrs. Susannah M., *86-7*, 90, 123, 127, 155.
Guy Fawkes. (*See* Ainsworth.)
Guy Rivers. (*See* Simms, W. G.)

Haferkorn, Reinhard, 58.
Haidenmauer. (*See* Cooper, J. F.)
Halfpenny, Jos., 28.

Hanway, Mrs. Mary Ann, 30, 146, 166.
Hardy, Thos., 205, 215.
Haunted Cavern. (*See* Palmer, J.)
Haunted Priory. (*See* Cullen.)
Hawthorne, N., 200-1, 207-9.
Headsman. (*See* Cooper, J. F.)
Hearne, T., 28.
Hedgeland, Isabella (Kelly), 14, 19, 131, 137.
Heiresse di Montalde. (*See* Ker, A.)
Hellman, G. S., 198.
Helme, Mrs. Elizabeth, 139.
Henry, Robert, 28, 132.
Henry Fitzowen. (*See* Drake, N.)
Herbert Lodge. (*See* Warne.)
Hernon, G. D., 140.
Hero, 166.
Heroine. (*See* Barrett, E. S.)
Hervey, Mrs. Elizabeth, 126, *159-60*, 169.
Heseltine, Wm., 186-7.
Hill, John, 75.
History of Eliza Warwick, 90.
History of Joshua Trueman, 66.
History of Lady Barton. (*See* Griffith, Mrs. E.)
History of Lord Belford and Miss Sophia Woodley, 90-1.
History of Miss Indiana Danby, 86.
History of Miss Meredith. (*See* Parsons.)
History of Miss Pamela Howard, 67.
History of Ophelia. (*See* Fielding, Sarah.)
History of the Carrils and the Ormes. (*See* Brown, C. B.)
History of the Countess of Dellwyn. (*See* Fielding, Sarah.)
Holcroft, Thos., 13.
Home, John, 55.
Honor O'Hara. (*See* Porter, A. M.)
Horrid Mysteries. (*See* Grosse, K. Von.)
House of the Seven Gables. (*See* Hawthorne.)
Houses of Osma and Almeria. (*See* Roche.)
Hubert de Sevrac. (*See* Robinson, M.)
Humphry Clinker. (*See* Smollett.)
Hunting's End. (*See* Eberhard.)
Hurd, Bishop, 50.

Husband's Resentment, 92.
Hussey, Christopher, 12.
Hutchinson, Wm., 90.
Huxley, Aldous, 214.
Hypatia. (*See* Kingsley, C.)

Infidel. (*See* Bird, R. M.)
Invisible Enemy. (*See* Lathy, T. P.)
Irving, Washington, 4, 165, 198, 207.
Italian. (*See* Radcliffe, A.)
Ivanhoe. (*See* Scott, Walter.)

Jack Sheppard. (*See* Ainsworth.)
James, G. P. R., 184, 187.
James, Henry, 215.
Jewett, Sarah Orne, 168, 202.
Johnson, Dr. Samuel, 2, 47, 56, *71-2*, 79, 143, 150, 157.
Johnstone, Mrs., 167.
Johnstone, Charles, 21, 147-8.
Journey's End. (*See* Forster, E. M.)
Julia. (*See* Williams, H. M.)
Julia di Roubigné. (*See* Mackenzie, H.)
Juliana, 90.
Juvenile Indiscretions. (*See* Bennett, A. M.)

Kahlert, F. C., 76.
Kelly, Mrs. (*See* Hedgeland.)
Kendall, A., 53, 149.
Kenilworth. (*See* Scott, Walter.)
Ker, Mrs. Anne, 129.
Kingsley, Charles, 151.
Knight, Ellis Cornelia, 150, 157.
Kruitzner. (*See* Lee, H.)

Lady Jane Grey, 171.
Lamb, Charles, 207.
Langhorne, John, 155, 168.
Langley, Batty, 32.
Last Days of Pompeii. (*See* Bulwer-Lytton.)
Last of the Lairds. (*See* Galt, J.)
Last of the Plantagenets. (*See* Heseltine, Wm.)
Lathom, Francis, 53, 77, 137, 191.
Lathy, T. P., 11, 174.
Lauder, T. D., 184, 188.
Lee, Harriet, 10, 64, 107, 133.
Lee, Sophia, 77, *84-6*, 94-5, 97, 107-8, 133, 170, 173.
Lefanu, Alicia, 166.

Novels and Authors

Leila. (*See* Bulwer-Lytton.)
Leland, Thos., *72-4*, 170.
Lennox, Mrs. Charlotte, 75.
LeRoy, Julian, 27.
Lewis, M. G., 2, 22, 53, 131, 132, 137, 198, 207.
Lidora, 123.
Life and Adventures of Indiana. (*See* Collyer.)
Life of Harriot Stuart. (*See* Lennox.)
Literary Hours. (*See* Drake, N.)
Little Dorrit. (*See* Dickens.)
Lochandhu. (*See* Lauder, T. D.)
Lockhart, John, 150-2.
Logan. (*See* Neal, J.)
Longsword. (*See* Leland, Thos.)
Louisa. (*See* Hervey, Mrs. E.)
Louisa. (*See* Hernon, G. D.)
Loves of Othniel and Achsah. (*See* Tooke.)
Lucas, Charles, 53, 127, 163.
Lucretia. (*See* Bulwer-Lytton.)
Lucy. (*See* Parsons.)
Lydia. (*See* Shebbeare.)

McHenry, James, 194.
McIntyre, Clara, 30, 118-9, 154.
Mackenzie, Henry, 62, 68, 87, 132.
Mackenzie, W. M., 179.
Macpherson, James. (*See* Ossian.)
Magdalen. (*See* Helme, Mrs. E.)
Major, Thomas, 27.
Mallock, W. H., 214.
Man of Feeling. (*See* Mackenzie, H.)
Man of the World. (*See* Mackenzie, H.)
Mansfield Park. (*See* Austen, J.)
Manwaring, E., 12, 119.
Marble Faun. (*See* Hawthorne.)
Marchmont. (*See* Smith, Mrs. C.)
Maria. (*See* Blower.)
Maria. (*See* Stabback.)
Marius the Epicurean. (*See* Pater.)
Marlowe, Christopher, 55.
Marsh, Mrs., 207.
Mason, Wm., 59.
Masquerades, 90, 94.
Mathews, Mrs. C., 141.
Maturin, C. R., 21, 140, 146, 176.
Meeke, Mrs. Mary, 137.
Melincourt. (*See* Peacock, T. L.)

Melissa and Marcia. (*See* Hervey, Mrs. E.)
Mellichampe. (*See* Simms, W. G.)
Melmoth. (*See* Maturin, C. R.)
Melville, Lewis, 9.
Memoirs of a Man of Honour, 74.
Memoirs of Mary. (*See* Gunning, S. M.)
Memoirs of Sir Roger de Clarendon. (*See* Reeve, C.)
Mercedes of Castile. (*See* Cooper, J. F.)
Middleton, Thos., 55.
Midnight Bell. (*See* Lathom.)
Milesian Chief. (*See* Maturin.)
Millenium Hall. (*See* Scott, Mrs. Sarah.)
Milner, John, 28.
Milton, John, 50, 56, 58.
Misfortunes of Elphin. (*See* Peacock, T. L.)
Mitchell, Isaac, 195.
Mitford, Miss M. R., 207.
Modern Chivalry. (*See* Brackenridge.)
Modern Novel Writing. (*See* Beckford.)
Monk. (*See* Lewis, M. G.)
Montalbert. (*See* Smith, Mrs. C.)
Moore, Geo., 132.
Moore, Thos., 150.
More Ghosts. (*See* Patrick.)
Morgan, Lady S. O., 21, 140, 147, 150, 174.
Morlands. (*See* Dallas.)
Morley Ernstein. (*See* James, G. P. R.)
Mosse, Henrietta R., 174.
Mount Henneth. (*See* Bage.)
Munster Cottage Boy. (*See* Roche.)
Munster Village. (*See* Walker, Lady M.)
Murphy, James, 28-9.
Mutability of Human Life, 68, 93.
Mysteries of Udolpho. (*See* Radcliffe, A.)
Mysterious Warning. (*See* Parsons.)
Mystic Castle, 131, 133.

Neal, John, 194, 196-7.
Necromancer of the Black Forest. (*See* Kahlert.)
New Republic. (*See* Mallock.)

228 Novels and Authors

Nightmare Abbey. (*See* Peacock.)
Nocturnal Visit. (*See* Roche.)
Northanger Abbey. (*See* Austen, J.)
Novice of St. Dominick. (*See* Morgan, Lady S. O.)

O'Donnel. (*See* Morgan, Lady S.O.)
O'Halloran. (*See* McHenry, J.)
Old Curiosity Shop. (*See* Dickens.)
Old English Baron. (*See* Reeve, C.)
Old Gentleman of the Black Stock. (*See* Page, T. N.)
Old Mad House. (*See* De Morgan.)
Old Manor House. (*See* Smith, Mrs. C.)
Old St. Paul's. (*See* Ainsworth.)
O'Neill, E., 215.
Orlando and Seraphina, 156, 174.
Orphan of the Rhine. (*See* Sleath.)
Orphan Sisters, 127, 158.
Ossian, *58-63,* 65, 75, 78, 82, 108, 127.
Our Mutual Friend. (*See* Dickens.)

Packet. (*See* Gunning, Miss E.)
Page, T. N., 202, 219.
Palmer, John, 53.
Pamela. (*See* Richardson.)
Paraclete. (*See* Lathy, T. P.)
Parsons, Mrs. Eliza, 20-1, 69, 77, 123, 125, *128-9,* 137, 149.
Partisan. (*See* Simms, W. G.)
Pater, Walter, 151, 206.
Pathfinder. (*See* Cooper, J. F.)
Patrick, Mrs. F. C., 163-4.
Paul Jones. (*See* Cunningham.)
Peacock, T. L., 167, 213.
Peep at our Ancestors. (*See* Mosse, H. R.)
Percy, Thomas, 63-5.
Perry, Francis, 28.
Philip Augustus. (*See* James, G. P. R.)
Pioneers. (*See* Cooper, J. F.)
Piozzi, Hester T., 30, 154.
Pirate. (*See* Scott, Walter.)
Pitaval, Gayot de, 120.
Plain Sense, 126.
Pope, Alexander, 2, 57, 75.
Porter, Anna Maria, 15, 175.
Porter, Jane, *174-5,* 184, 188.
Precaution. (*See* Cooper, J. F.)
Price, Uvedale, 188.
Prickett, Miss, 173.
Privilege. (*See* Sadleir, M.)

Prodigious!!!, 166.
Quentin Durward. (*See* Scott, Walter.)
Radcliffe, Anne, 2, 16-8, 22-3, 29-30, 49, 53, 54, 59, 62, 68-9, 76-7, 86, 94-5, *106-21,* 129, 132-7, 138-9, 140, 142-5, 149, *153-5,* 158, 168, 173-4, 176-9, 181-5, 189, 191, 194, 198-9, 201, 204-5.
Rameses. (*See* Upham.)
Randolph. (*See* Neal, J.)
Ranspach, 13.
Rasselas. (*See* Johnson, Dr. S.)
Recess. (*See* Lee, S.)
Redgauntlet. (*See* Scott, Walter.)
Red Rover. (*See* Cooper, J. F.)
Reeve, Clara, 49, 77, *83-4,* 94, 124, 132, 171, 177.
Reuben and Rachel. (*See* Rowson.)
Revett, Nicholas, 27.
Richardson, Samuel, 2, *65-70,* 75.
Richelieu. (*See* James, G. P. R.)
Rienzi. (*See* Bulwer-Lytton.)
Ringan Gilhaize. (*See* Galt, J.)
Rival Friends, 20, 82, 94.
Robinson, Mrs. Mary, 30, 53, *129-30,* 133, 149, 154-5, 158, 174.
Roche, Mrs. Regina M., 15, 19, 21, 53, 58, 62, 77, 125, *127-8,* 137, 141, 158.
Rogers, Samuel, 22.
Rogers, W. H., 166.
Romance of the Forest. (*See* Radcliffe, A.)
Rookwood. (*See* Ainsworth.)
Rothelan. (*See* Galt, J.)
Rowson, Mrs., 193.
Ruins of Avondale Priory. (*See* Hedgeland.)
Ruins of Tivoli. (*See* Clifford, F.)

Sadleir, Michael, 16, 166, 214-5.
St. Botolph's Priory. (*See* Curties.)
St. Herbert, 195.
St. Leon. (*See* Godwin.)
Salathiel. (*See* Croly.)
Satanstoe. (*See* Cooper, J. F.)
Scarlet Letter. (*See* Hawthorne.)
School for Widows. (*See* Reeve, C.)
Scott, Geoffrey, 220.
Scott, Mrs. Sarah, 67, 74.
Scott, Sir Walter, 4, 81, 95, 121, 165, 168, 173, *175-89,* 199, 207, 213, 218.

Scottish Chiefs. (*See* Porter, Jane.)
Scottish Legend. (*See* Curties.)
Scout. (*See* Simms, W. G.)
Secrecy. (*See* Fenwick.)
Secrets in Every Mansion. (*See* Anne of Swansea.)
Selden, Catherine, 19, 53, 58, 131, 149.
Sentimental Spy, 27, 148.
Septimius Felton. (*See* Hawthorne.)
Seymour Castle, 122, 152.
Shakespeare, Wm., 2, *50-5,* 58, 75-7, 108.
Shebbeare, John, 27, 148.
Shoshonee Valley. (*See* Flint, T.)
Sicilian Mysteries. (*See* Anne of Swansea.)
Sicilian Romance. (*See* Radcliffe, A.)
Siege of Kenilworth. (*See* Stanhope, L. S.)
Simms, W. G., 201.
Sir Bertrand. (*See* Aikin, J.)
Sir Charles Grandison. (*See* Richardson.)
Sir Reginald du Bray, 82.
Sir Roger de Clarendon. (*See* Reeve, C.)
Sleath, Mrs. Eleanor, 53, 62, 68, 77, 132.
Smith, Mrs. Charlotte, 14, 16, 20, 30, 49, 53, 57-8, 63, 64, 76-7, *94-108,* 110, 118-21, 132-3, 135-7, 142, 144, 148-9, 155, *161-3,* 173-4, 177, 183, 191.
Smith, Horace, 150-1, 184, *186-7.*
Smith, John, 130.
Smollett, Tobias, 70, 89, 92, 168-9.
Solitary Castle, 122, 126.
Solitary Wanderer. (*See* Smith, Mrs. C.)
Solyman and Almena. (*See* Langhorne.)
Southey, Robert, 186.
Southward Ho! (*See* Simms, W. G.)
Spenser, Edmund, 50, 55-6, 70, 76-7, 203.
Sprite of the Nunnery. (*See* Trapp, J.)
Spy. (*See* Cooper, J. F.)
Stabback, Thos., 158.
Stanhope, Louisa S., 57, *138-40,* 166, 173, 189.
Step-Mother. (*See* Wells, H.)

Sterne, L., 162.
Stevenson, R. L., 207.
Story of Lady Juliana Harley. (*See* Griffith, Mrs. E.)
Strathallan. (*See* Lefanu.)
Stratton Hill. (*See* Carne, J.)
Striking Likenesses. (*See* Stanhope, L. S.)
Stuart, James, 27, 29, 107.

Talba. (*See* Bray, A. E.)
Tale of the Times. (*See* West, Mrs. J.)
Tasso, 70.
Tennyson, A., 2, 143.
Teuthold, Peter, 76.
Theodore Cyphon. (*See* Walker, G.)
Thomson, James, 50, 56, 58, 77.
Thorpe, John, 29, 132.
Tom Jones. (*See* Fielding, Henry.)
Tompkins, J. M. S., 30.
Tooke, Wm., 156.
Tower of London. (*See* Ainsworth.)
Toynbee, Paget, 38.
Trapp, Jos., 156.
Two on a Tower. (*See* Hardy, Thos.)

Upham, Edward, 150-1.

Valerius. (*See* Lockhart.)
Vancenza. (*See* Robinson, M.)
Vasconselos. (*See* Simms, W. G.)
Vathek. (*See* Beckford.)
Vaughan, Thos., 48, 148, 168.
Vicar of Lansdowne. (*See* Roche.)
Victory. (*See* Conrad, J.)
Vivian Gray. (*See* Disraeli.)

Waldron, Geo., 180.
Walker, Geo., 175.
Walker, Lady M., 48.
Waller, Edmund, 56.
Walpole, Horace, 3, 8, 12, 20, 22-3, 25, 28, *31-42,* 44-7, 49, 55, 57, 65, *77-81,* 83, 86, 94, 123, 132, 142, 176-7, 180, 182-3, 198, 207, 218.
Walter Colyton. (*See* Smith, Horace.)
Wanderer. (*See* Burney.)
Wanderer of the Alps, 77, 131.
Warbeck. (*See* D'Arnaud.)
Warne, Miss, 20.

Warner, Richard, 20.
Warton, Jos., 50, 77.
Warton, Thos., 28, 50, 77.
Warwick Castle. (*See* Prickett.)
Water Witch. (*See* Cooper, J. F.)
Waugh, Evelyn, 214.
Waverley. (*See* Scott, Walter.)
Webster, John, 55-6.
Week at a Cottage. (*See* Hutchinson, W.)
Wells, Helena, 193.
Wept of Wish-ton-Wish. (*See* Cooper, J. F.)
West, Mrs. Jane, 125.
White, Jas., 156, *170-1*.
White Hoods. (*See* Bray, A. E.)
Wieland. (*See* Brown, C. B.)
Wild Irish Boy. (*See* Maturin.)
Wild Irish Girl. (*See* Morgan, Lady S. O.)
Wilkinson, Mrs. Sarah, 138.
Will, P., 76.
Williams, Helen Maria, 122-3.

Wilmot, 158.
Windsor Castle. (*See* Ainsworth.)
Wing-and-Wing. (*See* Cooper, J. F.)
Winter's Tale. (*See* Brewer, J. N.)
Witch of Aysgarth. (*See* Golland.)
Woman. (*See* Morgan, Lady S. O.)
Wood, Robert, 27, 29.
Woodland Cottage, 122-3.
Woodlanders. (*See* Hardy, Thos.)
Woodstock. (*See* Scott, Walter.)
Wuthering Heights. (*See* Brontë, Emily.)
Wyandotté. (*See* Cooper, J. F.)

Yemassee. (*See* Simms, W. G.)
Young, Arthur, 30.
Young, Mary Julia, 166.
Young Philosopher. (*See* Smith, Mrs. C.)
Yvon, Paul, 40.

Zanoni. (*See* Bulwer-Lytton.)
Zillah. (*See* Smith, Horace.)

YALE STUDIES IN ENGLISH

I. The Foreign Sources of Modern English Versification. CHARLTON M. LEWIS, Ph.D. $0.50. (Out of print.)

II. Ælfric: A New Study of his Life and Writings. CAROLINE LOUISA WHITE, Ph.D. $1.50.

III. The Life of St. Cecilia, from MS. Ashmole 43 and MS. Cotton Tiberius E. VII, with Introduction, Variants, and Glossary. BERTHA ELLEN LOVEWELL, Ph.D. $1.00. (Out of print.)

IV. Dryden's Dramatic Theory and Practice. MARGARET SHERWOOD, Ph.D. $0.50.

V. Studies in Jonson's Comedy. ELISABETH WOODBRIDGE, Ph.D. $0.50.

VI. A Glossary of the West Saxon Gospels, Latin-West Saxon and West Saxon-Latin. MATTIE ANSTICE HARRIS, Ph.D. $1.50.

VII. Andreas: The Legend of St. Andrew, translated from the Old English, with an Introduction. ROBERT KILBURN ROOT, Ph.D. $0.50.

VIII. The Classical Mythology of Milton's English Poems. CHARLES GROSVENOR OSGOOD, Ph.D. $1.00.

IX. A Guide to the Middle English Metrical Romances dealing with English and Germanic Legends, and with the Cycles of Charlemagne and of Arthur. ANNA HUNT BILLINGS, Ph.D. $1.50. (Out of print.)

X. The Earliest Lives of Dante, translated from the Italian of Giovanni Boccaccio and Lionardo Bruni Aretino. JAMES ROBINSON SMITH. $0.75.

XI. A Study in Epic Development. IRENE T. MYERS, Ph.D. $1.00.

XII. The Short Story. HENRY SEIDEL CANBY, Ph.D. $0.30.

XIII. King Alfred's Old English Version of St. Augustine's Soliloquies, edited with Introduction, Notes, and Glossary. HENRY LEE HARGROVE, Ph.D. $1.00.

XIV. The Phonology of the Northumbrian Gloss of St. Matthew. EMILY HOWARD FOLEY, Ph.D. $0.75.

XV. Essays on the Study and Use of Poetry by Plutarch and Basil the Great, translated from the Greek, with an Introduction. FREDERICK MORGAN PADELFORD, Ph.D. $0.75.

XVI. The Translations of Beowulf: A Critical Bibliography. CHAUNCEY B. TINKER, Ph.D. $0.75.

XVII. The Alchemist, by Ben Jonson, edited with Introduction, Notes, and Glossary. CHARLES M. HATHAWAY, JR., Ph.D. $2.50. Cloth, $3.00. (Out of print.)

XVIII. The Expression of Purpose in Old English Prose. HUBERT GIBSON SHEARIN, Ph.D. $1.00.

XIX. Classical Mythology in Shakespeare. ROBERT KILBURN ROOT, Ph.D. $1.00. (Out of print.)

XX. The Controversy between the Puritans and the Stage. ELBERT N. S. THOMPSON, Ph.D. $2.00. (Out of print.)

XXI. The Elene of Cynewulf, translated into English Prose. LUCIUS HUDSON HOLT, Ph.D. $0.30. (Out of print.)

XXII. King Alfred's Old English Version of St. Augustine's Soliloquies, turned into Modern English. HENRY LEE HARGROVE, Ph.D. $0.75.

XXIII. The Cross in the Life and Literature of the Anglo-Saxons. WILLIAM O. STEVENS, Ph.D. $0.75.

XXIV. An Index to the Old English Glosses of the Durham Hymnarium. HARVEY W. CHAPMAN. $0.75. (Out of print.)

XXV. Bartholomew Fair, by Ben Jonson, edited with Introduction, Notes, and Glossary. CARROLL STORRS ALDEN, Ph.D. $2.00. (Out of print.)

XXVI. Select Translations from Scaliger's Poetics. FREDERICK M. PADELFORD, Ph.D. $0.75. (Out of print.)

XXVII. Poetaster, by Ben Jonson, edited with Introduction, Notes, and Glossary. HERBERT S. MALLORY, Ph.D. $2.00. Cloth, $2.50.

XXVIII. The Staple of News, by Ben Jonson, edited with Introduction, Notes, and Glossary. DE WINTER, Ph.D. $2.00. Cloth, $2.50.

XXIX. The Devil is an Ass, by Ben Jonson, edited with Introduction, Notes, and Glossary. WILLIAM SAVAGE JOHNSON, Ph.D. $2.00. Cloth, $2.50. (Out of print.)

XXX. The Language of the Northumbrian Gloss to the Gospel of St. Luke. MARGARET DUTTON KELLUM, Ph.D. $0.75. (Out of print.)

XXXI. Epicœne, or the Silent Woman, by Ben Jonson, edited with Introduction, Notes, and Glossary. AURELIA HENRY, Ph.D. $2.00. Cloth, $2.50.

XXXII. The Syntax of the Temporal Clause in Old English Prose. ARTHUR ADAMS, Ph.D. $1.00. (Out of print.)

XXXIII. The Knight of the Burning Pestle, by Beaumont and Fletcher, edited with Introduction, Notes, and Glossary. HERBERT S. MURCH, Ph.D. $2.00. (Out of print.)

XXXIV. The New Inn, by Ben Jonson, edited with Introduction, Notes, and Glossary. GEORGE BREMNER TENNANT, Ph.D. $2.00.

XXXV. A Glossary of Wulfstan's Homilies. LORING HOLMES DODD, Ph.D. $1.00. (Out of print.)

XXXVI. The Complaint of Nature, translated from the Latin of Alain de Lille. DOUGLAS M. MOFFAT, M.A. $0.75.

XXXVII. The Collaboration of Webster and Dekker. FREDERICK ERASTUS PIERCE, Ph.D. $1.00. (Out of print.)

XXXVIII. English Nativity Plays, edited with Introduction, Notes, and Glossary. SAMUEL B. HEMINGWAY, Ph.D. $2.00. Cloth, $2.50. (Out of print.)

XXXIX. Concessive Constructions in Old English Prose. JOSEPHINE MAY BURNHAM, Ph.D. $1.00. (Out of print.)

XL. The Tenure of Kings and Magistrates, by John Milton, edited with Introduction and Notes. WILLIAM TALBOT ALLISON, Ph.D. $1.25.

XLI. Biblical Quotations in Middle English Literature before 1350. MARY W. SMYTH, Ph.D. $2.00.

XLII. The Dialogue in English Literature. ELIZABETH MERRILL, Ph.D. $1.00. (Out of print.)

XLIII. A Study of Tindale's Genesis, compared with the Genesis of Coverdale and of the Authorized Version. ELIZABETH WHITTLESEY CLEAVELAND, Ph.D. $2.00.

XLIV. The Presentation of Time in the Elizabethan Drama. MABLE BULAND, Ph.D. $1.50.

XLV. Cynthia's Revels, or, the Fountain of Self-Love, by Ben Jonson, edited with Introduction, Notes, and Glossary. ALEXANDER CORBIN JUDSON, Ph.D. $2.00. (Out of print.)

XLVI. Richard Brome: A Study of his Life and Works. CLARENCE EDWARD ANDREWS, Ph.D. $1.25.

XLVII. The Magnetic Lady, or, Humors Reconciled, by Ben Jonson, edited with Introduction, Notes, and Glossary. HARVEY WHITEFIELD PECK, Ph.D. $2.00.

XLVIII. Genesis A (sometimes attributed to Cædmon), translated from the Old English. LAWRENCE MASON, Ph.D. $0.75.

XLIX. The Later Version of the Wycliffite Epistle to the Romans, compared with the Latin Original: A Study of Wycliffite English. EMMA CURTISS TUCKER, Ph.D. $1.50.

L. Some Accounts of the Bewcastle Cross between the Years 1607 and 1861. ALBERT STANBURROUGH COOK. $1.50.

LI. The Ready and Easy Way to Establish a Free Commonwealth, by John Milton, edited with Introduction, Notes, and Glossary. EVERT MORDECAI CLARK, Ph.D. $1.50.

LII. Every Man in his Humour, by Ben Jonson, edited with Introduction, Notes, and Glossary. HENRY HOLLAND CARTER, Ph.D. $4.00.

LIII. Catiline, his Conspiracy, by Ben Jonson, edited with Introduction, Notes, and Glossary. LYNN HAROLD HARRIS, Ph.D. $2.00.

LIV. Of Reformation, touching Church-Discipline in England, by John Milton, edited with Introduction, Notes, and Glossary. WILL TALIAFERRO HALE, Ph.D. $2.00.

LV. Old English Scholarship in England from 1566 to 1800. ELEANOR N. ADAMS, Ph.D. $2.00.

LVI. The Case is Altered, by Ben Jonson, edited with Introduction, Notes, and Glossary. WILLIAM EDWARD SELIN, Ph.D. $2.00.

LVII. Wordsworth's Theory of Poetic Diction: A Study of the Historical and Personal Background of the Lyrical Ballads. MARJORIE LATTA BARSTOW, Ph.D. $1.50.

LVIII. Horace in the English Literature of the Eighteenth Century. CAROLINE GOAD, Ph.D. $3.00.

LIX. Volpone, or, The Fox, by Ben Jonson, edited with Introduction, Notes, and Glossary. JOHN D. REA, Ph.D. $2.50.

LX. The Mediæval Attitude toward Astrology, particularly in England. THEODORE OTTO WEDEL, Ph.D. $2.50.

LXI. Purity: A Middle English Poem, edited with Introduction, Notes, and Glossary. ROBERT J. MENNER, Ph.D. $3.00.

LXII. Ann Radcliffe in Relation to her Time. CLARA FRANCES MCINTYRE, Ph.D. $1.50.

LXIII. The Old English Physiologus: Text and Prose Translation by ALBERT STANBURROUGH COOK; Verse Translation by JAMES HALL PITMAN. $0.80.

LXIV. The Life and Work of Joanna Baillie. MARGARET S. CARHART, Ph.D. $2.00.

LXV. The Influence of Robert Garnier on Elizabethan Drama. ALEXANDER M. WITHERSPOON, Ph.D. $2.00.

LXVI. Goldsmith's Animated Nature: A Study of Goldsmith. JAMES HALL PITMAN, Ph.D. $2.00.

LXVII. The Riddles of Aldhelm: Text and Verse Translation, with Notes. JAMES HALL PITMAN, Ph.D. $1.00.

LXVIII. The American Indian in English Literature of the Eighteenth Century. BENJAMIN BISSELL, Ph.D. $2.00.

LXIX. The Life and Poems of Nicholas Grimald. L. R. MERRILL, Ph.D. $4.50.

LXX. Christ and Satan: An Old English Poem, edited with Introduction, Notes, and Glossary. MERREL DARE CLUBB, Ph.D. $2.00.

LXXI. Oliver Goldsmith's The Citizen of the World: A Study. HAMILTON JEWETT SMITH, Ph.D. $2.00.

LXXII. St. Erkenwald: A Middle English Poem, edited with Introduction, Notes, and Glossary. HENRY L. SAVAGE, Ph.D., $2.00.

LXXIII. Eastward Hoe, by Chapman, Jonson, and Marston, edited with Introduction, Notes, and Glossary. JULIA HAMLET HARRIS, Ph.D. $2.00.

LXXIV. The Life and Poems of Richard Edwards. LEICESTER BRADNER, Ph.D. $2.00.

LXXV. The Life and Works of Edward Moore. J. HOMER CASKEY, Ph.D. $2.00.

LXXVI. Sir Walter Scott's Novels on the Stage. H. A. WHITE, Ph.D. $2.50.

LXXVII. Nathan Field, The Actor-Playwright. ROBERTA FLORENCE BRINCKLEY, Ph.D. $2.50.

LXXVIII. Thomas Heywood: A Study in the Elizabethan Drama of Everyday Life. OTELIA CROMWELL, Ph.D. $2.50.

LXXIX. Melanthe: A Latin Pastoral Poem of the Early Seventeenth Century. JOSEPH S. G. BOLTON, Ph.D. $2.50.

LXXX. The Dramatic Work of Samuel Foote. MARY MEGIE BELDEN, Ph.D. $2.50.

LXXXI. Thomas Southerne, Dramatist. JOHN WENDELL DODDS, Ph.D. $2.00.

LXXXII. Carlyle and German Thought: 1819-1834. CHARLES FREDERICK HARROLD, Ph.D. $2.50.

LXXXIII. Architecture in English Fiction. WARREN HUNTING SMITH, Ph.D. $2.50. Cloth, $3.00.